COGNITIVE APPROACHES TO HUMAN PERCEPTION

COGNITIVE APPROACHES TO HUMAN PERCEPTION

Edited by
Soledad Ballesteros
Universidad Nacional de Educación a
Distancia, Madrid, Spain

LEA
LAWRENCE ERLBAUM ASSOCIATES, PUBLISHERS
1994   Hillsdale, New Jersey   Hove and London

Lawrence Erlbaum Associates, Inc., Publishers
365 Broadway
Hillsdale, New Jersey 07642

Library of Congress Cataloging-in-Publication Data
Cognitive approaches to human perception / Soledad Ballesteros (ed.).
    p. cm.
    Includes bibliographical references and index.
    ISBN 0-8058-1043-9
    1. Perception. 2. Form perception. 3. Visual perception.
    4. Mental representation. 5. Cognitive psychology.
    I. Ballesteros, Soledad.
    BF311.C55115 1993
    153.7—dc20   93-6805
                                                CIP

Books published by Lawrence Erlbaum Associates are printed on acid-free paper, and their
bindings are chosen for strength and durability.

Printed in the United States of America
10 9 8 7 6 5 4 3 2 1

To Pepe, Ana, and Jose Luis Andres

Contents

Preface

The aim of this volume is to examine the current state of the research in perception, stressing contributions in visual information processing, and to give an original and timely account of recent results obtained in this and other related areas of cognitive psychology. To achieve this goal, I convened a group of specialists in perception and cognition and asked them to write about topics in which they have been active during the last few years.

The scope of the book is intended to be broad, at least in two senses. First, it contains many state-of-the-art contributions from a number of outstanding researchers in the field; and second, contributors from different parts of the world, including the United States, Europe (Spain) and Australia.

The volume, of course, does not intend to cover all the important issues that comprise this broad and complex field. Nevertheless, I hope it will provide the reader with some of the more recent developments in perception and related areas of cognitive psychology. A book like this must be selective in some way. My intention is to update areas of considerable theoretical implication and active experimental investigation in this broad field called the Psychology of Perception.

This volume has been prepared specifically for graduate and advanced undergraduate students in psychology and cognitive science. Its main purpose is to highlight a selected number of important theoretical and empirical topics from a cognitive position that deal with some critical issues in perception and other high-level, related cognitive processes such as attention, mental representation, memory, word naming, and semantic categorization. The studies reported in this volume were designed trying to answer some of the following questions: Is the global precedence effect due to low- or high-level processing? Furthermore, is it a unitary phenomenon? Can veridical and illusory perception be explained by the same theory? Is there a certain parallelism between feature extraction and feature weighting in connectionist models and human processes that mediates form recognition? Do pattern recognition processes, embodied in artificial networks, have psychological reality? What is the relationship between attention and perception? Is it possible to achieve perceptual organization without attention? Is perceptual organization an attentional or preattentional process? How is irrelevant information processed by the visual system? Is perception direct or is it an inferential process? How can this be investigated and isolated experimentally from different functions of the underlying representations of visual objects? What type of information is preserved in such representations? How are different aspects of these representations retrieved when we remember consciously or unconsciously visual objects and patterns? What mechanisms are involved in picture and word naming and categorization? What are the variables responsible for the facilitatory and inhibitory effects found in picture and word processing? How can word and picture processing be modeled?

These and other important questions have guided the research programs of the contributors to this book. Their answers to questions like these just formulated seek to unite theoretical perspectives on very important areas of cognitive psychology such as attention, perception, representation of visual objects and words, and human memory.

Plan of the Book

The introductory chapter focuses on the particular contributions to this book, trying to place them along current lines of inquiry in cognitive psychology.

Part I of the book is dedicated to important aspects of attention and information processing. The chapters discuss several experimental paradigms used to investigate the implications of attentional processes in perceptual organization and the influence of context and irrelevant information in the visual processing of relevant, "to be attended" information.

Rock and Mack present a new experimental method developed to try to clarify whether the well-known phenomena of Gestalt grouping and texture segregation can be achieved without attention. A second line of inquiry focuses on which aspects of the stimulation are given preattentively and which ones required attention. They create experimental conditions that ascertain that no attention was allocated to a series of perceptual organization phenomena. Under this situation, texture segregation, pop-out, and perceptual grouping was not perceived. As Rock and Mack point out, the finding that grouping requires attention fits quite nicely with the idea that it occurs at a late postconstancy level of processing.

Ballesteros and Manga consider the way in which nonlinguistic and linguistic stimuli are processed when irrelevant information is present in the experimental display. Two types of experimental situations are considered. In a situation, two nonlinguistic stimuli created by the orthogonal combination of two physical dimensions, one relevant and the other irrelevant, are presented for a very short period of time, and the subject has to discriminate as to whether they are "same" or "different" in the relevant dimension, trying to ignore the irrelevant one. In the other situation, three linguistic stimuli appear immersed in different contexts in order to investigate the influence of several contexts in the processing of the physical and name identity of the letters. In both cases, we were interested in showing how the irrelevant information present in the experimental display affects the processing of the relevant stimuli; that is, we wanted to know whether selective attention to the relevant information is possible when irrelevant information is also present in the experimental situation.

Part II is concerned with important topics in form perception considered from different perspectives. Lovegrove and Pepper present in their chapter new experimental evidence that shows the influence of low-level processing in the perception of hierarchically constructed visual patterns. Their results also seem to support the idea that different mechanisms at different levels are responsible for the two commonly reported effects found in the global precedence effect (GPE). Low-level processes seem to be responsible for the perceptual priority of global over local information, whereas high-level mechanisms seem to be implicated in the interference effect.

Latimer and Stevens explore the psychological plausibility of single-layer connectionist models in the perception of geometric forms. They proposed that the segmentation of geometric shapes is mediated by the extraction and differential weighting of local features. The experimental strategy consisted of comparing the performance of artificial networks and human subjects during the process of form recognition. They used eye movements and fixation indices as valid indicator of feature extraction and feature weighting assigned to these features by human subjects.

Pomerantz, Carson and Feldman present experimental results using several selective attentional techniques in order to discover the psychological reality of visual parts.

Part III is concerned with topics such as the mental representation of visual objects and its underlying memory systems, and patterns of facilitation and inhibition in the processing of visually presented pictures of common objects and its corresponding words. Mayor and González Marqués provide a theoretical and methodological overview of the research conducted in naming and categorization tasks of words and pictures. After reviewing several current models that have been proposed to explain word and picture processing, a new model is tested experimentally.

Cooper, from a different perspective, presents experimental evidence from an ongoing program of investigation, which tries to uncover the underlying representational systems that support priming and recognition of novel three-dimensional objects. She reports a number of important behavioral dissociations found in implicit and explicit memory tests related to the structural and semantic aspects of visual objects. Those results are used to infer the existence of two different representational systems, one related to the codification of structural information of visual objects and the other in charge of the representation of its episodic characteristics (object's meaning).

Cooper and Hochberg, in their joint and last chapter in Part III, provide an interesting account of the theoretical stance that underlines each of their programs of research on object perception and representation. They make clear the importance of considering mental representations of objects for visual cognition. Cooper and Hochberg further argue that mental representation has to be considered as a necessary tool for studying visual cognition. In the second part of this chapter, they present several examples that challenge the idea that those mental representations of objects and events reflect the internalization of properties of the physical world. These cases, in which a noncorrespondence between mental representations and physical objects in the world is present, are the most important cases to study.

Finally, *Part IV* deals with some fundamental issues in perceptual theory and in normal and illusory perception. Day proposes a general theory, which tries to explain under the same framework, both veridical and nonveridical (illusory) perception. He argues that many features of the proximal patterns are correlated with a particular property of a situation in the physical world. When researchers varied and contrived these cues systematically, nonveridical perception was the result. He concludes that perception appears to be direct (and results from the correlation of integrated stimuli); but at the same time, it seems mediated, due to the specific subject's experience, as some of these attributes become more salient than others.

Hochberg convincingly differentiates theories concerned with proximal properties of the stimulation from those dealing with distal properties. He considers that early visual theories concerning the study of proximal stimulation and late visual theories of perception are, despite several efforts, totally unrelated. Hochberg argues that earlier theories can be useful in demonstrating how the receptive machinery works; however, these theories do not contribute to explain how visual perception and visual cognition operate.

ACKNOWLEDGMENTS

The editor wishes to acknowledge the contributions of a number of people to this book. Firstly, I am very grateful to Larry Erlbaum who was interested in the project of this book when I outlined the plan to him. Secondly, I am deeply in debt to Judy Amsel, Vice President, Editorial, at Lawrence Erlbaum Associates for her help throughout all the stages of the book, and to Editorial Associate, Kathleen Dolan, for her kind advice during the production process, and to Kathryn M. Scornavacca for her help during all the book production process. Thirdly, I am very grateful to the contributors without whom this book would not have been published.

I would like to express my appreciation to Jose Luis Fernández Trespalacios, Head of the Basic Psychology Department (UNED), who encouraged me to apply for the DGICYT grant, which made possible my first stay at Columbia University in 1989 as visiting scholar.

Finally, I am deeply indebted to Lynn A. Cooper, Head of the Psychology Department at Columbia University, who invited me to her laboratory and provided me with friendship, support, and the necessary scientific climate during my stay at Columbia. I also wish to thank my family for their understanding during all this time.

The research reported by me in different parts of the book was supported by CAICYT (1985 grant), a DGICYT foreign country research grant (1989), and an UNED sabbatical leave support grant (1990–1991). The current work in haptic perception and memory is supported by DGICYT grant PB90-0003 and by two UNED "Ayudas de Infraestructura de Investigación" awarded in 1991 and 1992, respectively.

—Soledad Ballesteros

1 Cognitive Approaches to Human Perception: Introduction

Soledad Ballesteros
Universidad Nacional de Educación a Distancia, Madrid, Spain

The study of perception has appealed to psychologists for more than a century and philosophers and neurologists even earlier (for a review, see Hochberg, 1988). The purpose of this introductory chapter is to consider how important topics in perception are approached in the chapters that follow, trying to place them along current lines of inquiry in cognitive psychology.

The cognitive approach to the study of mental processes, specifically attention, perception, mental representation, and memory, is the theoretical stance favored throughout the chapters of this book. This approach, however, is not the only theoretical position that can be adopted in the study of perception but only one of the various ways of addressing it (Dretske, 1990). Since the beginning of experimental psychology, psychophysical investigation equipped with a rigorous and sophisticated methodology has studied how human perception is influenced by the systematic variation of different stimulus variables. As Hochberg points out (this volume), even though this kind of research is very useful in showing how the receptive structures of the visual system function, this line of work provides little support in explaining human perception and constructing useful theories that could be used to understand a wide variety of perceptual phenomena. Hochberg recognizes, however, that recently, a number of important conceptual tools such as sensory networks and acquisitive neural nets have appeared that can help in such an effort.

There are other positions as well, one of which is the behavioristic approach, which focuses only on observable behavior. This theoretical stance, no longer in vogue, dominated practically all research conducted in experimental psychology during the first half of this century (see Amsel, 1989; Bechtel, 1988).

A more updated approach, however, characterizes mental activities as the underlying neural processes. Neuropsychological studies focusing on people who suffer different kinds of brain injuries have proved very useful in understanding not only impaired perception but normal perception as well (e.g., Farah, 1990; Humphreys & Riddoch, 1984; Lamb, Robertson, & Knight, 1990; Shimamura & Squire, 1987; Squire & McKee, 1992). These studies in conjunction with other investigations consisting of single-cell recording in the visual cerebral cortex and visual pathways in animals (especially in monkeys) have provided important information for knowing how normal visual perception works (e.g., Cowey & Gross, 1970; Desimone, Albright, Gross, & Bruce, 1984; Gross, 1978; Plaut & Farah, 1990).

Today, the neural approach is a very active field of investigation that provides a way of testing theories constructed from data obtained with normal as well as impaired populations. At the same time, this approach can be very valuable in proposing new hypotheses about cognitive functioning (e.g., Biederman & Cooper, 1992; Desimone & Ungerleider, 1986; Ellis & Young, 1988; Farah, 1990; Nadel, Cooper, Culicover, & Harnish, 1989; Shimamura & Squire, 1987; see Cooper, chapter 8, this volume).

The cognitive approach, by contrast, is characterized by its interest in identifying mental states functionally, considering their causal interactions with other mental states as a way of overcoming the strictures of behaviorism. At the same time, these mental states can be thought of independently of their material realization in the brain. This characteristic ensures the necessary independence of psychology from neuroscience.

Cognitive scientists investigate the nature of the human mind and its underlying structures and processes. For this purpose they try to understand the nature of the mental representations that underly perception and other cognitive processes that support our interactions with the external world. Much of the recent research in the field has been directed at the understanding of the inferential or computational character of perception and to the study of the main qualities that perception exhibits. Are those qualities comparable to those of reason and intelligence? Are perceptual processes top–down, directed by reason, or are they bottom–up, directed by the data? Does the perceptual system postulate hypothesis or solve problems? These are just some of the questions that arise in the field of human perception and are addressed in this volume.

Following Helmholtz's tradition, a large number of researchers maintain that the correspondence between proximal and distal stimulation is never perfect (e.g., Gregory, 1978; Hochberg, 1988, chapter 11, this volume; Rock, 1983; Ulman, 1980). Hochberg, (chapter 11, this volume) distinguishes between two kinds of theories: (a) theories about edges, contours, motions, and so on (the attributes of the retinal image); and (b) theories about visual perception. The latter are concerned with the distal properties of the stimuli, whereas the former are interested in its proximal attributes. Because there is never a total (1:1) correspondence between proximal and distal properties of stimulation, higher processes are supposed to do the job.

Others scientists, like Gibson (1950, 1966, 1979; Michaels & Carello, 1981), however, challenged this position and defended that all the information necessary to specify the distal object is on the stimulus. That is, the stimulus carries out enough information to determine the character of the distal object. Contrary to constructivist theorists, following Gibson's leadership direct perception psychologists discard all kinds of intervening cognitive variables from the act of perception. Constructivist scientists, however, believe that the sensory stimulation carries a great burden of ambiguity because a large variety of distal stimuli could be responsible for the same pattern of stimulation (see Hochberg, chapter 11, this volume). Immersed in this ambiguous situation, the perceiver has to add further information to the stimulus in order to achieve a meaningful percept.

Attending, recognizing, remembering, and reasoning about the environment is something that people do quite easily, but we are still very far from achieving a complete understanding of how these processes work. The main interest today rests on understanding and explaining the structure of mental representations underlying these psychological processes, as well as how these processes are carried out by the human perceiver. The chapters throughout this volume deal directly with these two issues.

SELECTED TOPICS AND THEORETICAL ISSUES

Most of the relationships that we establish with the environment are carried out through perception, especially visual perception. Vision is very important for human beings because it provides the perceiver with crucial information about individual objects and spatial layout. Vision helps human perceivers to distinguish a friend from a stranger, a hostile landscape from a familiar space, novel visual forms and objects from familiar ones, and so on. Nevertheless, other perceptual modalities such as audition and touch are also very important in our daily relationship with the external world. Lets take haptic perception as an example. Through purposive touch the haptic perceiver can obtain accurate and valid information about objects and surfaces, some of which can not be captured through other perceptual systems (Klatzky, Lederman, & Metzger, 1985; Loomis & Lederman, 1986; Millar, 1978). Important volumes in tactual (Heller & Schiff, 1991; Katz, 1989) and auditory perception (Bregman,

1990; Buser & Imbert, 1992) have been published in recent years, and the interested reader will find in these books important studies about the properties, characteristics, and capabilities of touch and audition.

Cognitive scientists have as a goal the understanding of human minds, and a good way to achieve this goal is to formulate hypotheses and test theories about how attentional and perceptual mechanisms work, as well as to try to discover the nature of representations underlying object perception and memory. This understanding will eventually help us in building machines provided with similar capabilities that could be used in industry and by disabled populations in their interactions with the world.

Attention and Visual Perception

The chapters in Part I of this volume deal with fundamental issues in attention and its relation to perceptual organization. Most of the recent developments in attention are due to research trying to determine the locus of the attentional bottleneck. Traditionally, the two most important issues in attentional investigation have been: (a) the problem of the limited capacity of attention, also called the limitation of resources; and (b) where the locus of selection in the information processing system must be located, that is, the problem of early versus late selection.

This line of enquiry started with the pioneering work of Broadbent (1958), who argued that there is a selective filter working at an early stage of the sensory analysis of the stimuli, before perceptual recognition or categorization of the stimuli takes place. According to Broadbent, the main purpose of this filter is to avoid overload inside the limited capacity mechanism. Some physical characteristics of the sensory input are processed in parallel until its arrival to this filter, but information not selected at this point is excluded from further analysis. This excluded information is neither recognized nor categorized. Soon after the publication of Broadbent's work, some investigators, proposed based on empirical results, that the filtering occurs quite late, after categorization, or even not at all (for reviews, see Johnston & Dark, 1986; Kahneman & Treisman, 1984).

It is well accepted that phenomena such as perceptual organization and figure-ground segregation based on the detection of homogenous regions and discontinuities may occur automatically (or preattentively) at the beginning of a visual presentation (e.g., Shiffrin, 1988). However, in addition, these phenomena seem to be affected by attentional processes, as results show in chapter 2 of this volume by Rock and Mack. These findings can be taken as new evidence that when perceptual patterns are viewed without attention, perceptual grouping does not seem to take place.

Rock and Mack's results pose two main problems for previous research.

The first problem is how to reconcile these negative results on perceptual organization with those obtained from the search paradigm indicating parallel processing. The second problem is how to explain the early stage of preattentively visual field organization if it is not based on Gestalt laws. Rock and Mack, in an attempt to reconcile these two sets of evidence, assume the existence of three different levels of attentional processing: (a) a nonattentional level at which some stimulus properties may be perceived without attention or intention to perceive; (b) a distributed attentional level in which multiple elements can be detected in parallel over the visual field; and (c) a highest level in which focal attention to the stimuli is necessary.

In summary, Rock and Mack, taking into account new findings from a number of recent studies reported in their chapter, as well as on previous results, argue that shape perception always requires attention and without it perception cannot be achieved (Rock 1983; Rock & Gutman, 1981).

Ballesteros and Manga (chapter 3) try to understand the way in which irrelevant information present in the experimental situation influences the processing of relevant characteristics of the stimulus. In other words, the question is whether selective attention to the relevant information is possible when irrelevant information is also present in the visual field. Several lines of research are presented that seem to support the idea that various types of information about the stimulus, or the context in which the stimulus appeared, are available to the perceiver shortly after the stimulus presentation.

Nevertheless, after years of investigation the controversy is still present (see Allport, 1989; Broadbent, 1991; Shiffrin, 1988). At the moment, it seems reasonable to propose that the extraction of information is carried out by attentional processes prone to limitations that may appear at any stage of processing.

Form Perception

Chapters in Part II are mainly concerned with several important issues in form perception. Pomerantz, Carson, and Feldman present several lines of experimental results related to the diagnosis of the psychologically real parts of visual forms. The leading hypothesis is that if two elements function as separate parts, the perceiver should be able to attend to each element selectively, otherwise interference will occur. Pomerantz, Carson, and Feldman (chapter 6, this volume) present differences between Garner and Stroop interference, asymmetries of interference, and how perceptual interactions can be diagnosed in the laboratory by performance in visual information processing tasks.

The Processing of Global and Local Information in Form Perception.
An old but still pervasive topic in visual perception and cognition is
whether the recognition of a global, overall pattern precedes the recognition
of its component elements.

Throughout the history of experimental psychology opposed positions
over this issue have appeared. In the early times, structuralists such as
Titchener (1909) proposed that the extraction of components in a visual
pattern is carried out first, followed by the building up of the total percept
from these elementary units. According to the structuralist position, the
processing of local units takes place first. In contrast, Gestalt psychology
holds that the perceptual whole is qualitatively different from the composition of its individual parts or units, maintaining a holistic view.

More recently, cognitive researchers presented experimental results that
are in agreement with the idea that perceptual processes proceed from
global to local, that is, from more general to more detailed extraction of
information. This is known as the global precedence hypothesis, first
proposed by Navon (1977). The common way of testing this proposal has
been to observe the effect of hierarchically constructed patterns over
behavioral measures such as the reaction times.

The visual forms are usually large letters composed of a certain number
of smaller letters. In a typical experiment, participants are asked to respond
to the global or to the local level of the perceptual pattern according to
experimental conditions. The results obtained by Navon and others favored
a global-to-local order of processing. Global letters are processed before its
component local elements (the global precedence effect); and global information produces an inhibitory effect in the condition of local directed
attention when global conflicting information is present in the display (the
interference effect). On the contrary, local conflicting information does not
affect the processing of global information. These two effects taken
together were interpreted by Navon (1977) as a sufficient demonstration of
the inevitability of global precedence in visual information processing. This
interpretation, however, has been questioned on several grounds, for
example, attributing the results either to the differential salience of the
stimuli (Garner, 1983; Pomerantz, 1983) or stating that the phenomenon is
not perceptual in nature but postperceptual (e.g., attentional and response
competition; Boer & Keuss, 1982; J. Miller, 1981).

More recent studies (Navon, 1991), however, have focused on whether
the global precedence effect would be stationary throughout the entire
processing period, thus considering the possibility of an increase in the local
consistency effect at different SOAs. Nevertheless this effect did not appear
in several experiments. Instead, global precedence under conditions of
focused, divided, and diffuse attention was found. These results led Navon
to the conclusion that attention to global stimuli is either involuntary or the

locus of global precedence is preattentive. In both cases he interpreted the advantage as perceptual.

A topic of recent research is whether the global processing is obligatory. A series of experiments conducted by Paquet (1992) confirm previous results by Paquet and Merikle (1988) that showed global processing dominance in nonattended objects even when local information directs the selection of the attended objects. Furthermore, these results also showed that even when local categorization occurs, it does not produce local processing dominance.

It is important to note, however, that during the last few years researchers have started to question the commonly accepted idea that both effects, global advantage and interference, always appear together. Lamb, Robertson, and their associates (e.g., Lamb & Robertson, 1988, 1989; Lamb, Robertson, & Knight, 1990) challenged this well-accepted view. As Lamb and Robertson (1988) observed, important changes in reaction times can occur without any change in interference. Data from brain-injured patients showed a dissociation between these two effects, suggesting that different anatomical structures intervene in the processing of hierarchical patterns. Global precedence effect and local interference, they reasoned, may be caused by different mechanisms and simply do not reflect global-to-local processing. Even in normal participants, global RTs advantage and interference do not necessarily occur together (Lamb & Robertson, 1989; Navon & Norman, 1983).

The processing of the local structure is associated with the left superior temporal lobe, whereas the right posterior superior temporal lobe favors the processing of global structure. On the other hand, the integration of information from global and local structure is disrupted in patients with lesions in the superior posterior temporal lobe or in the afferent pathways to this area. The speed of processing local and global levels of structure seems to be modulated by attentional mechanisms associated with the rostral inferior temporal lobe (Lamb et al., 1990)

Lovegrove and Pepper, chapter 4, this volume, reach a quite similar conclusion from results obtained in their studies with normal university students. They argue that different processes at different levels seem responsible for the global advantage effect and the interference effect. According to their results, low-level processes seem responsible for the global precedence effect. However, the inconsistency (inhibitory) effect, they argue, may be the result of higher order processes.

In summary, Lovegrave and Pepper's results as well as neuropsychological ones (Lamb & Robertson, 1989; Lamb, Robertson, & Knight, 1989) point to the idea that the two effects associated with the GPE (global advantage and local interference) are quite different in nature. As Lovegrove and Pepper point out, if further research confirms the results reported in this volume, a main revision of perceptual theories that defend either the involvement of high-level processes in the GPE or the covariation of interference and relative speed measures will be necessary.

Psychological Reality of Connectionist Modeling.   The origin of neural networks relies on the pioneer work of McCulloch and Pitts (1943), Hebb (1949), and Rosenblatt (1962), among others. But Connectionism, as an active program of research trying to apply its principles to extended areas of psychological functioning, has started much more recently (see Rumelhart, MacClelland et al., 1986). Nevertheless, before researchers can be certain of its value it will be necessary to prove the validity of this class of modeling. A book edited by Nadel, Cooper, Culicover and Harnish (1989) addressed important questions in connection with the psychological adequacy and the neurological plausibility of the connectionist approach. Contrary to the classical architecture inspired in the von Neumann tradition of serial computing, connectionist models are neurally inspired and motivated by the idea that in the near future the computer metaphor could be replaced by a new one inspired by the functioning of the brain (see Rumelhart, 1989). Knowledge in connectionist models is stored in the connections among the units of the system instead of being stored in the units of the system as in the classical models (Ballesteros, 1992). Furthermore, connectionist models operate in parallel, which seems more in line with the way the brain functions. According to these new models, cognitive functioning takes place in networks that operate in parallel. These are nonsymbolic models of mind in which activity arises from the strength of the connections among the units of the system instead of from symbols stored and coded inside the system as has been proposed by traditional models (symbolic models) of the mind.

In chapter 5, Latimer and Stevens ask precisely whether pattern recognition processes embodied in artificial networks have psychological reality. They test the hypothesis that the recognition of geometric forms is mediated by the extraction and differential weighting of local features using eye movements and fixations in visual forms as reliable and valid indices of recognition processes and simple artificial networks to model them. The main idea is that artificial neural networks that learn to recognize visual forms employ feature extraction and feature weighting processes that may mediate human recognition. The main question addressed in their research is whether or not human perceivers assign more weight to the more discriminating features of geometric forms when they learn to distinguish a standard geometric form from a set of distractors. To test this hypothesis, Latimer and Stevens trained a single-layer artificial network to distinguish a standard form from a set of comparison forms and looked up its feature-weighting comparing it to the performance of human participants trained to do the same task. In conclusion, connectionist models of form perception of the type tested here as well, as more complex neural networks (Hummel & Biederman, 1992), have received some support and seem to conform to empirical results. Well-trained participants and neural networks of the form tested by Latimer and Stevens seem to assign weight to the same informative regions of the geometrical forms.

Mental Representation of Visual Objects, Words, and Pictures

During the last decade, priming studies have flourished in cognitive psychology. Priming refers to a facilitation in accuracy and/or reaction time as a consequence of a previous encounter with the same material. A very interesting phenomenon is that priming occurred without conscious knowledge of previous experience with the items. Operatively, a better performance with the old items (or targets, those previously studied) in comparison with the new items is the signal that shows that priming has occurred. Furthermore, important behavioral dissociations have been found between implicit memory or priming (indirect memory tasks) and explicit memory tasks (direct memory tasks). Implicit memory refers to the unintentional retrieval of previous experiences measured by a facilitation in performance with previously presented stimuli compared to new ones. On the contrary, explicit memory supposes the conscious recollection of recent experience, usually measured by standard memory tests of recognition and recall (for recent reviews, see Richardson-Klavhen & Bjork, 1988; Schacter, 1987; Tulving & Schacter, 1990).

The theoretical importance of the investigation in priming and interference rely in its significance in trying to unite extensive areas of cognition as a way to overcome the title of "dismembering" science that cognitive psychology has suffered for many years (G. A. Miller, 1986). In this sense, priming studies on words and pictures can be interpreted as providing a way to connect important areas in the psychology of language and perception with the field of mental representation of words and pictorial information. At the same time, studies on perceptual priming and mental representation of novel objects and patterns are seeking to establish a wide bridge between areas of perception, mental representation, and memory.

Early studies on priming used verbal materials as stimuli (words, non-words, pair-associated). However, more recently researchers' interest has turned to the investigation of priming and dissociations between implicit and explicit memory using nonverbal visual objects and patterns. For reviews on nonverbal priming see Schacter, Delaney, and Merikle (1990), and on priming and interference effects in picture naming see Glaser (1992).

A large number of studies in the field have used pictures, photographs, and line drawings representing familial objects and its corresponding words as a way to study picture/word transfer (see Glaser, 1992; Schacter et al., 1990). Since the first study reported by Winnick & Daniel (1970), the usual pattern of results has pointed to an important dissociation between direct and indirect tests of memory: Priming on word identification was larger after studying a word than a picture, but free recall (a direct or explicit memory test) was higher after studying a picture than a word. An important feature that emerges from this and other studies (e.g., Durso & Johnson, 1979; Kirsner, Milech, & Stumpfel, 1986; Scarborough, Gerard, & Cortese, 1979; Weldon & Roediger, 1987) is that there is smaller and sometimes no priming at all from intermodal presentation (word–picture or picture–word transfer) than from intramodal presentation (word–word or picture–picture). These results are consistent with the interpretation that the physical components of the stimuli are the important features in priming and are interpreted as a sign of the closeness between priming and perception (but see Brown, Neblett, Jones, & Mitchell, 1991).

Mayor and González-Marqués, in chapter 7, study facilitatory and interference effects in picture naming and semantic categorization of picture–picture, word–word, picture–word, and word–picture stimuli under different SOAs conditions. They propose and test a model for word and picture processing that consists of three main distinguishable yet interconnected central systems: a linguistic processor containing a surface linguistic processor for graphemic–phonemic codification and a lexicon processor for lexical codification; an iconic, pictorial system containing a surface iconic processor in charge of processing structural and formal information about pictorial stimuli; and an amodal linguistic system of semantic processing.

A consistent pattern of priming effects and important dissociations between implicit and explicit memory tests on pictures, photographs, and line drawings of familiar objects using an object-naming task have also been reported by Biederman and his associates (e.g., Biederman & Cooper, 1991, 1992) among others (e.g., Mayor & González-Marqués, chapter 7, this volume; Mitchell & Brown, 1988; Snodgrass & Feenan, 1989; Warren & Morton, 1982). But see Schacter, Delaney, and Merikle (1990) for a discussion on the theoretical implications of using familiar materials with preexisting representations for interpreting the nature of the mental representations that support priming.

Important theoretical questions arise concerning the underlying structure of the memory system: Is there just a unique memory system or are there several memory systems? Do different types of representations mediate priming and recognition? Which stimulus dimensions are preserved in those mental representations? Can priming be explained by the activation of previously existing representations? In chapter 8, Cooper answers explicitly these and other important questions, presenting the results obtained in her ongoing collaborative research program with Schacter and associates on object representation and types of memory for novel three-dimensional objects. Cooper reports consistent priming effects and important behavioral dissociations between implicit and explicit memory tasks for three-dimensional novel objects (e.g., Cooper, Schacter, Ballesteros, & Moore, 1992; Schacter, Cooper, & Delaney, 1990). In short, Schacter, Cooper, and Delaney (1990) did find significant and important dissociations between implicit and explicit memory measures. Priming was observed following encoding conditions that supposably required the construction of the three-dimensional structure of the studied objects (right/left judgments). However, under encoding conditions that enhanced the local components of the objects (counting the number of vertical and horizontal lines) or their semantic interpretation (thinking of a familiar objects that each object reminded them of) priming was not found. Nevertheless, recognition memory was significantly enhanced after elaborative or semantic encoding. In these and other experiments priming was never found for impossible objects. They interpreted this result as indicative of the impossibility of constructing a mental three-dimensional structure for impossible objects. This pattern of results led Schacter and associates (Cooper et al., 1992; Schacter et al., 1990;) to propose that priming is supported by the construction of a three-dimensional representation of the visual object, whereas explicit memory is enhanced under conditions that require the semantic codification of the individual objects.

In another series of experiments, Cooper et al., 1992 explored the nature of the proposed representational systems that support implicit and explicit memory for unfamiliar three-dimensional objects. The idea behind the experiments is that if only structural information concerning relations among components of the objects is preserved in the structural description system that by hypothesis supports the observed priming, the experimental manipulation of aspects of visual information irrelevant to the encoding of such relations should preserve priming effects. In those experiments the effects of changing the size and overall reflection of the objects from study to test were assessed by implicit and explicit memory tests (see Cooper, chapter 8, this volume). The results showed that priming was intact despite the physical transformations of size and reflection. In contrast, recognition was significantly impaired by these transformations. Those results led Cooper et al. (1992) to propose that the structural description system constructs some abstract representation of the objects in which certain properties such as size and reflection are not represented, whereas a different episodic system encodes these transformations in memory.

Perceptual Priming of Two-Dimensional Patterns.   Some recent studies have used two-dimensional novel dot or line patterns for studying priming effects and memory dissociations in neuropsychological patients (Gabrieli,

Milberg, Keane, & Corkin, 1990) as well as in normal adults (Musen, 1991; Musen & Treisman, 1990). In these studies priming was assessed by an implicit drawing task in which respondents had to draw each briefly presented pattern. Priming, as well as important dissociations between implicit and explicit memory tests, were found. But, as Musen and Treisman (1990) pointed out, factors such as rapid decay and output interference could have differential influences in old and new patterns.

In a study conducted by Ballesteros and Cooper at Columbia University, two-dimensional symmetric and asymmetric novel line patterns were used. In this study, Ballesteros and Cooper (1992) showed priming for novel two-dimensional line patterns using a perceptual task instead of a drawing task as a measure of implicit memory in an attempt to avoid motor implications. Participants started with a study phase in which 12 symmetric (six exhibiting vertical symmetry and six oblique symmetry) and 12 asymmetric patterns were studied for 5 seconds under the right–left structural encoding condition devised by Schacter Cooper, and Delaney (1990). Different groups of respondents participated in the perceptual and in the recognition task. In these two tasks, 12 symmetric and 12 asymmetric new patterns were added to the 24 previously presented at the encoding phase. In the case of the implicit memory task the new patterns were used to calculate the baseline and, in the explicit memory task, to perform the surprise "old–new" recognition discrimination.

Respondents participating in the perceptual task were asked to discriminate as to whether the pattern briefly presented on the computer monitor, followed by a mask, was symmetric or asymmetric as quickly and accurately as possible. The results of this experiment for respondents participating in the implicit memory task showed priming for novel two-dimensional patterns. Facilitation of symmetrical–asymmetrical judgements of studied over nonstudied patterns was obtained for both symmetric and asymmetric patterns, with the priming effect being larger for symmetric patterns.

As half of the symmetric patterns had vertical symmetry and half oblique symmetry, we were able to analyze data corresponding to symmetrical patterns only, collapsing over vertical and oblique symmetry. Substantial priming was shown by patterns with oblique symmetry. Although performance on studied patterns was fairly similar for both types of symmetry, performance at baseline (nonstudied patterns) was much higher for patterns with vertical symmetry than for those with oblique symmetry. We interpreted this result as a confirmation of the "easy-to-perceive account" of patterns exhibiting a vertical axis of symmetry compared to patterns exhibiting an oblique axis of symmetry. Explicit recognition, which required the identification of patterns as "old" or "new" under identical encoding conditions, showed higher levels of recognition for symmetrical than for asymmetrical patterns.

A new line of research conducted at Ballesteros' laboratory is seeking to generalize present findings to another perceptual system: the haptic system (Ballesteros, 1991; Ballesteros, in press; Ballesteros & Reales, 1992). Priming effects of nonverbal stimuli and dissociations between implicit and explicit memory tests have been mostly studied using visually presented objects and patterns. I would like to emphasize the importance of extending current results to the haptic system, which is much less investigated. Haptic studies, as well as intermodal (visual and haptic) studies, would advance theorizing in the area of the mental representation of objects perceived visually and haptically, and would contribute to a better understanding of the unity and/or diversity of the perceptual systems and the underlying representational mechanisms as well.

One important goal of this research is to study the effects of different coding strategies on haptic performance in implicit and explicit memory tasks as a way to further characterize the properties and special characteristics of active tactual perception. A second goal of this research is to gather further information about the different tactual exploratory procedures used during coding, perceptual, and recognition tasks. The third main goal is to obtain further information on the functional organization that supports the haptic representational systems.

Which mechanisms support priming? Is there a single memory system carrying different psychological processes or are there multiple-memory systems, each one in charge of dealing with the codification of different types of information? Questions such as these are of extreme theoretical importance in order to explain the underlying structures and processes that support object representation and memory. Three main theoretical accounts have tried to explain the behavioral and neurological dissociations reported in implicit–explicit memory literature. One of the oldest theories of visual priming was proposed by Warren and Morton (1982). This theory, however, has been largely disconfirmed by behavioral data obtained from research with novel, unfamiliar objects and patterns. According to Warren and Morton, priming of familiar objects is due to the temporary activation of preexisting representations of objects. As discussed earlier, the well-documented finding, that novel objects for which previous representations do not exist in memory produce a significant and consistent priming, seems to disconfirm this theoretical interpretation (e.g., Ballesteros & Cooper, 1992; Cooper et al., 1992; Kroll & Potter, 1984; Musen, 1991; Musen & Treisman, 1990, Schacter et al., 1990).

Two other general groups of theories have been proposed to account for much of the results in the area: The multiple, separable memory systems approach advocated by Schacter Cooper, Delaney (1990), Cooper et al., (1992), Squire and McKee (1992), Tulving and Schacter (1990) and the single memory system account based on the transfer-appropriate processing mechanism proposed by Roediger and associates (Roediger & Blaxton, 1987; Roediger & Challis, 1992; Roediger, Weldon, & Challis, 1989; Srinivas & Roediger, 1990). The basic assumptions underlying this approach are: (a) memory tests are better performed when operations required at test are the same as the operations carried out during the learning phase, and (b) explicit memory tests are conceptually driven whereas implicit memory tests are data driven.

As Cooper points out, experimental results reported by Schacter, Cooper, and associates seem to be more compatible with the multiple-system explanation discussed above. On the other hand, a recent paper by Brown, Neblett, Jones, and Mitchell (1991) reported a series of studies using a picture and word-naming task. This study evaluated the effect of stimulus format (word vs. picture) and type of response (overt vs. covert) on repetition or direct priming. According to the transfer-appropriate explanation, repetition priming on picture naming should be higher when using pictures as primes than words. At the same time, they predicted no differences between overt and covert responses because of the same mental process underlying both modes of response (name retrieval). Results were in disagreement with this theoretical interpretation. Brown et al. concluded that their results are more in agreement with a multiple-memory system than with the transfer-appropriate processing model. See also Mayor and González-Marqués (chapter 7, this volume) for a multiple system proposal.

An important theoretical issue in visual cognition relates to whether or not it is necessary to infer any mental representational concept and, more precisely, whether mental representations are needed in object perception. Cooper and Hochberg, chapter 9, this volume, defend the necessity of postulating at a conceptual level a "mentally represented object" as a way to study visual cognition. They further ask about which properties of the physical world are internalized in these mental representations. A good way to start, they say, could be to think that objects represented in the mind retain the properties of physical objects existing in the real world. That is, what human perceivers internalize is a mental analog of a physical structure (Ballesteros, 1993). This is true in many cases. Cooper and Hochberg, however, present several examples of empirical evidence that does not reflect a precise correspondence between properties of perceived representations of objects and properties of these objects in the physical world. Their conclusion is that for the advance in visual cognition it is important to carefully study precisely those cases in which the analogy between mental representations of objects and physical objects cannot be applied.

Perceptual Theories and Illusory Perception

The last two chapters that compose Part IV by Day and Hochberg provide two current approaches to perceptual theory. However, whereas Day's chapter tries to unite the direct and empirical traditions, Hochberg clearly advocates a more cognitive approach.

Illusions of length, size, and shape are a pervasive and well-known phenomenon not only in visual perception (Ames, 1951; Day & Duffy, 1988; Day, Watson, & Jolly, 1986; Gregory & Harris, 1974, 1975) but in haptic perception as well (Avery & Day, 1969; Day, 1990; Révész, 1950; Rudel & Teuber 1963). For a review, see Coren and Girgus (1978).

The existence of illusory perception is a serious challenge for those psychological theories that try to explain perception as a direct information "pickup." Direct-perception theorists argue that in normal viewing conditions the optic array conveys sufficient information so as to provide a moving viewer with enough information to perceive the world adequately (Gibson, 1979). From this perspective, illusions occur only in impoverished viewing conditions and artificial situations, such as line-drawing stimuli, and not in free viewing of normal three-dimensional objects and events (Gibson, 1950, 1966, 1979; Michaels & Carello, 1981). But the fact is that robust, very frequent, and systematic illusions are reported in the literature, not only under those two-dimensional impoverished conditions, but also with solid three-dimensional objects under ordinary viewing conditions, as have recently shown DeLucia and Hochberg (1991) among others. Those errors present a serious challenge for direct perception theories and also for empiricist theories, which maintain that perception is the result of perceptual learning of the regularities in the world (Hochberg, 1988). If this is so, why does such experience make us perceive in an erroneous way?

Day (chapter 10, this volume) tries to bring together the two most important traditions in perceptual theory, the direct and the empirical as a way to explain both veridical and illusory perception. He states that under conditions of normal perception, multiple features of the stimulus array (cues) are correlated with one property of the physical world. Under normal perception conditions those correlates undergo a process of integration, providing the perceiver with a veridical representation. In these circumstances, perceptual representations are veridical and correspond closely to the physical properties of the stimuli. However, when manipulations of those stimulus correlates of physical properties of objects and events are produced, illusions appear.

Hochberg, in the last chapter of this volume, takes a more cognitive approach and proposes the concept of mental structures as standing between sensory information and visual cognition. He describes the classical theory outlined by Helmholtz a century ago as the theoretical position advocated by most of the current perception researchers. This line of thinking makes use of concepts such as mental representations, mental operations, and cognitive processes for explaining perceptual phenomena.

Hochberg discards the theories based on attributes of retinal image as theories of visual perception. Simply, these theories deal with proximal properties, whereas theories of visual cognition deal with distal properties of the stimulus and, as Hochberg shows, there is not a perfect correspondence between these two classes of properties. However, we have learned to match these two sets of properties. According to Hochberg, two important problems arise when we try to use mental structures as the explanation from sense to experience. The first is to specify the characteristics of these structures so that they can be tested in the laboratory; the second is to explain how these mental structures combine with other cognitive processes such as thinking or remembering. He argues that once these problems are solved, the constructs of mental structures should be replaced by specific theories.

ACKNOWLEDGMENTS

The research reported in this chapter by S. Ballesteros was supported by a 1989 Spanish DGICYT grant to conduct research in a foreign country and a Sabbatical Leave Grant from the UNED (1990-1991). The research on haptics is currently supported by Grant PB90-0003 from the DGICYT.

REFERENCES

Allport, A. D. (1989). Visual attention. In M. I. Posner (Ed.), *Foundations of cognitive science* (pp. 631–682). Cambridge, MA: MIT Press.

Ames, A. (1951). Visual perception and the rotating trapezoidal window. *Psychological Monographs Series, 65.*

Amsel, A. (1989). *Behaviorism, neobehaviorism, and cognitivism in learning theory.* Hillsdale, NJ: Lawrence Erlbaum Associates.

Avery, G. C., & Day, R. H. (1969). The basis of the horizontal vertical illusion. *Journal of Experimental Psychology, 81,* 376-380.

Ballesteros, S. (1991, November). *Haptic perception and forms of memory for three-dimensional objects and two-dimensional patterns: A project.* Paper presented at the annual meeting of the Tactile Research Group, San Francisco, CA.

Ballesteros, S. (1992). La representación del conocimiento en los sistemas conexionistas (The representation of knowledge in connectionist systems). *Psicothema, 2,* 343-354.

Ballesteros,S. (in press). La percepción háptica de objetos y patrones realzados [Haptic perception of objects and two-dimensional patterns: A revision]. *Psicothema, 5* (2).

Ballesteros, S. (1993). Representaciones analógicas en percepción y memoria: Imágenes, transformaciones mentales y representaciones estructurales [Anological representations in perception and memory: Imagery, mental transformations and structural representations]. *Psicothema, 5* (1), 7-19.

Ballesteros, S., & Cooper, L. A. (1992, July). *Perceptual priming for two-dimensional patterns following visual presentation.* Paper presented at the 25th International Congress of Psychology, Brussels, Belgium.

Ballesteros, S., & Reales, J. M. (1992, November). *The perception of symmetric and asymmetric patterns by touch and vision.* Paper presented at the 33rd Annual Meeting of the Psychonomic Society, St. Louis, MO.

Bechtel, W. (1988). *Philosophy of mind. An overview for cognitive science.* Hillsdale, NJ: Lawrence Erlbaum Associates.

Biederman, I., & Cooper, E. E. (1991). Priming contour-deleted images: Evidence for intermediate representations in visual object recognition. *Cognitive Psychology, 23,* 393–419.

Biederman, I., & Cooper, E. E. (1992). Size invariance in visual object priming. *Journal of Experimental Psychology: Human Perception and Performance, 18,* 121–133.

Boer, L. C., & Keuss, P. J. C. (1982). Global precedence as a posperceptual effect: An analysis of speed-accuracy trade-off functions. *Perception & Psychophysics, 31,* 358–366.

Bregman, A. S. (1990). *Auditory scene analysis: The perceptual organization of sound.* Cambridge, MA: MIT Press.

Broadbent, D. E. (1958). *Perception and communication.* London: Pergamon.

Broadbent, D. E. (1991). Early selection, late selection, and the partitioning of structure. In G. R. Lockhead & J. R. Pomerantz (Eds.), *The perception of structure* (pp. 169–181). Washington, DC: American Psychological Association.

Brown, A. S., Neblett, D. R., Jones, T. C., & Mitchell, D. B. (1991). Transfer of processing in repetition priming: Some inappropriate findings. *Journal of Experimental Psychology: Learning, Memory, and Cognition, 17,* 514–525.

Buser, P., & Imbert, M. (1992). *Audition.* Cambridge, MA: MIT Press.

Cooper, L. A., Schacter, D. L., Ballesteros, S., & Moore, C. (1992). Priming and recognition of transformed three-dimensional objects: Effects of size and reflection. *Journal of Experimental Psychology: Learning, Memory, and Cognition, 18,* 43–57.

Coren, S. C., & Girgus, G. (1978). *Seeing is deceiving: The psychology of visual illusions.* Hillsdale, NJ: Lawrence Erlbaum Associates.

Cowey, A., & Gross, C. G. (1970). Effects of foveal prestriate and inferotemporal lesions on visual discrimination by rhesus monkeys. *Experimental Brain Research, 11,* 128–144.

Day, R. H. (1990). The Bourdon illusion in the haptic space. *Perception & Psychophysics, 47,* 400–404.

Day, R. H., & Duffy, F. M. (1988). Illusions of time and extent when the Muller-Lyer figure moves in an aperture. *Perception & Psychophysics, 44,* 205–210.

Day, R. H., Watson, W. L., & Jolly, W. J. (1986). The Poggendorff displacement effect with only three dots. *Perception & Psychophysics, 39,* 351–354.

DeLucia, P. R., & Hochberg, J. (1991). Geometrical illusions in solid objects under ordinary viewing conditions. *Perception & Psychophysics, 50,* 547–554.

Desimone, R., Albright, T. D., Gross, C. G., & Bruce, C. (1984). Stimulus selective properties of inferior temporal neurons in the macaque. *Journal of Neuroscience, 4,* 2051–2062.

Desimone, R., & Ungerleider, L. G. (1986). Multiple visual areas in the caudal superior temporal sulcus of the macaque. *Journal of Comparative Neurology, 248,* 164–189.

Dretske, F. (1990). Seeing, believing, and knowing. In D. N. Osherson, S. M. Kosslyn, & J. M. Hollerbach (Eds.), *Visual cognition and action: An Invitation to cognitive science* (Vol. 2., pp. 129–148). Cambridge: MA: MIT Press.

Durso F. T., & Johnson, M. K. (1979). Facilitation in naming and categorizing repeated pictures and words. *Journal of Experimental Psychology: Human Learning and Memory, 5,* 449–459.

Ellis, A. W., & Young, A. W. (1988). *Human cognitive neuropsychology.* Hillsdale, NJ: Lawrence Erlbaum Associates.

Farah, M. J. (1990). *Visual agnosia. Disorders of object recognition and what they tell us about normal vision* Cambridge, MA: MIT Press.

Gabrieli, J. D. E., Milberg, E., Keane, M. M., & Corkin, S. (1990). Intact priming of patterns despite impaired memory. *Neuropsychologia, 8,* 417–428.

Garner, W. R. (1983). Asymmetric interactions of stimulus dimensions in perceptual information processing. In T. J. Tighe & B. E. Shepp (Eds.), *Perception, cognition, and development: Interactional analysis* (pp. 1–37). Hillsdale, NJ: Lawrence Erlbaum Associates.

Gibson, J. J. (1950). *The perception of the visual world*. Boston: Houghton Mifflin.

Gibson, J. J. (1966). *The senses considered as perceptual systems*. Boston: Houghton Mifflin.

Gibson, J. J. (1979). *An ecological approach to visual perception*. Boston: Houghton Mifflin.

Glaser, W. R. (1992). Picture naming. *Cognition, 42*, 61–105.

Gregory, R. L. (1978). Illusions and hallucinations. In E. C. Carterette & M. P. Friedman (Eds.), *Handbook of perception: Vol. IX. Perceptual processing* (pp. 337–357). New York: Academic Press.

Gregory, R. L., & Harris, J. P. (1974). Illusory contours and stereo depth. *Perception & Psychophysics, 15* 411–416.

Gregory, R. L., & Harris, J. P. (1975). Illusion destruction by appropriate scaling. *Perception, 4*, 203–220.

Gross, C. G. (1978). Inferior temporal lesions do not impair discrimination of rotated patterns in monkeys. *Journal of Physiological Psychology, 92*, 1095–1109.

Hebb, D. O. (1949). *The organization of behavior: A neuropsychological theory*. New York: Wiley.

Heller, M. A., & Schiff, W. (Eds.). (1991). *The psychology of touch*. Hillsdale, NJ: Lawrence Erlbaum Associates.

Hochberg, J. (1988). Visual Perception. In K. C. Atkinson, R. J. Hernstein, G., Lindzay, & R. D. Luce (Eds.), *Steven's handbook of experimental psychology* (pp. 195–275). New York: Wiley.

Hummel, J. E., & Biederman, I. (1992). Dynamic binding in a neural network for shape recognition. *Psychological Review, 99*, 480–517.

Humphreys, G. W., & Riddoch, J. (1984). Routes to object constancy: Implications from neurological impairments of object constancy. *Quarterly Journal of Experimental Psychology, 36A*, 385–415.

Johnston, W. A., & Dark, V. J. (1986). Selective attention. *Annual Review of Psychology, 37*, 43–75.

Kahneman, D., & Treisman, A. M. (1984). Changing views of attention and automaticity. In. R. Parasuraman & D. R. Davies (Eds.), *Varieties of attention* (pp. 29–61). New York: Academic Press.

Katz, D. (1989). *The world of touch* (L. E. Krueger, Ed. and Trans.). Hillsdale, NJ: Lawrence Erlbaum Associates. (Original work published 1925)

Kirsner, K., Milech, D., & Stumpfel, V. (1986). Word and picture identification: Is representational parsimony possible? *Memory and Cognition, 14*, 398–408.

Klatzky, R. L., Lederman, S. J., & Metzger, V. A. (1985). Identifying objects by touch: An "expert system." *Perception & Psychophysics, 37*(4), 299–302.

Kroll, J. F., & Potter, M. C. (1984). Recognizing words, pictures, and concepts: A comparison of lexical, object, and reality decisions. *Journal of Verbal Learning and Verbal Behavior, 23*, 39–66.

Lamb, M. R., & Robertson, L. C. (1988). The processing of hierarchical stimuli: Effects of retinal locus, locational uncertainty, and stimulus identity. *Perception & Psychophysics, 44*, 172–181.

Lamb, M. R., & Robertson, L. C. (1989). Do response time advantage and interference reflect the order of processing of global and local level information?. *Perception & Psychophysics, 46*, 254–258.

Lamb, M. R., Robertson, L. C., & Knight, R. T. (1989). Attention and interference in the processing of global and local information: Effects of unilateral temporal-parietal junction lesions. *Neuropsychologia, 7*, 471–483.

Lamb, M. R., Robertson, L. C., & Knight, R. T. (1990). Component mechanisms underlying the processing of hierarchically organized patterns: Inferences from patients with unilateral cortical lesions. *Journal of Experimental Psychology: Learning, Memory, and Cognition, 16*, 471–483.

Loomis, J. M., & Lederman, S. J. (1986). Tactual perception. In K. Boff, L. Kaufman, & J. Thomas (Eds.), *Handbook of perception and human performance* (Vol. 2, pp. 31–41). New York: Wiley.

McCulloch, W. S., & Pitts, W. (1943). A logical calculus of the ideas immanent in neural nets. *Bulletin of Mathematical Biophysics, 5,* 115–137.

Michaels, C., & Carello, C. (1981). *Direct perception.* Englewood Cliffs, NJ: Prentice-Hall.

Millar, S. (1978). Aspects of memory for information from touch and movement. In G. E. Gordon (Ed.), *Active touch* (pp. 215–227). Oxford: Pergamon Press.

Miller, G. A. (1986). Dismembering cognition. In S. H. Hulse, & B. F. Green (Eds.), *One hundred years of psychological research in America: G. Stanley Hall and the Johns Hopkins tradition* (pp. 277–298). Baltimore: The Johns Hopkins University Press.

Miller, J. (1981). Global precedence in attention and decision. *Journal of Experimental Psychology: Human Perception and Performance, 7,* 1161–1174.

Mitchell, D. B., & Brown, A. S. (1988). Persistent repetition priming in picture naming and its dissociation from recognition memory. *Journal of Experimental Psychology: Learning, Memory, and Cognition, 14,* 213–222.

Musen, G. (1991). Effects of verbal labelling and exposure duration on implicit memory for visual patterns. *Journal of Experimental Psychology: Learning, Memory, and Cognition, 17,* 954–962.

Musen, G., & Squirre, L. R. (1992). Nonverbal priming in amnesia. *Memory & Cognition, 20,* 441–448.

Musen, G., & Treisman, A. (1990). Implicit and explicit memory for visual patterns. *Journal of Experimental Psychology: Learning, Memory, and Cognition, 16,* 127–137.

Nadel, L., Cooper, L. A., Culicover, P., & Harnish, R. M. (Eds.). (1989). *Neural connections, mental computations.* Cambridge, MA: MIT Press.

Navon, D. (1977). Forest before trees: The precedence of global features in visual perception. *Cognitive Psychology, 9,* 353–383.

Navon, D. (1991). Testing a queue hypothesis for the processing of global and local information. *Journal of Experimental Psychology: General, 120,* 173–189.

Navon, D., & Norman, D. A. (1983). Does global precedence really depend on visual angle? *Journal of Experimental Psychology: Human Perception and Performance, 9,* 955–965.

Paquet, L. (1992). Global and local processing in nonattended objects: A failure to induce local processing dominance. *Journal of Experimental Psychology: Human Perception and Performance, 18,* 512–529.

Paquet, L., & Merikle, P. M. (1988). Global precedence in attended and nonattended objects. *Journal of Experimental Psychology: Human Perception and Performance, 14,* 89–100.

Plaut, D. C., & Farah, M. J. (1990). Visual object recognition: Interpreting neuropsychological data within a computational framework. *Journal of Cognitive Neuroscience, 2,* 320–343.

Pomerantz, J. R. (1983). Global and local precedence: Selective attention in form and motion perception. *Journal of Experimental Psychology: General, 112,* 516–540.

Révész, G. (1950). *Psychology and art of the blind* (H. A. Wolff, Trans.). London: Longmans.

Richardson-Klavhen, A., & Bjork, R. A. (1988). Measures of memory. *Annual Review of Psychology, 36,* 475–543.

Rock, I. (1983). *The logic of perception.* Cambridge MA: MIT Press.

Rock, I., & Gutman, D. (1981). The effect of inattention on form perception. *Journal of Experimental Psychology: Human Perception and Performance, 7,* 275–285.

Roediger, H. L. III, & Blaxton, T. A. (1987). Retrieval modes produce dissociations in memory for surface information. In D. Gorfein & R. R. Hofman (Eds.), *Memory and cognitive processes: The Ebbinghaus Centennial Conference* (pp. 349–379). Hillsdale, NJ: Lawrence Erlbaum Associates.

Roediger, H. L., & Challis, B. H. (1992). Effects of exact repetition on free recall and primed word-fragment completion. *Journal of Experimental Psychology: Learning, Memory, and Cognition, 18,* 3-14.

Roediger, H. L. III, Weldon, M. S., & Challis, B. H. (1989). Explaining dissociations between implicit and explicit measures of retention: A processing account. In H. L. Roediger & F. I. M. Craik (Eds.), *Varieties of memory and consciousness. Essays in honour of Endel Tulving* (pp. 3-41). Hillsdale, NJ: Lawrence Erlbaum Associates.

Rosenblatt, F. (1962). *Principles of neurodynamics.* New York: Sparten.

Rudel, R. G., & Teuber, H. -L. (1963). Decrement of visual and haptic Müller-Lyer illusion on repeated trials: A study of crossmodal transfer. *Quarterly Journal of Experimental Psychology, 15,* 125-131.

Rumelhart, D. E. (1989). The architecture of mind: a connectionist approach. In M. I. Posner (Ed.), *Foundations of cognitive science* (pp. 133-159). Cambridge, MA: MIT Press.

Rumelhart, D. E., McClelland, J. L., and the PDP Research Group (1986). *Parallel distributed processing: Explorations in the microstructure of cognition.* (Vols. 1 & 2) Cambridge, MA: MIT Press.

Scarborough, D. L., Gerard, L., & Cortese, C. (1979). Accessing lexical memory: The transfer of word repetition effects across task and modality. *Memory and Cognition, 7,* 3-12.

Schacter, D. L. (1987). Implicit memory: History and current status. *Journal of Experimental Psychology: Learning, Memory, and Cognition, 13,* 501-518.

Schacter, D. L., Cooper, L. A., & Delaney, S. (1990). Implicit memory for unfamiliar objects depends on access to structural descriptions. *Journal of Experimental Psychology: General, 119,* 5-24.

Schacter, D. L., Delaney, S., & Merikle, E. P. (1990). Priming of nonverbal information and the nature of implicit memory. In G. H. Bower (Ed.), *The psychology of learning and motivation,* (Vol. 26, pp. 83-123). New York: Academic Press.

Shiffrin, R. M. (1988). Attention. In K. C. Atkinson, R. J. Hernstein, G. Lindzay, & R. Duncan Luce (Eds.), *Steven's handbook of experimental psychology: Vol. 2. Learning and cognition* (pp. 739-811). New York: Wiley.

Shimamura, A. P., & Squire, L. R. (1987). A neuropsychological study of fact memory and source amnesia. *Journal of Experimental Psychology: Learning, Memory, and Cognition, 13,* 464-473.

Snodgrass, J. C., & Feenan, K. (1989). Priming effects in Picture fragment completion: Support for the perceptual closure hypothesis. *Journal of Experimental Psychology: General, 119,* 276-296.

Squire, L. R., & McKee, R. (1992). Influence of prior events on cognitive judgments in amnesia. *Journal of Experimental Psychology: Learning, Memory, and Cognition, 18,* 106-115.

Srinivas, K., & Roediger, H. L. (1990). Testing the nature of two implicit memory tests: Category association and anagram solution. *Journal of Memory and Language, 29,* 389-412.

Titchener, E. (1909). *Experimental psychology of thought processes.* New York: MacMillan.

Tulving, E., & Schacter, D. L. (1990). Priming and human memory systems. *Science, 247,* 301-306.

Ulman, S. (1980). Against direct perception. *The Behavioral and Brain Sciences, 3,* 373-415.

Warren, C., & Morton, J. (1982). The effects of priming in picture recognition. *British Journal of Psychology, 73,* 117-129.

Weldon, M. S., & Roediger H. L. (1987). Altering retrieval demands reverses the picture superiority effect. *Memory & Cognition, 15,* 269-280.

Winnick, W. A., & Daniel, S. A. (1970). Two kinds of response priming in tachistoscopic recognition. *Journal of Experimental Psychology, 84,* 74-81.

ATTENTION AND VISUAL PERCEPTION

2 Attention and Perceptual Organization

Irvin Rock
University of California at Berkeley

Arien Mack
New School for Social Research, New York

Some entities *must* be present in the visual field prior to the deployment of attention to which we can attend or not as the case may be. Otherwise expressed, some kind of organization must be presumed to occur at a very early stage of processing, a belief that goes back to Gestalt psychology. Max Wertheimer (1923) provided us with principles of grouping, and it has been implicitly assumed or explicitly maintained ever since that perceptual organization is based on the preattentive operation of these principles.

However, the following thought experiment would seem to challenge this conclusion. Imagine an array in which the *un*attended ground of an attended figure is a Gestalt grouping pattern, as in Fig. 2.1. The participant is to attend to the red outline shape. The green pattern ought to be organized into columns by virtue of the law of proximity. It *is* for us as we look at it attentively. However, in an experiment with a similar display and procedure, in which two overlapping novel figures of differing colors are presented, as shown in Fig. 2.2, and the subject attends to one or the other, we found that the unattended figure was not recognized when subsequently shown. (See Rock & Gutman, 1981, and a replication by Butler & McKelvie, 1985.) In other words, if the organization into columns can be thought of as rather like shape perception, we ought to predict that it will not be perceived without attention. So, we have a conflict here between logic and intuition.

This issue then is the basis of our current research. It has been a collaboration between us with the participation of several students. Mack concentrated on the question of whether or not Gestalt grouping and texture segregation occurs without attention; and Rock focused on the

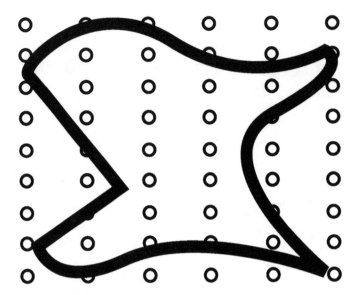

FIG. 2.1. Thought experiment. The participant attends to a colored figure. The grouping of the unattended background elements of a different color into columns may not be achieved.

question of what *is* and what is *not* given preattentively should it prove to be the case that grouping as described by Gestalt laws is not given preattentively.

A NEW METHOD

But first we needed a new method. The paradigm on which much of contemporary thinking is based, concerning what is preattentive and what is not, consists of a search task in a display of multiple elements. If pop-out or texture segregation occurs as quickly with many elements as with few (Treisman, 1988), or if it is effortless in brief exposures (Julesz, 1981), then the assumption is that processing occurs in parallel. If processing is parallel as is generally assumed, it must be preattentive because focused attention is assumed to be serial. Although these assumptions are plausible, participants are obviously attending to the array in this paradigm and searching for an odd item or a quadrant or region. Thus the participant is both attending and intending something. Therefore, one might ask what would be perceived if the entire array were to be presented under conditions in which attention is directed to something else and there is no intention to search for anything, only to report about the "something else."

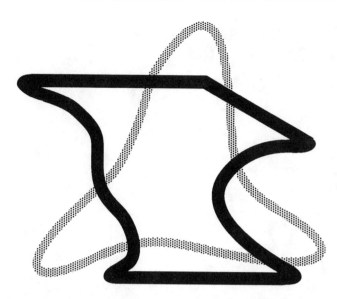

FIG. 2.2. When participants attend to one of the two colored figures the other overlapping figure of a different color is not recognized in a subsequent test. After Rock and Gutman (1981).

We devised the following method. While fixating on a central mark, the participant is shown a cross figure briefly (200 ms) and the task is to report which arm is longer. In some of our experiments, the presentation is followed by a pattern mask. After two or three such trials, something else unexpected is presented along with the cross figure. Immediately after reporting on line length, the participant is either questioned about what else if anything was seen, or given a recognition test. In Mack's experiments, the "something else" is a grouping pattern or texture array that fills the entire visible field around the cross figure. Figure 2.3 shows a texture segregation array in which the elements are vertical in one quadrant and horizontal in the other three. (Note that we are testing a tried-and-true type of element feature, namely orientation, and using the orientations for which we are known to be most sensitive, namely horizontal and vertical.)

To avoid a kind of shock effect on the critical trial when the background pattern appears along with the cross figure, we include a background pattern on the noncritical trials as well. However, it is a pattern that does not lead to any particular grouping or texture segregation, and the participant is not asked about it.

There is only the one critical, experimental trial because after being questioned about elements other than the cross on that trial, the participant is alerted to the possibility that something else besides the cross and random background pattern may be presented on subsequent trials, such as a texture

FIG. 2.3.   Texture segregation array used in an experiment in which the participant's task is to judge the relative lengths of the two arms of the cross.

segregation pattern. A repetition of a trial in which the grouping pattern appears is therefore more or less a *divided* attention trial. So following several more trials with only the cross and neutral background array shown, there is another critical trial in which a grouping or a texture pattern is shown. Following that, we introduce a control trial in which the cross figure is again shown along with a grouping pattern, but now the subject is told not to try to judge relative line length and only to report grouping or texture segregation in the surrounding pattern. Note then that the main data derive from only one pure inattention trial. To obtain meaningful data, we had to employ several hundred participants distributed over many experiments.

To summarize, the sequence of events in a typical experiment is shown in Fig. 2.4. The cross line-length task was explained to participants before testing began. Following the response to line length on the critical trials they were asked if they had seen anything else. If so and if necessary, the participants were asked whether one quadrant was different from the other three. When respondents reported correctly on critical trials that one

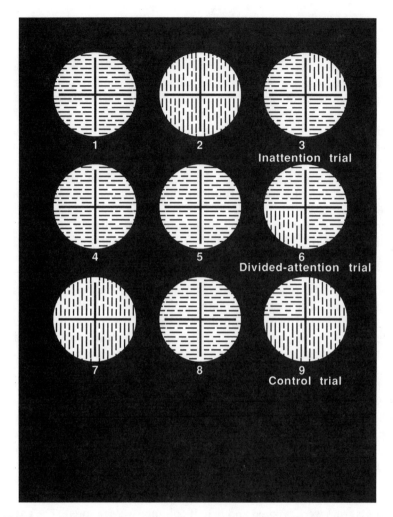

FIG. 2.4. Arrays presented on nine successive trials. On the third, sixth, and ninth trials the background is a texture segregation pattern in which one quadrant differs from the others. On all other trials the background is a uniform texture.

quadrant differed from the others, they were asked which one. We leave out further details about the procedure and stimuli because they are given elsewhere (Mack, Tang, Tuma, Kahn, & Rock, 1992).

TEXTURE SEGREGATION AND GROUPING

In one experiment on texture segregation, in which one quadrant was different, 20 respondents were run. In this experiment, a pattern mask was *not* used. As to the results for the line-judgment task, in this and most other experiments, respondents were correct about 75% of the time and improved over the first few trials so that on the critical inattention trial they performed even better. Thus it would seem that this task was sufficiently demanding to co-opt attention and to reduce the likelihood that participants might switch their attention on the critical trial. This is corroborated by finding that respondents don't perform any better on the cross task in a control experiment when no stimulus other than the cross is ever presented on any trial or in which a neutral background array appears on every trial, but there is no task associated with it. Hence, we can presume that they did not reallocate any attention from the cross to the critical stimulus, in this case the texture pattern, thus fulfilling the conditions of nonattention we hoped to establish.

Of the 20 respondents, on being questioned immediately after reporting on line length on the critical trial, 9 reported that one quadrant was different. However, given the two alternative responses, "same" or "different," this is no better than chance. Only 5 participants, or 25%, correctly identified the odd quadrant where chance *is* 25% given the four quadrants. On the divided attention trial, more respondents were able to identify the odd quadrant; and in the control trial with full attention to the texture pattern, 19 of 20 respondents reported that one quadrant was different and 18 of them got the quadrant right. This pattern of results was replicated in another experiment using slightly larger stimulus elements and an additional condition in which participants were asked to report the longer arm of the cross *as well as* the odd quadrant if there was one. Participants performed both tasks with no significant decrement in the number of correct line-length responses. Thus with attention, both texture segregation and the longer arm of the cross are perceived correctly, whereas without attention, texture segregation is not perceived.

In another experiment, we examined grouping by proximity or lightness similarity, using the patterns on the critical trials shown in Fig. 2.5. In half the trials rows were favored and in half columns were favored. The patterns used on the noncritical trials did not favor any particular grouping and are shown in Fig. 2.6. On all trials in this experiment, the stimulus presented *was* followed by a pattern mask.

We ran into a problem in this experiment that is worth comment. Only about half the respondents achieved grouping in the *control* trial. This led us to investigate the question of whether or not many of the Gestalt grouping figures used by Wertheimer and illustrated in textbooks on perception ever since, lead to a *spontaneous* impression of grouping, for example, into columns, rows, and so on. It looks like they do not and we are now investigating whether it is based on a failure to *perceive* grouping spontaneously without the experimenter asking about it, or a failure to

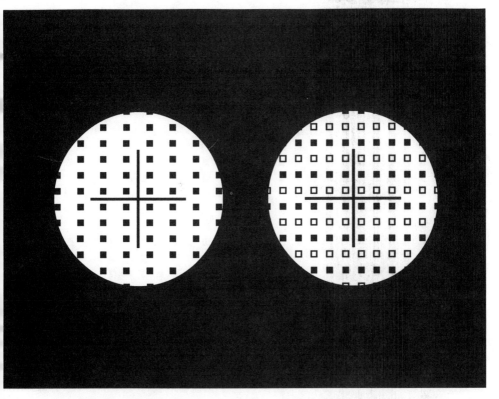

FIG. 2.5.   Grouping patterns used in an experiment. Left: proximity favors grouping into columns. Right: similarity favors grouping into rows.

report it spontaneously. Whatever the cause of this failure to report grouping, it led us to change the procedure in the experiment under discussion by first showing participants many different grouping patterns (including the critical test patterns that were to be used in the main experiment) until they correctly identified columns or rows in every figure. Following that, the experiment on grouping without attention was conducted with these participants.

In one experiment in which 10 participants were tested, on being questioned about what they had seen on the critical trial, only 1 correctly reported the grouping on the inattention trial whereas 7 did so in the control trial (chance in this experiment was not 50% because participants were not asked if they saw columns or rows, but only what they had seen in the background). For another 10 respondents, the control trial *preceded* the inattention trial. Despite the fact that this sequence could have had the effect of alerting respondents in the inattention trial to the possible presence of a pattern that would look like it contained rows or columns, only 2 of the

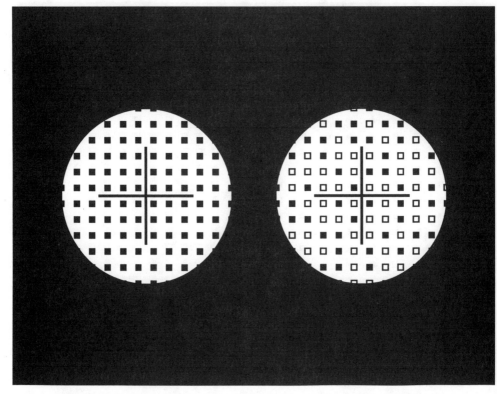

FIG. 2.6.   Uniform pattern (left) and random pattern (right) used on the noncritical trials of the experiment in which no particular grouping is favored.

10 correctly reported the grouping on this trial. All 10 respondents did so on the control trial. The pattern of results was similar for the proximity and similarity grouping arrays.

In a further experiment, the ratio of proximities between columns and rows or vice versa was increased to create a stronger grouping effect, as can be seen in Fig. 2.7. Nonetheless, grouping was never achieved in the inattention trial but was almost always achieved in the control trial. In still another experiment, the pattern mask was not used in an attempt to allow grouping a chance to manifest itself under conditions of inattention. This made no difference: Only 12% of the participants achieved grouping in the inattention trial, whereas 100% did so in the control trial. Finally, when a condition was added in which we instructed respondents to report both grouping and the longer arm of the cross, they were unable to perform both tasks adequately. The increased number of correct reports was offset by a significant decrease in the number of correct reports about the cross. This result suggests that

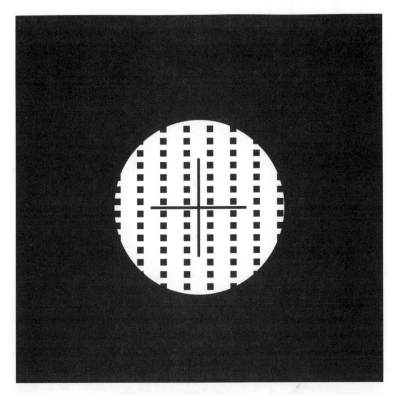

FIG. 2.7. Increased ratio of distances between elements in the vertical direction compared to distances in the horizontal direction, thereby creating a stronger pattern of grouping based on proximity.

grouping of the kind tested makes high attentional demands, higher than those required for texture segregation of the kind tested.

One further control experiment must be mentioned. Suppose we presented actual columns or rows instead of patterns that, via grouping, appeared as containing columns or rows. In other words, will black bars or alternating black and white bars such as in Fig.2.8 be perceived under our conditions of inattention? The prediction is not altogether clear because it depends on whether or not one believes that grouping is required to perceive actual bars just as it is to group elements *into* phenomenal columns. To assert that no grouping is required in this case is to commit the egregious sin the Gestaltists called the experience error. All perception of "things" or "units" requires a process of organization. However, the kind of principle of such organization would clearly be different for actual bars as compared to elements that were nearer to or more similar to one another in one direction versus another. At least one can safely say that grouping by proximity or similarity does not apply to the case of actual bars because there are no discrete elements here that can be said to be nearer or more similar to one another.

The critical stimulus figures shown in Fig. 2.8 were made simply by filling in the spaces between the square elements of the grouping patterns used in the main experiment. The background arrays for the noncritical trials were the evenly spaced black elements or the randomly arranged black and white elements, neither of which yielded any particular grouping. Of 20 respondents, on being questioned about what if anything they had seen on the critical trial, 12 perceived the bars and their orientation correctly. This 60% level is to be compared to the approximately 0 to 10% level for the patterns requiring grouping by proximity or similarity. In the control trial, as would be expected, all respondents perceived the bars correctly.

POP OUT

We also investigated the paradigm in which the participant searches for a single item among a number of distractors, the so-called pop-out effect. In

FIG. 2.8. Patterns of columns (left) or rows (right) used in control experiment in which the grouping of elements with one another is not required.

the most typical procedure, the odd item is embedded in an array of distractors, all of which are the same. Therefore, it is reasonable to assume that these items group on the basis of similarity as in the texture segregation paradigm. Because the single different item does not partake in this grouping, it stands out as unique. Assuming then that grouping must occur for pop out to occur, we sought to determine if such grouping occurs preattentively.

The procedure was very like the one we used for texture segregation. For the first three trials, the cross was seen in a background of all similar elements leading to no particular grouping. On the fourth trial, one element was different. In order to test for pop out under the optimum condition for it to occur, we used the feature of color. The odd element was red and all others green or vice versa. The elements were small circles subtending a visual angle of 0.5 degrees. These were larger than the elements used in most of our other experiments. They were bright on a dark screen and thus appeared luminous (see Fig. 2.9). With attention, the pop-out effect was very strong. For further details of conditions and procedure, see Linnett, Rock, and Mack (1991).

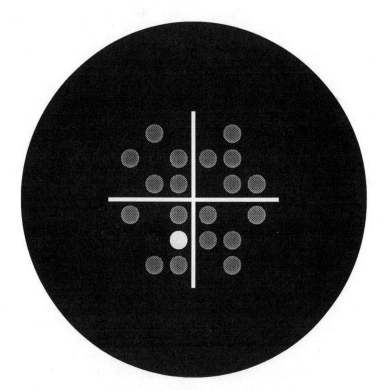

FIG. 2.9. The array used in experiment on search for the different element (pop out). The different element was red and the remainder green, or vice versa. The elements were bright on a dark screen and appeared luminous.

When respondents were asked directly after seeing the array (the fourth trial) whether or not all background elements were the same or different or, in a later variation, whether one element was of a color different from all others, about half of them said "different." This is what one would expect by chance if respondents guessed. In fact, in a control experiment in which all elements *were* the same on the fourth trial, about the same proportion said "different." Moreover, when those who said "different" in the experimental condition were asked in a recognition test about the color and location of the different item, performance was not significantly better than what one would expect from respondents who were guessing from the array of colors offered in the test or from the four quadrants. In the control trial in which participants no longer had to judge line length and were presumably attending to the array of elements, they always reported the correct color and quadrant. We obtained parallel results when the odd element was a circle and the rest a cross or vice versa.

WHAT IS PERCEIVED WITHOUT ATTENTION?

So much for a summary of our research on grouping, texture segregation, and pop out. When these patterns are viewed without attention, perceptual grouping of the elements with one another seems not to occur. (A similar finding concerning grouping has just been reported by Ben-Av, Sagi & Braun [1992] using an entirely different method.) If that is a correct conclusion, it leaves us with a serious problem: What principle or principles account for the organization of the visual field prior to the deployment of attention to the "things" that such organization achieves? In an attempt to answer this question, one of us, Rock and his coworkers, have been conducting research using the same method to eliminate attention. The main difference concerns *what* we present as the critical stimulus. See Rock, Linnett, Grant, and Mack (1992).

In the first experiment, the critical stimulus was a single small element, subtending a visual angle of 0.2 degrees. In the procedure, that element was presented on the fourth trial in one of the quadrants created by the cross figure. It was about 2 degrees from the fixation mark. All trials were of 200 ms duration and were followed by a pattern mask. On the seventh trial the element was presented again in a randomly selected quadrant and we consider this a divided-attention trial. On the eighth or control trial the respondent was told not to be concerned with the cross-length task. This experiment asks whether a single item will be seen and correctly localized when it is not expected and not attended to. It is about as simple a visual task as one can imagine. In all our experiments, respondents were forced to guess whenever they were uncertain or believed that they had not seen anything.

As in Mack's laboratory, these participants achieved about a 75% success rate on the cross task overall and improved slightly on the critical fourth trial. Of 12 respondents, 9, or 75% detected the element, and all of these localized its quadrant correctly. The remaining participants claimed to have seen nothing other than the cross figure. Their forced guesses were no better than chance. Although it may not be surprising that such a small element could be missed in a brief, masked, nonfoveal presentation, the fact is that it is always detected in the divided-attention and control trials, thus pointing clearly to inattention as the determinant of the "blindness" effect. Moreover, we have found that a large proportion of our participants, sometimes as high as 90%, fail to detect considerably larger or spatially distributed stimuli; and Mack has repeatedly found this "blindness" effect in her laboratory with grouping patterns when they are placed in one quadrant. We refer to this phenomenon as *Inattentional Blindness* and attach great importance to it. It suggests that perception may depend upon either voluntary, goal-directed attention (which our method surely eliminates) or stimulus-driven, attracted attention (which apparently our method sometimes prevents). In the absence of any attention then, perception fails to occur.

In further experiments, we presented elements of the same small size in more than one quadrant or a varying number of elements in one quadrant. By and large, in the critical inattention trial, our respondents correctly identified all the quadrants in which elements appeared and achieved a fairly good impression of numerosity when multiple elements were presented in one quadrant.

We then went on to test for form perception. We presented either a red, blue, or black rectangle, cross, or triangle. These figures averaged about 1 degree of visual angle and centered along the 45 degree virtual bisection of the quadrant angles no more than 2.3 degrees from the fixation mark. Figure 2.10 shows an example. Without bogging the reader down with details, the main result was that the correct shape was never selected beyond chance on the recognition test immediately following the critical trial. However, except for the usual number of "blindness" cases, respondents always perceived a "something" and identified the quadrant in which the shape had appeared and almost always perceived its color correctly. In the divided-attention and control trials, participants *did* perceive the shape correctly. There were five replications of this experiment checking on various possible explanations of the somewhat surprising result. They all confirmed the finding. Under our conditions of nonattention, shape is not perceived, and thus we also confirm the Rock and Gutman findings that were described at the outset using an entirely different method.

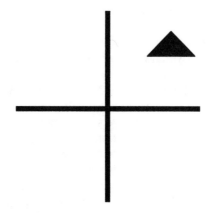

FIG. 2.10. Display used in experiment on form perception without attention. The figure was either a triangle, a rectangle, or a cross, and was either red, blue, or black.

CONCLUSIONS

So much for the data. We will now address two problems: (a) How to reconcile our negative findings on grouping and texture segregation with those of others using a search paradigm indicating a good deal of successful processing of multiple items in parallel, which many believe entail grouping, *and* (b) how to explain the early-stage, preattentive organization of the visual field if it is not based on the Gestalt laws of grouping.

As to reconciling our results with those from search experiments, it seems necessary to assume *three* levels of attention-related processing. At the first level, the nonattentional level, we perceive colored shapeless blobs in specific locations. (Other properties may be perceived as well). At this level no attention, expectation, or intention to perceive is required, but what *can* be perceived is therefore limited to the properties we have suggested. And occasionally the absence of attention can lead to a "blindness" effect. Alternately one might describe our method as eliminating voluntary, goal-directed attention, while allowing for the possibility of attention being captured by the unexpected stimulus. If this is correct, then the perception of colored shapeless blobs in specific locations or of moving blobs, requires attracted attention and, if that fails to occur, nothing at all is perceived (Inattentional Blindness). At the next level, which we designate as the distributed-attention level, voluntary attention to *the array* is necessary. At this level, multiple elements and their features can be detected in parallel, and various kinds of perceptual organization among elements can occur that permits grouping on the basis of similarity and the related phenomenon of segregation and pop out. At the highest level, focal attention to individual items is necessary, and this seems to require serial processing. It allows for the kind of combination of properties that Anne Treisman (1988) suggested requires such focused attention. Whether shape perception can only occur at this level, based, as Treisman and others suggest, on the combination of features, remains to be seen. However, an entirely different explanation has been suggested; namely that the process of description underlying shape perception requires attention (Rock, 1983; Rock & Gutman, 1981; Rock, Schauer, & Halper, 1976).

As to the second problem, namely the basis of an early stage or low-level nonattentional perceptual organization, we would like to suggest that it is based on a hitherto unrecognized principle that Stephen Palmer and Rock called *uniform connectedness* (Palmer & Rock, 1993). Regions of uniform stimulation of luminance, or wavelength, dots, lines, or more extended areas, are interpreted by the perceptual system as a single unit. It is not so much a matter of a grouping or putting together of separate elements (because often there are no such separate elements) as it is a matter of the *finding* of an interconnected homogeneous region. Viewed in this way, the principle is similar to those that have been advanced in the computer vision literature to account for the detection of uniform regions. Connectedness is a powerful organizational principle, as is evidenced in Fig. 2.11 in which it overpowers the combined effects of proximity and similarity. Wertheimer seems to have presupposed this principle because he offered no account of the perception of the elementary units in his displays *as units*. Perhaps he was guilty of the experience error in failing to realize that an explanation was needed for the perception of the spots and line elements *as such* in addition to their groupings with one another. In any event, connectedness can explain what we have found to be perceived under our conditions of no attention, namely individual blobs. It can also explain the perception of *bars* in Mack's experiment controlling for grouping.

There is another fact about grouping to be reckoned with. It concerns the level at which we should understand the Gestalt principles. For example, proximity or similarity can refer to distances or properties at the level of the proximal stimulus. Although the Gestaltists did not explicitly say so, one would think that grouping should be based on properties defined in this way if it is to account for the early spontaneous, autochthonous achievement of an organized world of discrete objects. But the proximity or similarity relevant to grouping can also refer to a higher level of *perceived* properties.

FIG. 2.11. Despite the proximity and similarity of the members of pairs of large circles and of small circles, one perceives grouping of large with small circles on the basis of a newly uncovered principle of organization, namely uniform connectedness. (After Palmer & Rock, 1992).

The evidence is mounting that grouping is based on such perceived properties and these in turn depend on depth perception and the achievement of constancy. We will not review this evidence here because such a review is given elsewhere (Palmer & Rock, 1992. See all Rock & Brosgole, 1964; Rock, Nijhawan, Palmer, & Tudor, 1992). The point is illustrated in Fig. 2.12, which demonstrates an effect uncovered by Palmer (in preparation). The half circles in the middle column tend to group with the full circles on the left rather than with the half circles on the right. That is obviously because the half circles in the middle are *perceived* to be amodally complete circles occluded by the vertical bar.

These findings about *level* or stage of processing fit perfectly with the conclusion we drew from the experiments described here on grouping. It is plausible that higher level processing and processing-requiring-attention go

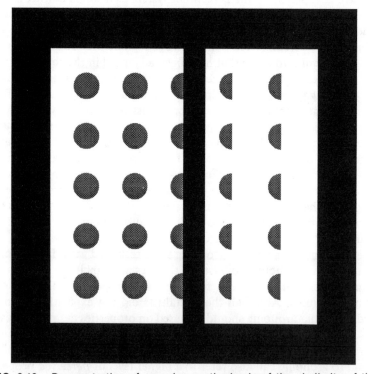

FIG. 2.12.   Demonstration of grouping on the basis of the similarity of the half circles in the center column to the complete circles in the two columns on the left. The process of completion of the center column occluded elements renders them as phenomenal circles, rather than as half circles. Thus, the grouping is *not* based on the similarity of the retinal images of the center column half circles to the half circle images of the elements in the two columns on the right.

hand in hand. So the finding that grouping based on similarity or proximity does not occur without attention fits the finding that such grouping occurs at a relatively late postconstancy level of processing. However, if *uniform connectedness* occurs on the basis of *proximal stimulus* uniformities, it fits our findings that individual blobs and regions are perceived without attention.

One can think of connectedness as yielding a basic level of organization such as a Mondrian-like array of regions each of which is a different luminance, color, or texture. From this, one can achieve either subordinate or superordinate units on the basis of Gestalt principles. So, for example, Fig. 2.13 shows line fragments that are interconnected, which, therefore, via connectedness, should be perceived as a single "thing." It *is*, but it also clearly has separated parts. The subdivision into four parts may be based on partitioning where deep concavities are present. Then the Gestalt law of good continuation can account for the grouping into two overlapping curves. Figure 2.14 shows an array that is first organized into three units on the basis of uniform connectedness: There are three separate uniform regions. However, on the basis of similarity and good continuation, two of these regions are grouped together as signifying one region occluded by the center rectangle. So here Gestalt grouping gives us a superordinate unit. If such Gestalt grouping into subordinate and superordinate units occurs on the basis of *perceived* rather than retinally defined properties, it can explain many of the facts of visual organization in daily life.

FIG. 2.13. A pattern that is first organized as a single entity on the basis of uniform connectedness (basic level organization) is then partitioned into four separate components by virtue of deep concavities. These in turn are grouped into two overlapping lines on the basis of the Gestalt principle of good continuation.

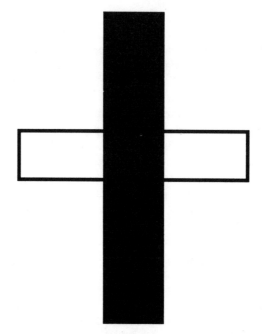

FIG. 2.14.   A pattern that is first organized into three separate regions on the basis of uniform connectedness (basic level organization) is then reorganized into two regions, a vertical bar and a partially occluded horizontal bar. The unification of the horizontal regions is achieved on the basis of the Gestalt laws of good continuation and similarity.

REFERENCES

Ben-Av, M., Sagi, D. & Braun, J. (1992) visual attention and grouping. *Perception & Psychophysics, 52*, 277–294,

Butler, L., & McKelvie, S. J. (1985). Processing of form: Further evidence for the necessity of attention. *Perceptual and Motor Skills, 61*, 215–221.

Julesz, B. (1981). Textures, the elements of texture perception and their interaction. *Nature, 290*, 91–97.

Linnett, C. M., Rock, I., & Mack, A. (1991). *Will pop-out occur without attention?* Poster presented at the Recent Advances in the analysis of Attention Conference, Davis, CA.

Mack, A., Tang, B., Tuma, R., Kahn, S., & Rock, I. (1992). *Perceptual organization and attention. Cognitive Psychology, 24*, 475–501.

Palmer, S. E. (in preparation). Late influences on perceptual grouping: Amodal completion.

Palmer, S., & Rock, I. (in press). Rethinking perceptual organization: The role of uniform connectedness. *Psychonomic Bulletin and Review.*

Rock, I. (1983). *The logic of perception.* Cambridge: Bradford Books, MIT Press.

Rock, I & Brosgole, L. (1964). Grouping based on phenomenal proximity. *Journal of Experimental Psychology, 67*, 531–538.

Rock, I. & Gutman, D. (1981). The effect of inattention on form perception. *Journal of Experimental Psychology: Human Perception and Performance, 7*, 275–285.

Rock, I., Linnett, C. M., Grant, P., & Mack, A. (1992). Perception without attention: *Results of a new method*. *Cognitive Psychology, 24,* 502–534.

Rock, I, Nijhawan, R., Palmer, S. E. & Tudor, L. (1992). Grouping based on phenomenal similarity of achromatic color. *Perception, 21,* 779–789.

Rock, I. Schauer, R., & Halper, F. (1976). Form perception without attention. *Quarterly Journal of Experimental Psychology, 28,* 429–440.

Treisman, A. (1988). A feature-integration theory of attention. *Cognitive Psychology, 12,* 97–136.

Wertheimer, M. (1923). Untersuchungen zur Lehre von Der Gestalt (Research on the theory of the Gestalt II. *Psychologische Forschung, 4,* 301–350.

3 The Influence of Irrelevant Information in Visual Perception

Soledad Ballesteros
Universidad Nacional de Educación a Distancia, Madrid, Spain

Dionisio Manga
Universidad Complutense, Madrid, Spain

The research described in this chapter relates to a series of experimental results that show how the human information-processing system perceives and compares linguistic and nonlinguistic visual patterns, while trying to ignore irrelevant information. This topic is closely related to visual attention and the topic of early versus late selection theories of attention.

To compare a pair of visual stimuli on a physical dimension irrespective of their variation on another physical dimension or in the physical context that surrounds the critical stimuli seems to be a relative easy task for human observers. Nevertheless, human perceivers cannot always ignore irrelevant information.

From a theoretical point of view, the way in which people deal with irrelevant information is a very important issue, directly related to selective attention. The main theoretical question is whether the selection of attended stimuli takes place during the "early" or "late" stages of processing. Nevertheless, the way in which irrelevant or unattended stimuli, or stimulus dimensions, are processed by humans has proved to be controversial and is far from being resolved. In this chapter we present results from a series of different experimental paradigms and consider how these results fit into the theoretical positions that have been proposed.

The first section of the chapter deals with how normal adult perceivers process information contained in nonlinguistic stimuli. In the second section, we consider the conditions under which linguistic visual stimuli are processed when irrelevant information is also present.

IRRELEVANT INFORMATION AND VISUAL ATTENTION

Since the beginning of cognitive psychology the way in which unattended visual (and auditory) stimuli are processed by humans has been an area of considerable theoretical interest as well as a subject of active experimentation. Nevertheless, controversy has always accompanied this issue. In the debate that followed this controversy, two main theoretical approaches and some intermediate positions have been proposed. The first, due to Broadbent (1958, 1982), assumes that the human information-processing system selects stimuli as soon as they come into the system, before semantic analysis takes place. According to this proposal, only attended stimuli will receive further perceptual analysis and will be processed at a higher semantic level. This early selection is made on the basis of physical dimensions. Whereas attended stimuli are further processed semantically, unattended stimuli are not.

The second account was proposed a few years later by Deutsch and Deutsch (1963) and is known as the *late selection theory*. According to this account, all the stimuli that arrive at the information processing system are automatically processed to a semantic level where recognition takes place. More recently, Duncan (1980) argued that all visual objects are categorized preattentively, but attended objects are selected for action rather than for identification.

The dispute concerning early versus late selection is still far from being resolved, but theorists have reached a certain consensus about the importance of space on visual attention (Broadbent, 1982; Driver & Baylis, 1989; Posner, Snyder, & Davidson, 1980). Today, it is widely accepted that there is a limit of approximately 1 degree of visual angle when attention is focused. Only stimuli that appear in this area can be fully processed (Eriksen & Hoffman, 1972b; Hoffman & Nelson, 1981). This model is known as the *spotlight model*, and several variations of the model exist. The fact that the interfering effects of distractors diminish as the distance from the target increases suggests that visual attention works by enlightening contiguous regions of the visual field. There are several experimental paradigms that provide considerable support for this theory, including the response competition model (Eriksen & Hoffman, 1973), spatial precuing (Posner, 1980), the visual search (Treisman & Gelade, 1980) and the illusory conjunction paradigm (Treisman & Schmidt, 1982).

An alternative account to spatial attention models is the perceptual group model (Driver & Baylis, 1989) or the model of object-based attention (Duncan, 1984; Humphreys & Bruce, 1989; Rock & Gutman, 1981). According to this point of view, attention is directed to perceptual groups in the Gestalt tradition. However, it is not easy to distinguish between these proposals because proximity is an important grouping factor. Nevertheless, it is possible that attention is directed to objects rather than to regions of space. For example, Duncan (1984) showed that it was easier to perceive two attributes pertaining to the same object than two attributes pertaining to different objects. Duncan's results are not totally opposed to the spotlight model because attention is still directed to contiguous regions of the visual field. A promising way to disentangle the effects has been provided by Driver and Baylis (1989), who showed that grouping of target and distractors by motion was more influential than their proximity.

An important study by Rock and Gutman (1981) also provided strong support for object-based theories of attention (see also Rock & Mack, chapter 2, this volume). They presented two overlapping novel shapes drawn in different colors and participants attended to one or the other in each pair. The main result was that memory was good for the attended shapes but not better than chance for the nonattended ones. The fact that the two objects in each pair appeared overlapping in the same visual space indicates that the participant did not attend to space but to objects.

An alternative to the two extreme theoretical positions of early selection and late selection emerged, according to which early selection of unattended stimuli is based on their physical properties, but unattended stimuli are not completely blocked from further processing (Treisman, 1964, 1969). This compromise model is more in accord with experimental results that will be considered later in this chapter.

EFFECTS OF IRRELEVANT INFORMATION IN OBJECT AND PATTERN PERCEPTION

According to early selection theories, unattended information should neither facilitate nor interfere with the processing of the relevant information because the system filters out irrelevant information as soon it arrives. Nevertheless, a large number of studies have shown that irrelevant information does influence perceptual processing. It is difficult to know whether unattended stimuli, backgrounds and stimulus dimensions, facilitate or interfere with the processing of relevant information because of the difficulty of finding neutral conditions for comparison (Flowers & Wilcox, 1982; Jonides & Mack, 1984).

In the first part of this chapter we review research related to the influence of contextual scenes and stimulus dimensions (irrelevant information) on object identification, pattern matching, and perceptual classification.

The second part considers results from studies on the perception of linguistic patterns. These also show that context and irrelevant stimuli influence visual processing. Irrelevant information cannot be ignored by the visual system, at least, at a certain level. Most experimental data are in contradiction with early selection theories.

Object Identification in Contextual Scenes

The differential effects of background information on object identification has been documented in studies concerning the influence of contextual scenes on the recognition of visually presented common objects. Experiments in this area have shown the beneficial influence on object identification when the object is presented in a coherent scene as well as its negative effect when objects are presented in inappropriate contexts (Biederman, 1972; Biederman, Glass, & Stacy, 1973; Palmer, 1975).

Recent theories of scene-context effects have attempted to determine the aspects of the scene producing the facilitation. In this respect, Biederman, Mezzanotte, and Rabinowitz (1982) favored the explanation that facilitation is due to the processing of a series of emergent features, and that global scene information facilitates object scene information. In this view, the identification of the relations that take place in the scene is the most important factor, and it is precisely this identification that provides accessing to a scene schema that produces facilitatory effects. The experimental paradigm of Biederman et al. (1982) consisted of presenting for 150 ms a series of scenes in which objects violated scene relations such as support, probability, size, interposition, and relation. They found that under such circumstances subsequent performance in object identification was impaired. This result led them to conclude that the perception of scene relations can be processed before object identification and that this perception is responsible for facilitation of object identification. Consistent with this account are the results of a more recent study conducted by Boyce, Pollatsek, and Rayner (1989). These researchers found that context scene facilitatory effects rely on global information provided by the scene background rather than local object information. Context effects were obtained even when diagnostic objects were not in the displays. This conclusion contrasts with Friedman's (1979) explanation, according to which the identification of an obligatory object in the scene activates the appropriate frame that is responsible for the facilitation obtained in object identification. According to Friedman, objects with a higher a priori probability of occurrence in a given context will facilitate the identification of other objects within the scene.

An important question is which mechanism is responsible for the observed facilitation. Again, on this point researches do not agree. Whereas for some (Antes, Penland, & Metzger, 1981; Biederman et al., 1982; Friedman, 1979) the facilitation is due to the activation of a certain scheme, for others (Henderson, Pollatsek, & Rayner, 1987) the facilitation is due to the spreading of activation through a semantic network. This point needs further investigation.

Perceptual Interference in Perceptual Classification

Several types of perceptual interference have been reported, such as the orthogonal interference (also called the Garner interference by Pomerantz, Pristach, & Carson, 1989), the Stroop interference, and the interference found in multidimensional same–different comparison tasks.

Garner and Stroop Interference. The orthogonal or Garner interference (Garner & Felfoldi, 1970) occurs when two integral dimensions are combined in a speeded classification task and the participant is asked to sort out, for example, color chips that vary in value and chroma. In this case orthogonal variations in chroma (irrelevant dimension for the classification) interfere with the sorting outcome in value (relevant dimension). When the same classification is performed with separable dimensions like size of the circle and angle of the radius, or form and color, orthogonal interference does not appear. Although a set of converging operations treats integral and separable dimensions as independent categories, results have favored the existence of a continuum of analyzability from the integral to separable (Ballesteros, 1989b; Foard & Kemler-Nelson, 1984; Garner, 1974). The problem is that most studies have used stimulus dimensions that vary only in two levels of disparity, so the influence of graded interference cannot be studied.

The Stroop phenomenon (Stroop, 1935) is a clear and widely cited example that shows that unattended stimuli are processed semantically at least to a certain extent. In the standard Stroop paradigm the naming of the ink in which a word is printed slows down performance when the color word is incompatible with the color of the ink (e.g., the word BLUE printed in red ink). At the same time, facilitatory effects have also be found when the color of the word and the ink coincide. Whereas Garner interference arises from the variation of information across trials, Stroop interference arises from the information content of the irrelevant stimuli. Garner interference occurs when performance in the filtering task where the irrelevant dimension varies randomly is lower than performance in control tasks where it is constant across trials. On the other hand, Stroop interference is shown by worsening of performance when the irrelevant dimension is incongruent with the relevant dimension (for a comprehensive discussion of the differences between both types of interference, see Pomerantz, Pristach, & Carson, 1989; see also, Pomerantz, Carson, & Feldman, Chapter 6, this volume). In both cases, attention to irrelevant stimuli or stimulus attributes has been repeatedly observed and are clear examples of the limitation of selective attention.

Interference has also be found in multidimensional "same–different" comparison tasks. This paradigm has proved useful in investigating stimulus encoding because it requires little perceptual recognition (Dixon & Just, 1978; Hawkins & Shigley, 1972; Miller & Bauer, 1981). Using this paradigm it has usually been found that disparity on an irrelevant dimension increases the time it takes to decide that the two stimuli are the same on the relevant dimension.

The Influence of Irrelevant Information in Speeded Classification and Comparison of Multidimensional Patterns: The Normalization Hypothesis

Empirical work has shown that when perceivers have to compare two stimuli that differ in several steps in different dimensions but only one of these dimensions is relevant for the perceptual comparison, the presence of the irrelevant information produces slower reaction times. What are the effects of the irrelevant information on the matching task? How is the matching task being performed by the perceiver? Dixon and Just (1978) assumed that the visual system performs a continual transformation in which subjects first equate the two patterns to be compared in the irrelevant dimension, and then, compare these patterns in the relevant dimension. This process has been called *normalization* and has been supposed to be responsible for a number of transformations such as mental rotation, size scaling, or even color scaling. Normalization is, according to this view, the usual way of processing information that human perceivers cannot ignore. Unfortunately, the normalization account is limited in generality (Ballesteros, Crespo, Manga, & Fernandez Trespalacios, 1988; Besner, 1983; Besner & Coltheart, 1976; Kubovy & Podgorny, 1981; Santee & Egeth, 1980).

Nevertheless, the theoretical importance of the existence of this normalization process should be highlighted because it is directly related to the problem of the internal representation of knowledge. This would show that the representation is isomorphic to its physical referent in a spatial sense, as was proposed by Shepard (1981).

The main prediction derived from the normalization model is that reaction times corresponding to "same" and "different"judgments will show a linear trend increasing with the number of steps of discrepancy existing in the irrelevant dimension. But, as has been pointed out earlier, this transformational explanation has not received complete support. Along with results that showed a linear increase of the reaction times with the graded increase of the number of steps in the irrelevant dimension (Bundesen & Larsen, 1975; Bundesen, Larsen, & Farrell, 1981; Larsen,

1985; Larsen & Bundesen, 1978), others studies have not confirmed this linear trend (Ballesteros et al., 1988; Besner, 1983; Besner & Coltheart, 1976; Kubovy & Podgorny, 1981; Santee & Egeth, 1980).

The lack of experimental support for the normalization hypothesis is especially evident in "different" judgments, when the two patterns to be compared are formed by different stimuli instead of reflected images of the same pattern.

Some Experimental Results.   In a series of experiments we investigated the scope of the normalization hypothesis. Our view was that the position of the irrelevant dimension in the continuum of intergrality–separability might be related to the need to perform the normalization process while the participants try to achieve the required comparison. In two of these experiments we tested whether the mean reaction times increase across the several steps of variation in an irrelevant dimension for same as well as for different comparisons. The stimuli used were ellipses that varied in four levels of inclination (45, 90, 135, and 180 degrees, starting from the horizontal position) and in four levels of size (the ellipses' major axes were 1.4, 1.8, 2.2 and 2.6 cm, and the ellipses' minor axes were 0.8, 1.0, 1.2 and 1.4cm). It is known from previous research that inclination and length are intermediate dimensions located closer to the separable end of the integrality–separability continuum (Ballesteros, 1989a, 1989b; Smith & Kilroy, 1979).

On each trail two ellipses were tachistoscopically displayed at the center of the screen for 200 ms, one at each side of the fixation point, and the participant decided whether the two ellipses had the same or different size (Exp. 1), or inclination (Exp. 2). The visual angles subtended by the ellipses varied from 1.43 to 2.66 degrees for small and large ellipses, respectively. The results of Experiment 1 for same and different judgments are shown in Fig. 3.1.

This figure presents the reaction times averaged over 8 respondents completing 96 trials of same and different comparisons. As predicted by the normalization hypothesis there was a large and significant effect of steps of irrelevant disparity in inclination over the time necessary to report that the two ellipses were the same in size, even though the linear trend was not significant. Nevertheless, the time required to perform different matches in size, the relevant dimension (control condition), or in both dimensions (experimental condition), diminished with the increase of the number of steps of discrepancy in inclination (irrelevant dimension). The trend for same and different matches was opposite. These results are difficult to accommodate in the normalization model.

In a second experiment we asked participants to report if the two ellipses were the same or different in inclination irrespective of size. We found again that the trends for both types of responses differed (Fig. 3.2).

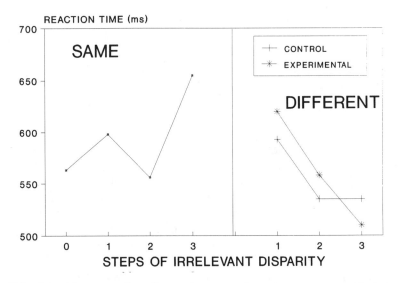

FIG. 3.1. Mean reaction times for correct responses averaged over subjects and replications on same (left panel) and different comparisons (right panel) as a function of steps of irrelevant disparity. The relevant dimension was size and the irrelevant was inclination of the ellipsis.

Same reaction times increased with increase in size disparity (irrelevant dimension) whereas different reaction times were not influenced by irrelevant disparity.

Reaction times in both experiments increased with the amount of disparity in the irrelevant dimension but the trend was not linear. We interpreted these nonlinear effects (obtained when the relevant dimension was size of the ellipses and the irrelevant one was inclination) due to the facilitation produced by the symmetric configuration of the two ellipses in the two-steps condition that reduced considerably the reaction times in the two steps discrepancy condition (Palmer, 1985).

On the other hand, the time necessary to process inclination (when size was the irrelevant dimension) was influenced by the absolute magnitude of the irrelevant disparity in size (0.4 cm increase in the major axis and 0.2 cm increase in the minor axis for each step of discrepancy). Most of the research conducted in size scaling used ratio discrepancies between stimuli rather than size differences (Besner, 1983; Bundesen & Larsen, 1975; Dixon & Just, 1978; Jolicoeur & Besner, 1987). This result supports earlier results although a monotonic increase was not found. The normalization hypothesis seems to hold for same comparisons but it does not hold for different ones. These results are clearly in contradiction with the normalization hypothesis, which predicts graded interference for both types of comparisons. As was pointed out earlier, there is some indication that size and

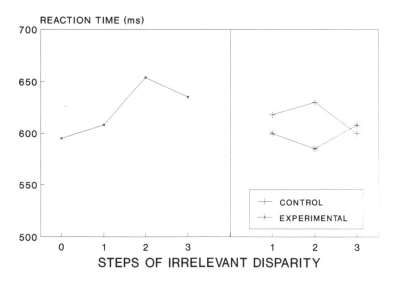

FIG. 3.2. Mean reaction times on same (left panel) and different comparisons as a function of steps of irrelevant disparity. The relevant dimension was inclination and the irrelevant was size.

inclination are dimensions located at some intermediate level in the integrality–separability continuum that could explain the results.

In the following experiment we used as visual patterns rectangles 2 cm long by 1.2 cm wide, generated by the orthogonal combination of four levels of brightness (levels 3, 4, 5, and 6 in the Value Munsell scale; Hue was constant at 5 PB, and Chroma at 8) and four levels of inclination (0, 30, 60, and 90 degrees from the upright position, counterclockwise).

Studies using color as the irrelevant dimension have been rare. Dixon & Just (1978) reported an experiment in which the relevant dimension was always hue and the irrelevant one was tint and found that same reaction times increased with increase of disparity in the irrelevant dimension whereas different trials did not show any systematic trend.

In earlier research (Ballesteros & Gonzalez Labra, 1989), we found that brightness and size were quite separable when chroma and hue were kept constant. Our expectation in this experiment was that the increment in brightness disparity would not interfere with the processing of inclination.

As can be seen in Fig. 3.3, the graded disparity in brightness (irrelevant dimension) did not affect reaction times for same comparisons in inclination of the rectangles (relevant dimension). Nevertheless, steps of disparity for different comparisons were highly significant. As the number of steps of disparity increased reaction times also increased.

The results of these experiments fail to support the necessity of a normalization process in all cases. Experiments 1 and 2 showed that "same"

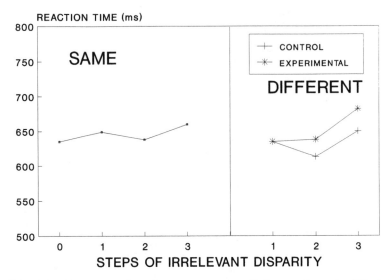

FIG. 3.3. Mean reaction times on same (left panel) and different comparisons as a functions of steps of irrelevant disparity. The relevant dimension was inclination and the irrelevant brightness of the rectangle.

reaction times increased with the amount of discrepancy in the irrelevant dimension; however, the data did not show a significant linear trend. These results are partially in agreement with those of Besner (1983), Besner and Coltheart (1976), Santee and Egeth (1980), and Simion, Bagnara, Roncato, and Umilta (1982). The lack of evidence for the existence of a normalization process seems to be the more common finding for those studies in which the two patterns to be compared are different patterns rather than the same patterns rotated 180 degrees (reflected patterns).

Normalization does not seem to be a necessary operation in all judgments. With more separable dimensions, like brightness and size of square patterns when the other two color dimensions (saturation and hue) are kept constant, normalization may not be obligatory even for same comparisons. We are currently pursuing this issue more closely trying to understand how the perceptual system performs comparisons when irrelevant graded information is present in the visual display. Nevertheless, selective attention to the relevant dimension was not always possible, specially in the same judgments, which shows the failure of early selectivity.

EFFECTS OF IRRELEVANT INFORMATION IN THE PROCESSING OF LINGUISTIC-LIKE PATTERNS

In the studies reviewed below we consider experimental results that show the failure of selective attention when the visual stimuli consist of well-learned linguistic-like patterns instead of visual patterns, geometric forms, or objects.

Context Effects in Letter Perception

First, experimental results that show the failure of selective attention when the visual stimuli consist of letters of the alphabet are considered. Very different experimental paradigms have shown the influence of context in letter perception even though the context is irrelevant for the task. These experimental results suggest that the early selection mechanism is not able to exclude completely the unattended material (e.g., other letters, geometric contexts, or color contexts that surround the attended letter).

The Flanker Compatibility Effect. The flanker compatibility effect (FCE) refers to the influence of irrelevant flanking letters in the perception of the relevant letter. Results have shown that the irrelevant flanking letters cannot be ignored and that they are semantically processed, at least, to some extent. The more common way of presenting the stimuli has been a linear display in which a series of three upper-case letters appear in the center of the visual field. The target or attended letter was usually the center letter, and the noise or unattended letters, called flankers, were usually located one on each side of the target (Eriksen & Schultz, 1979). Given fixation of the target on experimental trials, it has been argued that impairment of selective attention could have been due to the experimental display. Nevertheless, the effect still holds when circular displays and a cued task have been used, so that the target changes from trial to trial (e.g., Eriksen & St. James, 1986; Miller, 1991, Exp. 8). In these displays, 8 to 12 letters are presented in a circular arrangement and a line cues the target letter.

Importantly, results using either linear or circular displays do not support the idea that some early selection mechanism totally excludes the unattended letters (Broadbent, 1958, 1982).

Eriksen and colleagues (Eriksen & Eriksen, 1974; Eriksen & Hoffman, 1972a, 1972b; Eriksen & Schultz, 1979) studied the FCE phenomenon extensively. In a typical stimulus presentation, a relevant letter appears in the center (or above the fixation point) of the visual field while other noise letters (response compatible or incompatible at different between-letter spacing conditions) also appear flanking the attended letter. In all noise conditions incompatible letters produce slower reaction times than the compatible ones. At the same time, it is well established that reaction times decrease as the spatial separation between the letters increases. When target letters were assigned to two (e.g., Eriksen & Eriksen, 1974; Eriksen & Shultz, 1979) or to four response keys (as in Miller, 1988), and the respondent was asked to press the key assigned to the attended letter as soon as possible, the results were very similar. In all cases, the identity of the flanker letters produced important compatibility effects, showing that the respondent was aware of those letters even though they were supposedly unattended. When those unattended letters were targets assigned to the same response key as the attended letter, reaction times were faster than when the unattended letters were targets assigned to the opposite response.

More recently, Miller (1991) examined the boundary conditions that produce the FCE in an attempt to explain why early selection attenuates the influence of unattended stimuli instead of filtering them out completely. He explored the possibility of overriding this effect by manipulating different task conditions such as visual angle, attentional focus, visual transients, and perceptual load. These experiments showed that the flanker compatibility effect was still present after all such experimental manipulations. Miller concluded that human perceivers cannot completely exclude unattended stimuli. Some semantic processing of unattended visual stimuli exists. According to these results it is very difficult to rule out later selection theories. Even though researchers such as Yantis and Johnston (1990) employed optimal experimental conditions for early exclusion of unattended stimuli such as using highly valid location precues, allowing enough time for processing them, providing adequate spacing among letters, and permitting active reallocation of attention in each trial, small FCEs effects were still present.

The experimental results reviewed here seem to show that even though the processing of unattended stimuli can be attenuated with certain manipulations, it cannot be totally ruled out. It seems safe to conclude that even if early selection mechanisms exist, the location of the bottleneck occurs very late, as suggested by Duncan (1980, 1984).

Contexts in Letter Perception: Effects of Color and Geometric Frames. In a series of outstanding experiments, Posner and Mitchell (1967) showed that several nodes exist in letter processing. In these experiments the stimuli were always a pair of letters and the experimental conditions manipulated three levels of instructions. In the physical identity condition, participants were asked to report if the two letters had the same or different physical identity (e.g., AA would be same and aA would be different). In the name identity condition, participants had to report if the two letters were the same or different in name identity (e.g., Aa would be same, Ae would be different). In the third condition, the participant had to follow a rule identity. They would respond same if both letters were vowels or if both were consonants; in other cases, they would respond different. Based on the obtained RTs, Posner and Mitchell inferred three different processing nodes. The first node was based on *physical identity*, not influenced by previous learning. The responses to letters under the instruction of physical identity were 70 ms faster on the average than the responses under the name identity condition, and these were still faster than those in the rule identity condition. Comparison in the second node, based on *name identity*, had no obvious physical similarity and the respondent had to derive the name of the letter from memory storage prior to making the comparison. The third node proposed by Posner and Mitchell was based on *rule identity* (Are both letters vowels or consonants?).

In a number of experiments conducted in our laboratory (Ballesteros, Manga, Crespo, & Coello, 1989), we studied the effects of different kinds of irrelevant contexts on the visual processing of letters. In these experiments we used a modification of the Posner and Mitchell paradigm. Instead of presenting two letter in each trial, we presented three letters for 200 ms located at the three angles of an imaginary triangle. The letter appearing on the top was always the target that had to be compared to the two letters that appeared on the bottom, one on each side of the fixation point. One of the letters on the bottom was always equal to the target letter in physical or in name identity and the participant had to press the response key corresponding to the letter that was the same as the reference letter as quickly and accurately as possible. In this task there was always stimulus–response compatibility and the participant always made same judgments instead of same and different judgments as in Posner et al. studies.

In two experiments we studied the effects of color on letter matching, trying to find out if respondents were able to attend selectively to the letters without paying attention to the color that surrounded the letters or to the color of the letters. In other words, we asked if human perceivers were able to block out (completely) the information present in the context and attend selectively to the letters.

If participants were able to attend to the letters without taking color context into account, different context conditions would not influence reaction times or errors. In one experiment each letter was surrounded by a blue or green circular background, whereas in another there was no color context; instead the letters appeared printed in black or red tint, depending on the experimental condition. In both experiments, four experimental conditions were manipulated. In the *same neutral condition* the three letters — the target and the two comparison letters — were surrounded by the same color background (e.g., the three circular backgrounds were blue). In half of the trials the background was blue and in the other half the background was green. In the *favorable condition*, the target and the letter on the bottom that was the same as the target letter always appeared inside the same color background but the third letter was always surrounded by a different color background (e.g., the two matching letters appeared in a blue background and the different letter appeared in a green background).

In the *unfavorable condition* the target appeared in a color background different from the matching letter (e.g., the target was inside a circular blue patch, whereas the letter that was the same was inside a circular green patch and the different letter was inside a blue circular patch). The fourth condition was the *different neutral condition* in which the target was surrounded by a circular color patch different from the color that surrounded the two letters that appeared at the bottom (e.g., the target was inside a blue patch, whereas the two other letters were inside a green patch).

Figure 3.4 shows the mean reaction times for physical and name identity in each of the four experimental conditions averaged over participants and replications. The mean reaction time was significantly lower for the physical identity condition than for the name identity condition (669ms vs. 815 ms). More important, the effect of the context was also significant. The latency of the favorable condition was significantly faster than the latency of the same neutral condition. This result supports the idea that the color context facilitated letter processing. The interaction of identity by condition was also significant. Newman-Keuls tests showed that context had a significant influence only in the nominal identity condition but not in the physical identity condition. This was not expected on the basis of Posner and Mitchell's results. As shown in Fig. 3.5, name identity had shorter latencies in the favorable context condition than in the neutral condition (784 ms vs. 846 ms).

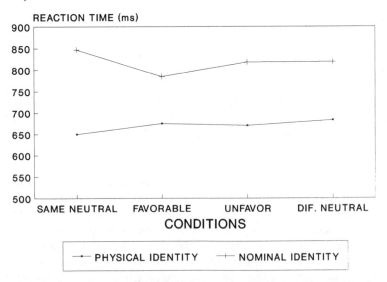

FIG. 3.4. Mean reaction times on physical and name identity in the four experimental context conditions (same neutral, favorable, unfavorable, and different neutral) when the letters appeared surrounded by a circular color patch.

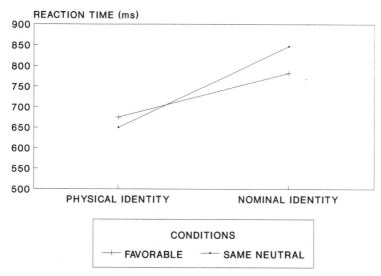

FIG. 3.5.   Interaction identity by condition.

In summary, we replicated the well known phenomenon of faster processing of physical than name identity. But more important was the context effect and the interaction that showed that the favorable context speeds up reaction times for name but not for physical identity relative to the same neutral condition.

The second experiment was designed to find out if these effects were present when the color background that surrounded the letter was the intrinsic color of the letters. In this experiment the color of the letters was manipulated using the same experimental design. The letters now appeared printed in red or in black and there was no color background surrounding them. Upper-case and lower-case letters also appeared in the same size in an attempt to rule out the influence of their different visual angles. The main results are shown in Fig.3.6.

Once again, type of identity was highly significant. Physical identity was 169 ms faster on average than name identity (566ms vs. 735 ms) even when the upper- and lower-case letters were of the same size. The important result here was that the manipulation of the color of the letters did not produce any significant effect. No other effect or interaction was significant.

The significant context effect found in the earlier experiment was due to the color context background. This effect dissapeared when the background was removed. It was also shown that the difference in size between letters in the physical and in the name identity did not account for the earlier results.

Two more experiments were designed to investigate the possible general-

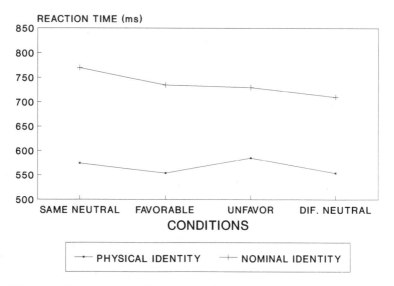

FIG. 3.6. Mean reaction times on physical and name identity in the four context conditions (same neutral, favorable, unfavorable, and different neutral) when the letters appeared printed in color.

ization of the context effects to other types of contexts. In the following two experiments a geometric background was used. In one experiment, the letters appeared inside a square or a circular geometric frame, spatially equivalent. In the other, a small geometric form appeared on top of the letters.

As before, physical identity was much faster than name identity (571 ms vs. 745 ms) and the effect of context was also significant.

Fig. 3.7 shows that when the two letters that were the same appeared inside the same geometric frame (context favorable condition) latency decreased compared to the context unfavorable condition; this occurred in the name identity condition only (715 ms vs. 789 ms).

In the following experiment, we asked if this context effect was present when the geometric form, instead of enclosing the letter, stood at the top of the letter. A small black triangle or square of equivalent size was located on the top of each letter. The procedure was the same as before.

Figure 3.8 shows the results. The effect of letter identity appeared again. Physical identity was 118 ms faster than name identity (645 ms vs. 763 ms), but no other effect nor any interaction achieved statistical significance.

When context was added at the top instead of enclosing the letter, the effect of context on name identity disappeared.

All the experiments showed the well-known effect of identity type (Posner & Mitchell, 1967). This effect was highly significant in all the context conditions manipulated in those experiments (color background,

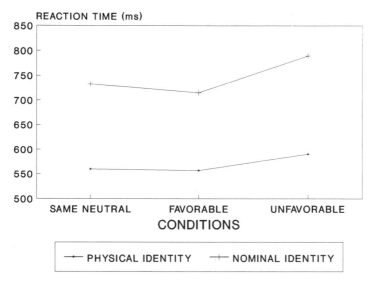

FIG. 3.7. Mean reaction times on physical and name identity matches in the three context conditions (same neutral, favorable and unfavorable) when the letters appeared inside a geometric frame.

color in the letter, geometric background, and geometric added background). In all cases physical matches were faster than name matches. These results suggest that the visual code can be accessed faster than the name or phonological code. In Posner's paradigm (Posner, 1978) it was about 70 ms faster to respond "same" to a pair of letters that were physically identical than it was to respond to a pair of letters that were the same in name. In our experiments the difference between both identities was larger (around 150 ms vs. 70 ms). In our case, participants were presented with three letters instead of the two and only "same" responses were required.

It has commonly been held that in visual letter perception an internal visual representation or code is formed first, which is then followed by a phonetic or name code representation. This finding was taken by Posner and associates as evidence favoring two different nodes of processing. The physical matching task required only the comparison between the letters at the level of the fast visual code (Node 1), whereas the name matching task required accessing to the slower name or phonetic code (Node 2).

However, further research has failed to support the role of the acoustic code in letter matching tasks and has challenged the proposed independence between visual and phonetic codes (Boles, 1986; Boles & Eveland, 1983; Carrasco, Kinchla, & Figueroa, 1988; Freides, Tupler, Hall, & Fowler, 1988). Boles and Eveland suggested that pairs like *Aa* are matched not through a common phonetic or name code, but rather through the detection of visual equivalence between alternate letter cases. Freides et al. recently

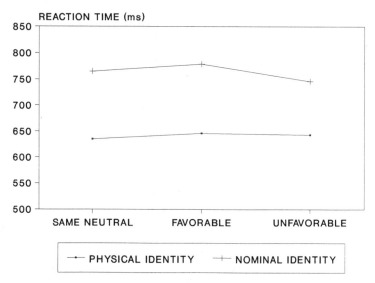

FIG. 3.8. Mean reaction times on physical and name identity matches in the three context conditions (same neutral, favorable, and unfavorable) when a small geometric figure appeared on top of the letter.

showed that the results obtained from college students, normal children at three school levels, and learning disabled children in both physical and nominal matches are not independent but highly correlated. These results challenge Posner's proposal that both types of matches are independent.

Nevertheless, the more striking finding in our experiments was that context manipulations of physical variables such as color (Experiment 1) or geometric frame (Experiment 3) had strong effects on name comparisons but no effect on physical comparisons. Note that Posner (1978) proposed the opposite. That is, physical matches can be affected by experimental manipulations of physical dimensions but not name matches.

As Keele (1986) pointed out, irrelevant background produces little interference with the processing of the relevant stimuli as long as the relevant dimensions are easy to perceive. This could be the case in Experiments 2 and 4 but not in the case of Experiments 1 and 3 in which the background clearly interferes with the processing of the letters when there is nominal identity. Keele also suggested that irrelevant information is often processed at a stage where it activates the information stored in memory. If that activated information represents an alternative interpretation in conflict with the relevant information, interference is likely to occur. We like the idea that context influences processing in a second stage after the physical information has been extracted. So the presence of a context does not influence the processing of the information contained in the physical code but it can produce facilitation or interference in a second stage in which the meaning of the letter has to be processed.

CONCLUSIONS

Our results, together with others from the FCE, the effects of contextual scenes on object detection, and Garner and Stroop interference, argue against early selection models and are more in accordance with late selection models of visual attention. There is something in the unattended visual field that cannot be excluded from further psychological processing. Egeth, Folk, and Mullin (1989) arrived at a similar conclusion in their work on spatial parallelism. In their study, participants were able to extract complex structural information in a spatially parallel fashion (e.g., lexical decision task) on independent channels.

For late selection theorists, selective attention occurs immediately before response selection. Therefore, irrelevant stimuli interfere with this selection. From this perspective, the response competition hypothesis has been proposed as the best way to explain distraction. According to this hypothesis an irrelevant attribute causes distraction when it is associated with responses incompatible with those of the relevant attributes. For example, in the word–color effect (Stroop effect) competition arises between oral response tendencies. Even though there are many arguments that favor this hypothesis, it is obvious that it does not explain all the available data. This hypothesis explains selective attention only in terms of postperceptual processes.

A question that naturally arises in this context is whether perceptual processing is only data driven or is also top–down controlled. According to the intraperceptual theory (Johnston & Dark, 1982, p. 409), "the top–down control of focused attention operates, at least in part, on perceptual processing." The seminal version of intraperceptual theory was Broadbent's (1958) original theory of early selection. The seminal version of extraperceptual theory was proposed by Deustch and Deutsch (1963). The locus of selective attention for Deustch and Deustch is subsequent to perceptual analysis; they proposed that a message will reach the same perceptual and discrimination mechanisms whether or not attention is directed to them. Selectivity of attention should take place after perceptual analysis of inputs. In Norman's (1968) model, all sensory inputs are analyzed and their memory representations are activated. Some of those inputs become pertinent; the combined sensorial and pertinence data determine which stimulus information is attended to. The model includes not only top–down processing (conceptually driven processing) but also bottom–up processing (data-driven processing).

The main point in the early versus late attention controversy is whether or not irrelevant stimuli undergo semantic analysis. Johnston and Dark (1986) concluded in a recent review that irrelevant stimuli sometimes undergo semantic analysis even though selection based on the physical properties of relevant stimuli is frequently superior to selection based on semantic properties. Nevertheless, sensory selection does not exclude semantic analysis of irrelevant stimuli. Today, theorists accept that selection is often guided by sensory features, but at the same time, irrelevant stimuli can be processed to semantic levels (e.g, Broadbent, 1982; Egeth et al., 1989).

In order to answer the question of whether relevant stimuli undergo more perceptual processing than irrelevant stimuli, it is important to rely on the neurophysiology of selective attention. From this perspective, selection of information is achieved by special facilitating mechanisms that transmit relevant stimuli and simultaneously block other irrelevant stimuli. According to many researchers these mechanisms of facilitation and blockage of sensory impulses work by controlling information inputs, changing excitability in specific pathways. A simultaneous redistribution of impulses occurs in polisensory nonspecific structures. These processes are now considered the main neurophysiological mechanisms of selective attention (e.g., Khomskaia, 1982). Neurophysiologists usually assign to the activity of a thalamic nonspecific system working jointly with its cortical projections, the selective transmission of relevant sensorial information, as well as the simultaneous inhibition of irrelevant competing input. Among the cortical mechanisms of selective action, two types of selective corticofugal influences are proposed: a direct effect from the cortical projection zones to the corresponding relay nuclei, and an indirect effect from the associative cortical zones to the specific relay nuclei, mediated by the activity of the nonspecific system. This nonspecific corticofugal effect originates primarily in the frontal cerebral lobe.

The screening of signals according to their novelty and significance for the perceiver is performed by a special cortical mechanism that analyzes all the stimulus parameters. According to Khomskaia (1982) and Sokolov (1963), the conduction of corresponding impulses is increased both in specific and in nonspecific pathways from the receptor to the cortex, due to the concentration of attention on new and significant stimuli. When the stimuli are irrelevant, the impulses are reduced by inhibition processes. At the same time, stimulus repetition and familiarity will produce habituation. In the first case, inattention due to distraction will occur because attention is engaged by more relevant stimuli. The underlying mechanism is inhibition and blockage of irrelevant stimuli versus facilitatory excitation that goes with relevant stimuli (Neill, 1977). In the second case, inattention due to habituation occurs. The mechanism underlying habituation is extinction of the arousal reflex in response to multiple repetitions of the same stimulus (Sokolov, 1963).

Intense research has developed lately trying to discover the mechanisms that underlie selective attention. In this context, excitatory and inhibitory mechanisms are studied within a model in which analysis of objects in a scene is carried out in parallel (Tipper, MacQueen, & Brehaut, 1988). Using a priming paradigm, Tipper and colleagues (e.g., Tipper & Cranston, 1985; Tipper & Driver, 1988) studied inhibitory mechanisms of selective attention suggesting that inhibition of conflicting irrelevant stimuli is confined to a central locus of processing between perception and action. On the other hand, habituation takes place when stimuli are repeatedly presented, so once habituation appears attention is not distracted by irrelevant stimuli. Looking for the mechanisms of habituation are Lorch and colleagues, among others (e.g., Lorch, Anderson, & Well, 1984; Lorch & Horn, 1986; Tipper, Bourque, Anderson, & Brehaut, 1989; see Cowan, 1988, for a review on habituation).

In conclusion, we favor the idea that information is processed in parallel during the first stages of processing, not only when the information is relevant but also when it is irrelevant. The point at which the conversion from parallel to serial processing takes place can be thought of as a bottleneck (as it has been previously proposed by others), which allows selection of messages and sends them to a serial processor, even after the information has been analyzed semantically. Conceptualized in this way, selective attention could be guided by semantic features. Taking into account neurophysiological research on selective attention, as well as Norman's pertinence model (Norman, 1968), we propose a moving bottleneck that can work at each point in the processing chain. Messages would be relevant when pertinence values were assigned to them in earlier processing stages. The pertinence value is changeable, and selective attention only works on messages with high pertinence values. On the other hand, due to habituation, the high pertinence value that stimuli acquire by means of novelty will diminish. This intermediate and more flexible explanation accounts for the manner in which systems that process in parallel until late stages elude overwhelming.

A better understanding of the flexibility with which the mechanisms operate in selective attention (excitation-inhibition, habituation) in conjunction with the importance that the stimuli might have acquired for the perceivers during development (pertinence value) will allow future research to use more adecuate approaches to study the role of irrelevant information when it interferes with the processing of relevant information.

ACKNOWLEDGMENT

This chapter was written for the most part while Soledad Ballesteros was a visiting scholar at Columbia University on sabbatical leave from the Universidad Nacional de Educación a Distancia. The support and resources of both institutions are gratefully acknowledged.

We thank A. Crespo for his help in collecting and analyzing some of the data reported here and in preparing the references for publication, Jose Manuel Reales for preparing the final figures, and Beryl E. Mckenzie for helpful comments on an earlier version of the chapter.

REFERENCES

Antes, J. R., Penland, J. G., & Metzger, R. L. (1981). Processing global information in briefly presented pictures. *Psychological Research*, *43*, 277–292.

Ballesteros, S. (1989a). Metric and perceived structures of lines varying in inclination and length. In D. Vickers & P. L. Smith (Eds.), *Human information processing: Measures, mechanisms, and models* (pp. 199–215). Amsterdam: North-Holland.

Ballesteros, S. (1989b). Some determinants of perceived structure: Effects of stimulus and tasks. In B. E. Shepp & S. Ballesteros (Eds.), *Object perception: Structure & Process* (pp. 235–266). Hillsdale, NJ: Lawrence Erlbaum Associates.

Ballesteros, S., Crespo, A., Manga, D., & Fernández Trespalacios, J. L. (1988, November). *Does normalization of irrelevant information exist in pattern matching?* Paper presented at the 29th Annual Meeting of the Psychonomic Society, Chicago.

Ballesteros, S., & Gonzalez Labra, M. J. (1989). Stimulus and observer determinants in the holistic and analytic processing. In H. Mandl, E. de Corte, N. Bennett, & H. F. Friedrich (Eds.), *Learning and instruction: European research in an international context* (Vol. 2.1, pp. 291–304). Oxford: Pergamon.

Ballesteros, S., Manga, D., Crespo, A., & Coello, T. (1989, November). *Context effects on letter matching.* Paper presented at the 30th Annual Meeting of the Psychonomic Society, Atlanta.

Besner, D. (1983). Visual pattern recognition: Size preprocessing re-examined. *Quarterly Journal of Experimental Psychology*, *35A*, 209–216.

Besner, D., & Coltheart, M. (1976). Mental size scaling examined. *Memory & Cognition*, *4*, 525–531.

Biederman, I. (1972). Perceiving real-world scenes. *Science*, *177*, 77–80.

Biederman, I., Glass, A. L., & Stacy, E. (1973). Searching for objects in real world scenes. *Journal of Experimental Psychology*, *97*, 22–27.

Biederman, I., Mezzanotte, R. J., & Rabinowitz, J. C. (1982). Scene perception: Detecting and judging objects undergoing relational violations. *Cognitive Psychology*, *14*, 143–177.

Boles, D. B. (1986). Confusion and visual effect in rhyme and name matching. *Perception & Psychophysics*, *39*, 123–128.

Boles, D. B., & Eveland, D. C. (1983). Visual and phonetic codes and the process of generation in letter matching. *Journal of Experimental Psychology: Human Perception and Performance*, *9*, 657–674.

Boyce, S. J., Pollatsek, A., & Rayner, K. (1989). Effect of background information on object identification. *Journal of Experimental Psychology: Human Perception and Performance*, *15*, 556–566.

Broadbent, D. E. (1958). *Perception and communication*. London: Pergamon.

Broadbent, D. E. (1982). Task combination and selective intake of information. *Acta Psychologica*, *50*, 253–290.

Bundesen, C., & Larsen, A. (1975). Visual transformation of size. *Journal of Experimental Psychology: Human Perception & Performance*, *1*, 214–220.

Bundesen, C., Larsen, A., & Farrell, J. E. (1981). Mental transformation of size and orientation. In A. Baddeley & J. Long (Eds.), *Attention & performance* (Vol. 9, pp. 279–294). Hillsdale, NJ: Lawrence Erlbaum Associates.

Carrasco, M., Kinchla, R. A., & Figueroa, J. G. (1988). Visual letter-matching and the time course of visual and acoustic codes. *Acta Psychologica, 69*, 1–17.

Coltheart, M. (1976). Mental size scaling examined. *Memory & Cognition, 4*, 525–531.

Cowan, N. (1988). Evolving conceptions of memory storage, selective attention, and their mutual constraints within the human information processing system. *Psychological Bulletin, 104*, 163–191.

Deutsch, J. A., & Deutsch, D. (1963). Attention: Some theoretical considerations. *Psychological Review, 70*, 80–90.

Dixon, P., & Just, M. A. (1978). Normalization of irrelevant dimensions in stimulus comparisons. *Journal of Experimental Psychology: Human Perception and Performance, 4*, 36–46.

Driver, J., & Baylis, G. C. (1989). Movement and visual attention: The spotlight metaphor breaks down. *Journal of Experimental Psychology: Human Perception & Performance, 15*, 448–456.

Duncan, J. (1980). The locus of interference in the perception of simultaneous stimuli. *Psychological Review, 87*, 272–300.

Duncan, J. (1984). Selective attention and the organization of visual information. *Journal of Experimental Psychology: General, 113*, 501–517.

Egeth, H. E., Folk C. L., & Mullin, P. A. (1989). Spatial parallelism in the processing of lines, letters, and lexicality. In B. E. Shepp & S. Ballesteros (Eds.), *Object perception: Structure and process* (pp. 19–52). Hillsdale, NJ: Lawrence Erlbaum Associates.

Eriksen, B. A., & Eriksen, C. W. (1974). Effects of noise letters upon the identification of a target letter in a nonsearch task. *Perception & Psychophysics, 16*, 143–149.

Eriksen, C. W., & Hoffman, J. E. (1972a). Some characteristics of selective attention in visual perception determined by vocal reaction time. *Perception & Psychophysics, 11*, 169–171.

Eriksen, C. W., & Hoffman, J. E. (1972b). Temporal and spatial characteristics of selective encoding from visual displays. *Perception & Psychophysics, 12*, 201–204.

Eriksen, C. W., & Hoffman, J. E. (1973). The extent of processing of noise elements during selecting encoding from visual displays. *Perception & Psychophysics, 14*, 155–160.

Eriksen, C. W., & Schultz, D. W. (1979). Information processing in visual search: A continuous flow conception and experimental results. *Perception & Psychophysics, 25*, 249–263.

Eriksen, C. W., & St. James, J. D. (1986). Visual attention within and around the field of focal attention: A zoom lens model. *Perception & Psychophysics, 40*, 225–240.

Flowers, J. H., & Wilcox, N. (1982). The effect of flanking context on visual classification: The joint contribution of interactions at different processing levels. *Perception & Psychophysics, 32*, 581–591.

Foard, C. F., & Kemler-Nelson, D. G. (1984). Holistic and analytic modes of processing: The multiple determinants of perceptual analysis. *Journal of Experimental Psychology: General, 113*, 94–111.

Freides, D., Tupler, L. A., Hall, J. M., & Fowler, T. E. (1988). On the independence of physical and nominal codes: A correlational analysis. *Brain and Cognition, 8*, 409–420.

Friedman, A. (1979). Framing pictures: The role of knowledge in automatized encoding and memory for gist. *Journal of Experimental Psychology: General, 108*, 316–355.

Garner, W. R. (1974). Dimensional and similarity structure in classification. In W. R. Garner (Ed.), *The processing of information and structure* (pp. 97–121). Hillsdale, NJ: Lawrence Erlbaum Associates.

Garner, W. R., & Felfoldy, G. L. (1970). Integrality of stimulus dimensions in various types of information processing. *Cognitive Psychology, 1*, 225–241.

Hawkins, H. L., & Shigley, R. H. (1972). Irrelevant information and processing mode in speeded discrimination. *Journal of Experimental Psychology, 96*, 389–395.

Henderson, J. M., Pollatsek, A., & Rayner, K. (1987). The effects of foveal priming and extrafoveal preview on object identification. *Journal of Experimental Psychology: Human Perception and Performance, 3,* 449–463.

Hoffman, J. E., & Nelson, B. (1981). Spatial selectivity in visual search. *Perception & Psychophysics, 30,* 283–290.

Humphreys, G. W., & Bruce, V. (1989). *Visual cognition. Computational, experimental and neuropsychological perspectives.* Hillsdale, NJ: Lawrence Erlbaum Associates.

Johnston, W. A., & Dark, V. J. (1982). In defence of intraperceptual theories of attention. *Journal of Experimental Psychology: Human Perception and Performance, 8,* 407–421.

Johnston, W. A., & Dark, V. J. (1986). Selective attention. *Annual Review of Psychology, 37,* 43–75.

Jolicoeur, P., & Besner, D. (1987). Additivity and interaction between size ratio and response category in the comparison of size-discrepant shapes. *Journal of Experimental Psychology: Human Perception and Performance, 13,* 478–487.

Jonides, J., & Mack, R. (1984). On the cost and benefit of cost and benefit. *Psychological Bulletin, 96,* 29–44.

Keele, S. W. (1986). Motor control. In K. R. Boff, L. Kaufman, & J. P. Thomas (Eds.), *Handbook of perception and human performance* (pp. 30-1/30–60). New York: Wiley.

Khomskaia, E. D. (1982). *Brain and activation.* New York: Pergamon.

Kubovy, M., & Podgorny, P. (1981). Does pattern matching require the normalization of size and orientation? *Perception & Psychophysics, 30,* 24–28.

Larsen, A. (1985). Pattern matching: Effects of size ratio, angular difference in orientation, and familiarity. *Perception & Psychophysics, 38,* 63–68.

Larsen, A., & Bundesen, C. (1978). Size scaling in visual pattern recognition. *Journal of Experimental Psychology: Human Perception and Performance, 4,* 1–20.

Lorch, E. P., Anderson, D. R., & Well, A. D. (1984). Effects of irrelevant information on speeded classification tasks: Interference is reduced by habituation. *Journal of Experimental Psychology: Human Perception and Performance, 10,* 850–864.

Lorch, E. P., & Horn, D. G. (1986). Habituation of attention to irrelevant stimuli in elementary school children. *Journal of Experimental Child Psychology, 41,* 184–197.

Miller, J. O. (1988). Response-compatibility effects in focused-attention tasks: A same-hand advantage in response activation. *Perception & Psychophysics, 43,* 83–89.

Miller, J. O. (1991). The flanker compatibility effect as a function of visual angle, attentional focus, visual transients, and perceptual load: A search for boundary conditions. *Perception & Psychophysics, 49,* 270–288.

Miller, J. O., & Bauer, D. W. (1981). Visual similarity and discrimination demands. *Journal of Experimental Psychology: General, 110,* 39–55.

Neill, W. T. (1977). Inhibition and facilitation processes in selective attention. *Journal of Experimental Psychology: Human Perception and Performance, 3,* 444–450.

Norman, D. A. (1968). Towards a theory of memory and attention. *Psychological Review, 75,* 522–536.

Palmer, S. E. (1975). The effects of contextual scenes on the identification of objects. *Memory & Cognition, 3,* 519–526.

Palmer, S. E. (1985). The role of symmetry in shape perception. *Acta Psychologica, 59,* 67–90.

Pomerantz, J. R., Pristach, E. A., & Carson, C. E. (1989). Attention and object perception. In B. E. Shepp & S. Ballesteros (Eds.), *Object perception: Structure & process* (pp. 53–89). Hillsdale, NJ: Lawrence Erlbaum Associates.

Posner, M. I. (1978). *Chronometric explorations of mind.* Hillsdale, NJ: Lawrence Erlbaum Associates.

Posner, M. I. (1980). Orienting of attention. *Quarterly Journal of Experimental Psychology, 32,* 3–25.

Posner, M. I., & Mitchell, R. F. (1967). Chronometric analysis of classification. *Psychological Review, 74*, 392–409.

Posner, M. I., Snyder, C. R. R. , & Davidson, B. (1980). Attention and the detection of signals. *Journal of Experimental Psychology: General, 109*, 160–174.

Rock, I., & Gutman, D. (1981). Effects of inattention on form perception. *Journal of Experimental Psychology: Human Perception and Performance, 7*, 275–285.

Santee, J. L., & Egeth, H. E. (1980). Selective attention in the speeded classification and comparison of multidimensional stimuli. *Perception & Psychophysics, 28*, 191–204.

Shepard, R. M. (1981). Psychophysical complementarity. In M. Kubovy & J. R. Pomerantz (Eds.), *Perceptual organization* (pp. 279–341). Hillsdale, NJ: Lawrence Erlbaum Associates.

Simion, F., Bagnara, S., Roncato, S., & Umilta, C. (1982). Transformation processes upon the visual code. *Perception & Psychophysics, 31*, 13–25.

Smith, L. B., & Kilroy, M. C. (1979). A continuum of dimensional separability. *Perception & Psychophysics, 25*, 285–291.

Sokolov, Y. N. (1963). *Perception and the conditioned reflex.* New York: Macmillan.

Stroop, J. R. (1935). Studies of interference in serial verbal reactions. *Journal of Experimental Psychology, 18*, 643–662.

Tipper, S. P., Bourque, T. A., Anderson, S. H., & Brehaut, J. O. (1989). Mechanisms of attention: A developmental study. *Journal of Experimental Child Psychology, 48*, 353–378.

Tipper, S. P., & Cranston, M. (1985). Inhibitory and facilitatory effects of ignored primes. *Quarterly Journal of Experimental Psychology, 37A*, 591–611.

Tipper, S. P., & Driver, J. (1988). Negative priming between pictures and words: Evidence for semantic analysis of ignored stimuli. *Memory & Cognition, 16*, 64–70.

Tipper, S. P., MacQueen, G. M., & Brehaut, J. O. (1988). Negative priming between response modalities: Evidence for the central locus of inhibition in selective attention. *Perception & Psychophysics, 43*, 45–52.

Treisman, A. (1964). Selective attention in man. *British Medical Bulletin, 20*, 12–16.

Treisman, A. (1969). Strategies and models of selective attention. *Psychological Review, 76*, 282–299.

Treisman, A., & Gelade, G. (1980). A feature-integration theory of attention. *Cognitive Psychology, 12*, 97–136.

Treisman, A., & Schmidt, H. (1982). Illusory conjunctions in the perception of objects. *Cognitive Psychology, 14*, 107–141.

Yantis, S., & Johnston, J. C. (1990). On the locus of visual selection: Evidence from focused attention tasks. *Journal of Experimental Psychology: Human Perception and Performance, 16*, 135–149.

11 FORM PERCEPTION

4 The Influence of Low-Level Processing in the Global Precedence Effect

William Lovegrove
Karen Pepper
University of Wollongong, New South Wales, Australia

The research reported in this chapter relates the known temporal properties of spatial frequency channels to the global precedence effect (GPE), which was studied in detail by Navon (1977). The general aim is to determine the extent to which the GPE and the inconsistency effect can be explained in terms of spatial frequency channels and the extent to which higher order mechanisms need to be invoked to explain the data. Both the GPE and the inconsistency effect are explained in detail shortly. Before that we discuss aspects of research on spatial frequency channels.

In the human visual system the rate of temporal processing decreases with increasing spatial frequency. This spatiotemporal interaction has been demonstrated with reaction time (Breitmeyer, 1975; Lupp, Hauske, & Wolf, 1976), visible persistence (Meyer & Maguire, 1977), critical duration (Watson & Nachmias, 1977), and cortical evoked potentials (Parker & Salzen, 1977; Vassilev, Manahilov, & Mitov, 1983; Vassilev & Stomonyakov, 1987). It has been shown that these temporal differences remain even when the different spatial frequencies are matched in apparent contrast with measures of reaction time (Breitmeyer, 1975; Lupp, Hauske, & Wolf, 1976) and visible persistence (Bowling, Lovegrove, & Mapperson, 1979).

These spatiotemporal interactions seem to reflect a global-to-local mode of visual information processing. The global, coarse configurational properties of the spatial stimulus are processed by fast-acting low spatial frequency mechanisms, and the local spatial details are subsequently processed by slower acting higher spatial frequency mechanisms. In other words, the visual system seems to process information about the forest before the trees. Little research, however, has been directed toward addressing this question with more natural stimuli than sine-wave gratings. Before continuing with this issue we briefly discuss some evidence for two subsystems within the visual system.

THE SUSTAINED AND TRANSIENT SUBSYSTEMS

It has been shown that spatial frequency channels also differ in their sensitivity to motion or flicker. In a typical experiment, participants are shown sine-wave gratings flickering at various rates. They are required to set contrast levels so that they just can see either flicker or pattern. When low spatial frequency gratings are moving quickly, participants characteristically see flicker at lower contrasts than pattern but experience the reverse at high spatial frequencies. Separate measures can be taken of sensitivity to flicker and pattern with a range of different spatial frequencies flickering at different speeds. Thus we can plot sensitivity functions for pattern and flicker thresholds at a range of spatial frequencies. With low spatial frequencies we are more sensitive to rapidly changing stimuli, but with high spatial frequencies we are more sensitive to stationary or slow-moving stimuli. The two functions obtained from such experiments are believed to measure two subsystems in the visual system, the transient and sustained subsystems. An extensive discussion of the properties of these systems and how they are identified can be found in Breitmeyer (1988). Breitmeyer also discussed the evidence indicating the physiological basis of these two systems.

The properties of these two subsystems have been identified and are shown in Table 4.1.

It has been proposed that the transient and sustained subsystems may be involved in global-to-local processing (Sestokas & Lehmkuhle, 1986; Sestokas, Lehmkuhle, & Kratz, 1987). It is possible that such a global-

TABLE 4.1
General Properties of the Sustained and Transient Subsystems

Sustained Subsystem	Transient Subsystem
Less sensitive to contrast	Highly sensitive to contrast
Most sensitive to high spatial frequencies	Most sensitive to low spatial frequencies
Most sensitive to low temporal frequencies	Most sensitive to high temporal frequencies
Most sensitive to the colors red and green	Most sensitive to the color blue
Slow transmission times	Fast transmission times
Responds throughout stimulus presentation	Responds at stimulus onset and offset
Predominates in central vision	Predominates in peripheral vision
The sustained system may inhibit the transient system	The transient system may inhibit the sustained system

to-local mode of visual processing is evident in higher order perceptual tasks, such as that devised by Navon (1977). In Navon's task respondents are shown large letters composed of smaller letters. The small and large letters may be consistent or inconsistent with each other. For example, respondents may be shown a large composite H or S constructed from a number of small Hs or small Ss (Fig. 4.1). Participants in the global identification condition are instructed to respond as soon as they can identify the larger letter as either an H or S. In the local identification condition they are asked to respond to the small component Ss and Hs. It was originally found (Navon, 1977) that participants are significantly faster in responding to the global composite than to the local component letters (the GPE). Furthermore, they respond more slowly to the inconsistent stimuli than to the consistent stimuli in the local condition but not the global condition. This is referred to as the inconsistency effect.

This effect has not always been found. Martin (1979) showed that with sparse stimulus components, local stimuli are processed more quickly than global stimuli. Kinchla and Wolfe (1977) showed that middle-range frequencies are processed more quickly than either high or low spatial frequencies. This raises the question of the extent to which the frequently reported global precedence effect is simply a reflection of low-level spatial frequency mechanisms.

A number of researchers have argued against this proposal by demonstrating that postperceptual processes (e.g., attention or response competition) clearly influence the magnitude of the global-precedence effect (Boer & Keuss, 1982; Garner, 1983; Miller, 1981; Shulman, Sullivan, Gish, & Sakoda, 1986; Shulman & Wilson, 1987). However, the global precedence effect remains to some extent when these processes are experimentally controlled (Hughes, 1986; Hughes, Layton, Baird, & Lester, 1984). The

(a).   (b).

```
H           H              S           S
H           H              S           S
H           H              S           S
H           H              S           S
H H H H H H                S S S S S S
H           H              S           S
H           H              S           S
H           H              S           S
H           H              S           S
```

FIG. 4.1.   Typical compound letter stimuli. Fig. 4.1 (a) shows a compound letter with consistent global and local letters, whereas Fig. 1(b) shows a compound letter with inconsistent global and local letters.

demonstration by Martin (1979) that local stimuli are sometimes processed more quickly than global stimuli clearly provides a further difficulty for an explanation of the global precedence effect in terms of low-level visual mechanisms.

If the low-level visual processes that contribute to the global precedence effect are the same processes revealed in psychophysical investigations of the influence of spatial frequency on reaction time, critical duration, visible persistence, and evoked potentials, the global precedence effect should be influenced by manipulations that are known to influence these psychophysical phenomena.

The general approach adopted in the research reported here has been to investigate the effect of a number of variables (with known influences on the perception of simple sine-wave stimuli) on the GPE. To the extent that these variables have similar effects on the GPE as they do on gratings, it is argued that the GPE reflects the involvement of spatial frequency channels.

The first series of experiments investigated Martin's findings that the GPE was not inevitable but depended on (amongst other things) stimulus sparsity. The second series considered the effect of color on the GPE. These were based on recent evidence suggesting that the transient and sustained subsystems are differentially influenced by color (Breitmeyer & Williams, 1990; Williams, Breitmeyer, & Lovegrove, 1990). The third series investigated the effects of color and spatial frequency adaptation on the GPE. The final series considered the role of low spatial frequency channels in the GPE. The involvement of low spatial frequency channels was reduced by the use of uniform-flicker masking and by high-pass filtering.

The general conclusion from these experiments is that low-level visual mechanisms play a major role in the GPE. This does not preclude the involvement of higher level processes but suggests that the latter may play a smaller role than had been argued previously.

THE EFFECT OF SPARSITY ON THE GPE

Martin (1979) demonstrated that the GPE could be reversed (i.e., local elements could be processed faster than global elements) simply by changing the density or sparsity of the stimuli. She did this by reducing the number of local letters present in the global stimulus. If her results are robust, they have important implications for the role of spatial frequency channels in more complex tasks.

Analysis of her experiments, however, shows that she not only changed stimulus sparsity but also stimulus size. In both the dense and the sparse conditions the global letter measured 4.1 × 2.8 degrees of visual angle. In the dense condition the global letter was made up of 0.35 × 0.49 degree local letters in a 7 × 5 letter matrix, whereas in the sparse condition the size of the local letters was increased to 0.68 × 0.51 degree in a 5 × 3 letter matrix. Kinchla and Wolfe (1979) showed that the strength and direction of the precedence effects can be affected by the retinal size of the stimuli. Consequently it is not clear whether stimulus sparsity or stimulus size or both are causing the reversal of the GPE. Furthermore, changing stimulus sparsity also changes the visibility of the stimulus. For example the local stimuli subjectively appear to be easier to see in the sparse condition than in the dense condition. Presumably there is less lateral masking in the sparse condition. The reverse appears to be true for the global stimuli. The first series of experiments, therefore, investigated the effects of target visibility and stimulus sparsity.

Experiment 1

Stimuli.   In the first of these experiments we controlled for the influence of stimulus size by using compound letter stimuli in which the global letters and the local letters always remained the same size. The global letters measured 4.4 × 2.8 degrees of visual angle for all conditions, and the local letters were 0.3 × 0.2 degrees. In the dense stimulus condition the local letters were arranged in a 9 × 7 letter matrix, whereas in the sparse stimulus condition they were arranged in a 5 × 4 letter matrix. This means that, unlike the stimuli used by Martin, there were wider gaps between the local letters in the sparse condition. (Fig. 4.2.)

Procedure.   The stimuli were generated by a computer program as white letters (E or H) against a black background, and were presented in a randomized order on the computer's monitor screen. Each compound letter was presented randomly to the left or right of the screen, so that the center of the global letter was 2.1 degrees of visual angle from a central fixation point. This prevents respondents from performing the task by fixating on a particular local feature of the displayed stimulus.

In each block of trials, the respondent was asked to attend selectively to either the global or the local letters, and to identify the relevant letter as either "E" or "H" by pressing one of two keys. The stimulus remained in view until the respondent made a response. The computer then recorded both the response time (RT) and the accuracy of each response. The participants were strongly encouraged to respond as quickly as possible without compromising accuracy. In each trial the compound letter stimulus was preceded by the presentation of a 3,000 ms central fixation point, and followed by a 1,000 ms random noise mask.

The experimental session began with 32 practice trials, followed by 160 test trials (4 trials for each stimulus type).

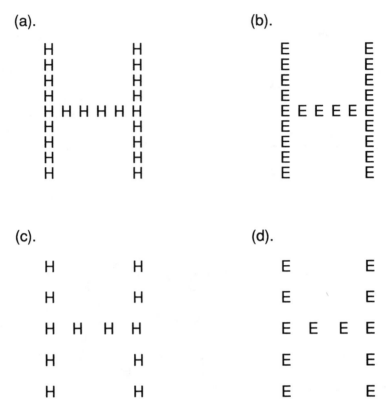

FIG. 4.2. Compound letter stimuli used in Experiment 1. Figures 4.2(a) and 4.2(b) are dense compound letters with consistent and inconsistent global and local letters, respectively. Figures 4.2(c) and 4.2(d) are sparse compound letters.

Participants. The participants were 14 undergraduate psychology students who participated in this experiment in order to earn extra credit points for their course. All had normal or corrected-to-normal vision and were aged from 18 to 53 years.

Results. The median RT for correct responses for each condition was calculated for each respondent. The means of these RT scores are shown in Fig. 4.3. These results show the normal pattern of the GPE in both the dense and the sparse stimulus conditions, although the GPE is not as strong in the sparse condition. Both the dense and the sparse conditions also produced an inconsistency effect, with a substantial increase in RT for local letters when the global letter was inconsistent with them.

These results were confirmed by submitting the RTs to an analysis of variance. The global letters were responded to significantly faster than the local letters [$F(1, 13) = 27.22, p < .002$]. Consistent letters at either global

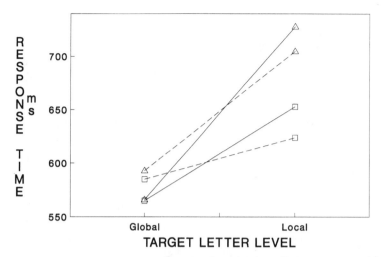

FIG. 4.3. Mean response time data for Experiment 1. Points connected by solid lines (———) represent the dense stimulus conditions, whereas points connected by dashed lines (- - - - -) represent the sparse stimulus conditions. Square symbols represent stimulus conditions with consistent global and local letters, whereas triangular symbols represent stimulus conditions with inconsistent letters.

or local level were more quickly responded to than inconsistent letters [$F(1, 13) = 15.99, p < .0015$]; and there was a significant interaction between letter level and letter consistency [$F(1, 13) = 48.32, p < .0001$]. There was no significant main effect for stimulus density [$F(1, 13) = 0.01, p > .94$], but there was a significant interaction between letter level and stimulus density [$F(1, 13) = 8.45, p < .012$]. The latter result reflects the weaker GPE in the sparse condition. There were no other significant effects. (Stimulus density $\times$ letter consistency interaction [$F(1, 13) = 0.45, p > .53$]; letter level $\times$ stimulus density $\times$ letter consistency interaction [$F(1, 13) < .01, p > .98$]).

All respondents showed a high degree of accuracy in their responses, with an average accuracy score of 98%.

Discussion. These results contradict Martin's (1979) finding of an apparent local precedence effect with a sparse stimulus configuration, but this leaves us with the question of why the GPE was weaker in the sparse stimulus condition. The sizes of the global and local letters were held constant, so size changes could not account for changes in the strength of the GPE in this case.

One possible explanation could be a difference in visibility between the global and local letters. In the dense stimulus condition, the local letters are very close to each other in space and so may be less visible due to lateral inhibition in the visual system. Conversely, the greater distance between local letters in the sparse condition may prevent lateral inhibition from coming into play, leaving the local letters more visible. At the same time, the sparsity of the local elements in the sparse conditions is likely to make the global letter less visible because of a lack of continuity of contour.

Hoffman (1980) found that if he distorted the shape of the global letter in a compound letter stimulus participants would display a local precedence effect, presumably because the global letter was now less visible. He argued that the GPE may be produced by the standard compound letter stimulus because the local letters here are somehow less visible than the global letter, and the better quality information about the global letter allows faster recognition.

Using compound geometric shapes, Navon (1983) found that the GPE could be weakened if the local elements were arranged in such a way that the "edges" of the global shape were not smooth. He also found that the GPE could be more difficult to produce if the global letter was made up of only a small number of local elements, regardless of their density. Boer and Keuss (1982) found that the GPE was lost if a few of the local letters in a compound stimulus were presented at a higher luminance than the rest, presumably making them more visible.

To investigate the role of visibility in the GPE a second experiment was carried out that attempted to equate the visibility of the stimulus components. This was done by manipulating the display duration for each type of stimulus until the respondent attained an equivalent degree of accuracy for each stimulus type.

Experiment 2

Stimuli.   The stimuli were the same as those used in Experiment 1.

Procedure.   The procedure was similar to that used in Experiment 1. However, in this case the compound letter stimulus was displayed for brief set durations of 10, 40, 70, and 100 ms, and followed immediately by a 1,000 ms random noise mask. Response time was measured from the onset of the letter stimulus.

Each participant was pretested for all stimulus conditions with all four durations. Thirty practice trials were followed by 448 test trials (14 trials for each condition). From these results we were able to determine, for each stimulus type, the duration that allowed participants to achieve at least 80% accuracy in their responses.

Each participant was then retested, with each stimulus type displayed for the optimal duration determined in the pretest stage for that particular participant. This should have ensured that all eight stimulus types—global and local, dense and sparse, consistent and inconsistent — were equally visible to the participant.

Participants. Participants were drawn from the same population as those in Experiment 1. Twelve participants were initially tested, but 4 were excluded because they failed to achieve the 80% accuracy criterion. The results shown below represent the remaining 8 participants.

Results. Response Times were determined for each participant as in Experiment 1, and the mean RTs for each condition are shown in Fig. 4.4. Despite the fact that all stimulus types should now be equally visible a significant GPE was found, with the global letters responded to more quickly than the local letter [$F(1, 7) = 7.93, p < .026$]. Once again there was no difference in RT between the dense and the sparse stimuli [$F(1, 7) = 0.08, p > .79$], although the weaker GPE in the sparse conditions produced a significant interaction between letter level and letter density [$F(1, 7) = 55.76, p < .0001$]. On the basis of these results, it seems unlikely that the GPE can be attributed solely to differences in visibility.

However, although the results of this experiment show a pattern suggesting an inconsistency effect, it was not statistically significant. (Main effect for letter consistency [$F(1, 7) = 1.64, p > .24$]; letter level × letter

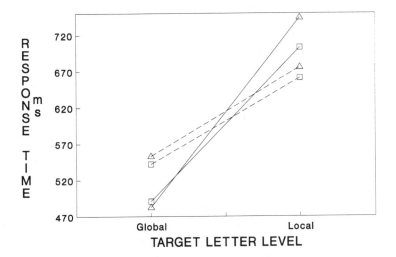

FIG. 4.4.   Mean response time data for Experiment 2. Points connected by solid lines (———) represent the dense stimulus conditions, whereas points connected by dashed lines (- - - - -) represent the sparse stimulus conditions. Square symbols represent stimulus conditions with consistent global and local letters, whereas triangular symbols represent stimulus conditions with inconsistent letters.

consistency interaction [$F(1, 7) = 3.05, p > .12$]). There were no other significant interactions.

Discussion.   Our results generally corroborate the findings of Hughes, Layton, Baird, and Lester (1984). In an experiment using equally visible horizontal and vertical compound line segments made up of small line segments, they found standard GPE and consistency effects. Interestingly, these researchers also discovered that the strength of the GPE decreased as luminance increased. Many of those studies that found little or no GPE had used high luminance stimuli (Kinchla & Wolfe, 1979; Martin, 1979; Pomerantz, 1983), so the luminance level may have played a part in producing the reversals in the GPE in such cases.

It has also been demonstrated that the location of the stimulus in the visual field can affect the strength and direction of precedence effects. Most of those experiments that have found a GPE, including our experiments, have used peripheral stimulus presentation (e.g., Navon, 1977, 1981b, 1983).

On the other hand, experiments using central presentation of stimuli have tended to find no GPE or even a local precedence effect (e.g., Boer & Keuss, 1982; Hoffman, 1980, Kinchla & Wolfe, 1979). In some cases, a GPE occurred with central presentation, but a bidirectional inconsistency effect was found, in which the RTs to both global and local letters were slowed by the presence of an inconsistent letter at the irrelevant level (e.g., Boer & Keuss).

Grice, Canham, and Boroughs (1983) compared the effects of presenting compound stimuli in the center and the periphery of the visual field. They found that only peripheral presentation produced a GPE, and an inconsistency effect for the local letters. There was no significant GPE with central presentation, but there was a bidirectional inconsistency effect for both global and local letters. In a similar experiment, Pomerantz (1983) also found that a strong GPE occurred with peripheral presentation only. These researchers have argued that peripheral presentation makes the local elements less visible because of the lack of acuity for fine detail in peripheral vision.

However, it could also be argued that central presentation makes the local elements more visible than the global elements. With most of the stimulus configurations used in these experiments (such as the letters E, H, and S) at least some of the local elements appear at or very close to the fixation point. This means that those local letters will fall in the high acuity foveal area of the visual field. The global letters, on the other hand, are likely to fall at least partly in the periphery. Significantly, Kinchla and Wolfe (1979) found that the GPE diminished in strength and eventually reversed as they increased the size of their centrally presented compound letter stimuli. The GPE disappeared when the compound letter was greater than about 6 degrees of visual angle. At this point, the boundaries of the global letter would have been more than 3 degrees from the central fixation point, and therefore encroaching on the less acutely perceived peripheral region of the visual field.

Navon and Norman (1983) addressed this problem by using compound stimuli composed of C and O shapes, so that the global and the local elements of the stimulus had equal eccentricity from the central fixation point. They used this configuration in sizes of 2 degrees (all foveal presentation) and 17.25 degrees (all peripheral presentation). Under both size conditions, the local and global elements of the stimulus should have been equally visible because they both fell in the same region of the visual field. They found both size conditions produced a significant GPE.

It is clear from these results that experiments must ensure that, as far as possible, both the global and local elements of the stimulus fall within the same region of the visual field. This is perhaps best done by presenting the entire stimulus at unpredictable locations around a central fixation point, in the periphery of the visual field. The stimulus might also be presented entirely in central vision, but in this case the compound letters have to be quite small and there would be a danger that the local element would be too small to be clearly visible.

The combined data from the experiments reported above demonstrate the robustness of the global precedence effect, while also demonstrating that it may be influenced by retinal position but only marginally by visibility.

THE EFFECT OF COLOR ON THE GPE

There is some evidence that the perception of color is connected with the transient and sustained visual subsystems. The perception of red and green has been associated with the sustained system, which is also involved in the detection of high spatial frequencies. The perception of blue seems to be connected with the transient system, which is also involved with the detection of low spatial frequencies (Breitmeyer & Williams, 1990; Williams, Breitmeyer, & Lovegrove, 1990). If low-level visual processes underlie the GPE, it is likely that the use of different colored stimuli should have a differential effect on the GPE. Specifically, the hypothesis predicts that the use of a blue stimulus should favor the perception of low spatial frequency stimuli such as the global letter in a compound letter, and slow the perception of high-frequency stimuli such as the local letter. Red and green stimuli, on the other hand, should favor the perception of high-frequency stimuli at the expense of the low-frequency stimuli. In short, blue stimuli should produce a stronger GPE than red or green stimuli. Our third experiment investigated this possibility.

Experiment 3

Stimuli. This experiment used only the set of dense compound letters from Experiment 1. However, in this case, each stimulus was either red, green or blue. The luminance and contrast of the three colors was matched at 15.8 cd/m².

Procedure   The procedure was the same as that used in Experiment 1. The three colors were presented in random order within each block of trials. The experimental session began with 24 practice trials followed by 240 test trials (20 trials for each condition).

Subjects.   Fourteen participants were drawn from the same population as that used in Experiment 1 (age range: 18–42 years).

Results.   Response Times were determined for each participant, as in Experiment 1, and the mean RTs are shown in Fig. 4.5. The results would

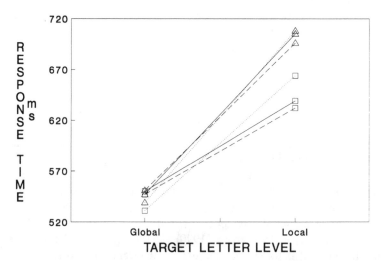

FIG. 4.5.   Mean response time data for Experiment 3. Points connected by solid lines (———) represent the red stimulus conditions, points connected by dashed lines (- - - - -) represent the green stimulus conditions, and points connected by dotted lines (........) represent the blue stimulus conditions. Square symbols represent stimulus conditions with consistent global and local letters, whereas triangular symbols represent stimulus conditions with inconsistent letters.

seem to indicate that blue stimuli produce a stronger GPE than red or green stimuli. This pattern of results is consistent with the hypothesis that faster perception of the global letter is mediated by the fast-transmitting transient visual system.

The results were confirmed by submitting the RTs for all conditions to a three-way analysis of variance. This revealed a significant overall GPE (main effect of letter level [$F(1, 13) = 91.28, p < .001$] inconsistency effect (main effect of letter consistency [$F(1, 13) = 66.2, p < .001$], and interaction of letter level and letter consistency [$F(1, 13) = 13.95$].

There was no significant main effect of color [$F(2, 26) = 0.26, p > .78$], so it was clear that no color was more visible than the others on average. However, there was a significant interaction between color and letter level [$F(2, 26) = 4.35, p < .023$], confirming that the different colors did differentially affect the strength of the GPE. There were no significant interactions of color with letter consistency [$F(2, 26) = 0.21, p > .81$], or color with letter level and letter consistency [$F(2, 26) = 0.92, p > .41$], indicating that the inconsistency effect was not affected by color.

Once again, the participants responded with a high level of accuracy ($M = 98\%$ accuracy).

This experiment provides further evidence for the involvement of low-level mechanisms in the GPE. The failure to find an effect of color on the inconsistency effect, however, suggests that this effect may reflect higher order processes.

THE EFFECTS OF SPATIAL FREQUENCY AND COLOR ADAPTATION ON THE GPE

It has been demonstrated that adaptation to gratings of a particular spatial frequency will selectively diminish the sensitivity of the visual system to other stimuli of the same and similar spatial frequencies for some time afterwards (e.g., Blakemore & Campbell, 1969; Graham & Nachmias, 1971; Pantle & Sekuler, 1968). Similarly, adaptation to gratings of a particular color should lower the visual system's sensitivity to stimuli of that color (Lovegrove & Over, 1972; McCollough, 1965).

If the GPE is brought about by the operation of low level processes such as spatial frequency and color channels, the GPE should be able to be modified by first adapting the participants to spatial frequencies and colors similar to those that occur in the compound letter stimuli. Our fourth experiment tested this hypothesis.

Experiment 4

Stimuli. The compound letter stimuli were the same as those used in Experiment 3, except that only the red and green stimuli were used. Two types of adaptation stimuli were used. The spatial frequency and color adaptation condition employed a red vertical square wave grating on a black background. The bars of the grating were the same width as the local letters in the compound letter stimuli (0.18 degrees of visual angle), which is equivalent to a spatial frequency of 2.8 cycles/degrees. The second was a control condition that employed a blank gray field with a luminance equal to the average luminance of a red grating stimulus.

Procedure.   The experiment was conducted in two separate sessions. The procedure was similar to that used in Experiment 3, apart from the inclusion in this experiment of adaptation stimuli prior to the presentation of the compound letter stimuli. In one session, the participants were asked to adapt to the red grating for 5 min before the test trials were run, and in the other (control) session they were asked to adapt to the blank gray field only. The adaptation was refreshed by 1-min presentations of the adaptation stimuli at about 4-min intervals throughout the experiment. The two sessions were held on separate days in order to prevent the adaptation from one session carrying over to the next. Each session began with 24 practice trials followed by 160 test trials (20 trials for each stimulus type).

Participants.   Eighteen participants were drawn from the same population used in the previous experiments (age range: 18–51 years.)

Results.   Rosponse Times were calculated for each participant as in the previous experiments, and the mean RTs are shown in Fig. 4.6. A four-way analysis of variance indicated that a GPE and inconsistency effect were present. (Main effect of letter level [$F(1, 17) = 145.86, p < .001$], main effect of letter consistency [$F(1, 17) = 32.36, p < .001$], interaction of letter level and letter consistency [$F(1, 17) = 21.75, p < .002$]).

Adaptation to the red grating seemed to slow response times in general (main effect of adaptation type [$F(1, 17) = 4.83, p < .042$]). However, the significant interaction between letter level and adaptation type [$F(1,17) = 6, 65, p < .02$] confirmed that adaptation to the grating differentially affected RT to the global and local letters. Specifically, adaptation to the grating seemed to increase substantially the RT to the global letter while having little effect on responses to the local letters, thus strengthening the GPE. Presumably, the grating that we used here was composed of spatial frequency components most similar to those comprising the global letter in the compound stimulus. Adaptation to the grating, however, seemed to have no significant effect on the inconsistency effect, (Interaction of adaptation type × letter consistency [$F(1, 17) = 2.55, p > .13$], interaction of adaptation type × letter level × letter consistency [$F(1, 17) = 1.62, p > .22$]).

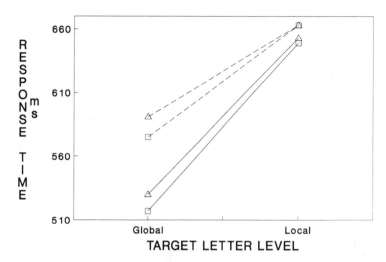

FIG. 4.6.   Mean response time data for Experiment 4. Points connected by solid lines (———) represent the stimulus conditions preceded by a blank gray adaptation field, whereas points connected by dashed lines (- - - - -) represent the stimulus conditions preceded by a red square-wave adaptation grating. Square symbols represent stimulus conditions with red letters, whereas triangular symbols represent stimulus conditions with green letters.

Strangely, it seems that the red letter stimuli were on average responded to slightly faster than the green letters despite the fact that they were equal in luminance and contrast. (Main effect of letter color [$F(1, 17) = 5.47, p < .03$]). However, adaptation to the color red seemed not to have any differential effect on perception of the compound letters. (Interaction of adaptation type × letter color [$F(1, 17) = 0.01, p > .94$], interaction of adaptation type × letter color × letter level [$F(1, 17) = 0.38, p > .55$], interaction of adaptation type × letter color × letter consistency [$F(1, 17) = 2.13, p > .16$], interaction of adaptation type × letter color × letter level × letter consistency [$F(1, 17) = 0.04, p > .85$]).

No other interactions were significant. The participants all maintained a high level of accuracy in their responses, with a mean accuracy of 99%.

Discussion.   The demonstration of spatial frequency adaptation of the GPE further implicates low-level mechanisms. The absence of color adaptation may be best understood in terms of the spatial frequency content of the adaptation stimuli used. It has been shown previously (Lovegrove & Badcock, 1981) that color selectivity in the tilt illusion is only found with high and not with low spatial-frequency stimuli. Again the failure of grating adaptation to influence the inconsistency effect suggests that it and the GPE probably reflect different mechanisms.

THE EFFECTS OF UNIFORM FIELD FLICKER AND
SPATIAL FREQUENCY FILTERING ON THE GPE

Adaptation to gratings is not the only way to manipulate the involvement of visual spatial frequency channels. The transient visual subsystem, which appears to mediate the perception of low spatial-frequency stimuli, is also sensitive to stimulus onset and offset, movement, and flicker. It has been demonstrated that the use of a uniform field flicker (UFF) mask can increase response times, evoked potential latencies and contrast detection thresholds for low spatial frequency stimuli, but does not increase them for high spatial frequency stimuli (Baro & Lehmkuhle, 1989, 1990; Breitmeyer, Levi, & Harwerth, 1981). If the GPE is partially the result of the involvement of the fast-transmitting transient system in perceiving the global aspect of the stimulus, we should be able to weaken or obliterate the GPE if we add a UFF mask to the compound stimulus.

In a study using compound letter stimuli, Lovegrove, Lehmkuhle, Baro, and Garzia (1991) found that the addition of a 12Hz UFF to the stimulus did indeed weaken the GPE. Uniform field flicker not only increased RT for the global letter but also decreased RT for the local letters, possibly because the masking of the low spatial frequency mechanisms had brought about a disinhibition of the high spatial frequency mechanisms involved in perceiving the local letters.

The involvement of high- and low-spatial frequency detection mechanisms can perhaps be most directly investigated using stimuli from which either the low spatial-frequency or high-spatial frequency components have been selectively filtered out. The study by Lovegrove et al. compared standard compound letter stimuli with compound letters that have had their high-spatial frequency components filtered out by the use of a diffusing screen, giving the stimuli a blurred appearance. These filtered stimuli produced a stronger GPE than the standard unfiltered stimuli, chiefly because the RT for the local letters was increased in the filtered condition. It seems that the lack of high-spatial frequency information in the filtered stimuli made the perception of the local elements more difficult.

A related study by Badcock, Whitworth, Badcock, and Lovegrove (1990) compared the RTs produced by standard compound letter stimuli with versions of the same stimuli that had had the low spatial frequency components filtered out. The standard stimuli produced the usual GPE and inconsistency effects. The filtered stimuli, however, greatly increased the RT for the global letter, while having little effect on RT to the local letters. The lack of low spatial-frequency information in the filtered stimuli appears to have a selectively detrimental effect on the perception of the global letters. The inconsistency effect also disappeared when the filtered stimuli were used.

THE ROLE OF HIGHER ORDER PROCESSES
IN THE GPE

Not all researchers have concluded that the GPE is a reflection of lower order processes. Miller (1981) reported an experiment in which participants were required to respond to the presence of a target letter in a compound letter stimulus. The target letter could appear in the global level only, in local level only, or in both the global and the local levels. He found that participants responded more quickly when the target letter was in the global level only than when it was in the local level only, which is consistent with previous findings. However, the participants responded even more quickly when the target letter appeared in both the global and local levels. Miller (1981) suggested that this indicates that the low-level visual processes transmit information about the global and local levels at equal speeds to a single decision mechanism. When this decision mechanism has received enough information about the stimulus it is able to make a decision about the presence or absence of the target letter. If the target letter is present at both global and local levels of the stimulus, the decision mechanism receives confirmatory information from two sources, allowing it to make a decision sooner. Miller accounted for the RT advantage of the global-only target letter over the local-only target letters by proposing that the global information has "greater strength" (p. 1171) or "more salience or more attention-grabbing power than local information" (p. 1164).

However, such an explanation leaves unanswered the question of why the global information has such "attention-grabbing power." Some quality or property of the low-level sensory information about the global level must have some influence on this "salience" or "attention-grabbing power," and one of these properties could be the relative speed of the transmission of information.

Navon (1981a) pointed out that Miller's (1981) results may be explained by using a parallel model of low-level visual processing in which there is a partial temporal overlap in the processing of global and local information, with the global information being processed slightly faster, rather than a serial model in which the processing of global information must be finished before local processing can begin. If the former model is correct, it is possible that some early information about the local level could be added to the almost complete information about the global level. In this case, the participant may be able to respond more quickly to a target letter that is present in both global and local levels of the stimulus. In a situation where the target is present at the global level only the participant would probably have to wait until the information about the global level alone was complete before making a response.

Ward (1982) also reported experimental results that suggest that attentional factors may play a part in the GPE. In his series of experiments two compound letters were displayed consecutively. In half the trials participants were required to identify the letters in either the global level or the local level of both compound letter stimuli. In the other half of the trials they had to identify the local letter in the first stimulus and the global letter in the second stimulus, or vice versa. The participants responded more quickly in those trials in which their attention was directed to the same level in both stimuli, and responded more slowly in those trials in which their attention was divided between levels. Most interestingly, RT was faster when the respondents had to identify the local letter in an undivided (local-and-local) attention trial than when they had to identify the global letter in a divided (local-and-global) attention trial. However, this result probably reflects the presence of a bidirectional inconsistency effect rather than a GPE.

Although it seems that the GPE is brought about chiefly by low-level visual processes, there is some evidence that the inconsistency effect that usually accompanies it may be connected with higher order processes. Kimchi and Palmer (1985) found that the same set of compound stimuli could produce different patterns of responses when different instructions were given to the respondents. The stimuli that Kimchi and Palmer used were squares and rectangles made up of much smaller black and white squares ("checkerboard") or rectangles ("stripes"). When participants were asked to identify the global form as either "square" or "rectangular" and the local forms as "checkerboard" or "stripes" no GPE or inconsistency effect was found. However, when another set of respondents were asked to identify the local forms, as well as the global forms, as "squares" or "rectangles" a bidirectional inconsistency effect was found. It seems that the use of the same names to denote the features of both global and local levels increased the interference caused by the content of the irrelevant stimulus level.

GENERAL CONCLUSIONS

The results of all of the experiments reported here indicate that low-level visual mechanisms have a strong involvement in the GPE. This necessitates a revision of many previous positions that have argued that the GPE was primarily a higher order effect. It does not eliminate the possibility of higher level processes in the GPE but shows that their functioning must be limited by the output of lower level mechanisms. At the same time the inconsistency effect did not show the same dependence on low-level visual processes. This suggests that it reflects a different mechanism, presumably a higher level mechanism.

REFERENCES

Badcock, J. C., Whitworth, F. A., Badcock, D. R., & Lovegrove, W. J. (1990). Low-frequency filtering and the processing of local–global stimuli. *Perception, 19*, 617–629.

Baro, J. A., & Lehmkuhle, S. (1989). The effects of a luminance-modulated background on grating-evoked cortical potentials in the cat. *Visual Neuroscience, 3*, 563–572.

Baro, J. A., & Lehmkuhle, S. (1990). The effects of a luminance-modulated background on human grating-evoked potentials. *Clinical Vision Science, 5*, 265–270.

Blakemore, C., & Campbell, F. W. (1969). On the existence of neurones in the human visual system selectively sensitive to the orientation and size of retinal images. *Journal of Physiology, 203*, 237–260.

Boer, L. C., & Keuss, P. J. (1982). Global precedence as a postperceptual effect: An analysis of speed-accuracy tradeoff functions. *Perception and Psychophysics, 31*, 358–366.

Bowling, A., Lovegrove, W., & Mapperson, B. (1979). The effect of spatial frequency and contrast on visible persistence. *Perception, 8*, 529–539.

Breitmeyer, B. G. (1975). Simple reaction time as a measure of the temporal response properties of transient and sustained channels. *Vision Research, 15*, 1411–1412.

Breitmeyer, B. G. (1988 August). *Reality and relevance of sustained and transient channels.* Paper presented to the 24th International Congress of Psychology, Sydney.

Breitmeyer, B. G., Levi, D. M., & Harwerth, R. S. (1981). Flicker masking in spatial vision. *Vision Research, 21*, 1377–1385.

Breitmeyer, B. G., & Williams, M. (1990). Effects of isoluminant-background color on metacontrast and stroboscopic motion: Interactions between sustained (P) and transient (M) channels. *Vision Research, 30*, 1069–1075.

Garner, W. (1983). Asymmetric interactions of stimulus dimensions in perceptual information processing. In T. Tighe & B. Shepp (Eds.), *Perception, cognition and development: Interactional analyses* (pp. 1–38). Hillsdale, NJ: Lawrence Erlbaum Associates.

Graham, N., & Nachmias, J. (1971). Detection of grating patterns containing two spatial frequencies: A comparison of single-channel and multiple-channel models. *Vision Research, 11*, 251–259.

Grice, G. R., Canham, L., & Boroughs, J. M. (1983). Forest before the trees? It depends where you look. *Perception and Psychophysics, 33*, 121–128.

Hoffman, J. E. (1980). Interaction between global and local levels of a form. *Journal of Experimental Psychology: Human Perception and Performance, 6*, 222–234.

Hughes, H. C. (1986). Asymetric interference between components of suprathreshold gratings. *Perception and Psychophysics, 40*, 241–250.

Hughes, H. C., Layton, W. M., Baird, J. C., & Lester, L. S. (1984). Global precedence in visual pattern recognition. *Perception and Psychophysics, 35*, 361–371.

Kimchi, R., & Palmer, S. E. (1985). Separability and integrality of global and local levels of hierarchical patterns. *Journal of Experimental Psychology: Human Perception and Performance, 11*, 673–688.

Kinchla, R. A., & Wolfe, J. M. (1979). The order of visual processing: "top-down," "bottom-up," or "middle-out." *Perception and Psychophysics, 25*, 225–231.

Lovegrove, W. J., & Badcock, D. (1981). The effect of spatial frequency on color selectivity in the tilt illusion. *Vision Research, 21*, 1235–1237.

Lovegrove, W. J., Lehmkuhle, S., Baro, J. A., & Garzia, R. (1991). The effects of uniform field flicker and blurring on the global precedence effect. *Bulletin of the Psychonomic Society, 29*, 289–291.

Lovegrove, W. J., & Over, R. (1972). Color adaptation of spatial frequency detectors in the human visual system. *Science, 176*, 541–543.

Lupp, U., Hauske, G., & Wolf, W. (1976). Perceptual latencies to sinusoidal gratings. *Vision Research, 16*, 969–972.

Martin, M. (1979). Local and global processing: The role of sparsity. *Memory and Cognition, 7*, 476–484.

McCollough, C. (1965). Color adaptation of edge-detectors in the human visual system. *Science, 149*, 1115–1116.

Meyer, G., & Maguire, W. (1977). Spatial frequency and the mediation of short-term visual storage. *Science, 198*, 524–525.

Miller, J. (1981). Global precedence in attention and decision. *Journal of Experimental Psychology: Human Perception and Performance, 7*, 1161–1174.

Navon, D. (1977). Forest before the trees: The precedence of global features in visual perception. *Cognitive Psychology, 9*, 353–383.

Navon, D. (1981a). Do attention and decision follow perception? Comment on Miller. *Journal of Experimental Psychology: Human Perception and Performance, 7*, 1175–1182.

Navon, D. (1981b). The forest revisited: More on global precedence. *Psychological Research, 43*, 1–32.

Navon, D. (1983). How many trees does it take to make a forest? *Perception, 12*, 239–254.

Navon, D., & Norman, J. (1983). Does global precedence really depend on visual angle? *Journal of Experimental Psychology: Human Perception and Performance, 9*, 955–965.

Pantle, A., & Sekuler, R. W. (1968). Contrast response of human visual mechanisms to orientation and detection of velocity. *Vision Research, 9*, 397–406.

Parker, D., & Salzen, E. (1977). Latency changes in the human visual evoked response to sinusoidal gratings. *Vision Research, 17*, 1201–1204.

Pomerantz, J. R. (1983). Global and local precedence: Selective attention in form and motion perception. *Journal of Experimental Psychology: General, 112*, 516–540.

Sestokas, A., & Lehmkuhle, S. (1986). Visual response latency of X-and Y-cells in dorsal geniculate nucleus of the cat. *Vision Research, 26*, 1041–1054.

Sestokas, A., Lehmkuhle, S., & Kratz (1987). Visual latency of ganglion X- and Y-cells: A comparison with geniculate X- and Y-cells. *Vision Research, 27*, 1399–1408.

Shulman, G. L., Sullivan, M. A., Gish, K., & Sakoda, W. J. (1986). The role of spatial frequency channels in the perception of local and global structure. *Perception, 15*, 259–273.

Shulman, G. L., & Wilson, J. (1987). Spatial frequency and selective attention to local and global information. *Perception, 16*, 89–101.

Vassilev, A., Manahilov, V., & Mitov, D. (1983). Spatial frequency and the pattern onset–offset response. *Vision Research, 23*, 1417–1422.

Vassilev, A., & Stomonyakov, V. (1987). The effect of grating spatial frequency on the early VEP-component CI. *Vision Research, 27*, 727–729.

Ward, L. M. (1982). Determinants of attention to local and global features of visual forms. *Journal of Experimental Psychology: Human Perception and Performance, 8*, 562–581.

Watson, A. B., & Nachmias, J. (1977). Patterns of temporal interaction in the detection of gratings. *Vision Research, 17*, 893–902.

Williams, M., Breitmeyer, B., & Lovegrove, W. (1990). *Metacontrast with masks varying in spatial frequency and wavelength.* Unpublished manuscript.

5 Eye Movement Measures and Connectionist Models of Form Perception

Cyril R. Latimer
Catherine J. Stevens
University of Sydney, Australia

The general hypothesis under scrutiny in this chapter is that the recognition of geometric forms, like other patterns, is mediated by the extraction and differential weighting of local features (Smith & Evans, 1989; Sutherland, 1968; Treisman, 1986; Uhr & Vossler, 1963). It is further proposed that eye movements and fixations on forms can provide potent indices of these otherwise unobservable recognition processes, and that mechanisms in the form of artificial neural networks may be a fruitful way to model them.

Research on form perception in general has been reviewed by Zusne (1970) and more recently by Pomerantz (1986) and Quinlan (1991b). The validity of eye movement indices of cognitive processes is now well established (Findlay, 1985; Just & Carpenter, 1976), and, in particular, results of the use of eye movement measures of form perception suggest that fixations, fixation time, and order of scan are indeed useful indices of underlying processes. For example, Baker and Loeb (1973) reported significant correlations between fixation duration on sections of geometric forms and respondents' ratings of the importance of these sections. In their examination of the role of eye movements in form perception, Bozkov, Bohdanecky, Radil-Weiss, Mitrani, and Yakimoff (1982) and Bozkov, Bohdanecky, and Radil-Weiss (1987) demonstrated that the majority of fixations on polygonal forms are located at angles and that the means of fixation distributions are most distant from acute than from obtuse angles.

The experimental work reported in this chapter follows a line of research developed by Pasnak (1971) and Pasnak and Tyer (1985, 1986), who presented evidence that, in form discrimination, respondents make most use of unique and idiosyncratic parts of the form. With experience, participants learn to attend to the regions of complex geometric forms that contain the most discriminating features.

A further guiding principle in the present study is the suggestion by Newell (1973) that an experimenter should know the methods that participants adopt when carrying out cognitive tasks (see also Barlow & Hersen, 1984, and Bush, 1963). In line with this suggestion, we make use of detailed analysis of data from individual respondents, and, in this way, development or acquisition of feature-extraction and weighting processes that mediate the ability to discriminate a standard from comparison forms is monitored closely.

CONNECTIONIST MODELS OF FORM PERCEPTION

Artificial neural networks that learn to distinguish and recognize visual forms employ the sorts of feature-extraction and feature-weighting processes that many psychologists believe may mediate human recognition. Bechtel and Abrahamsen (1991), Hinton (1981), Hrechanyk and Ballard (1982), McClelland and Rumelhart (1986) and Quinlan (1991a) provide examples of this approach. In the simplest case, a network may consist of an array of input units and a layer of output units that, when fully connected, have connection strengths (or weights on connections) that are initially random. A pattern is clamped onto the array of input units and the resulting input unit activations are transmitted forward to the output units. The activation of an output unit is usually the sum of its inputs multiplied by their weights minus a threshold value. The obtained activations of the output units are compared with desired activation and, if these differ, errors between desired and obtained outputs are generated. A learning rule then acts to reduce the errors by modifying weight on connections between inputs and outputs. The process of applying inputs and reducing error by modification of weights continues until the obtained outputs match the desired outputs, at which time the network is said to have learned how to discriminate between patterns of input. Essentially, this process is one of the network progressively assigning more weight to the more discriminating elements of patterns until it is able to give the desired outputs to particular patterns of input.

This chapter seeks evidence of possible parallels between the feature-extraction and weighting in connectionist models and the processes that mediate human form perception. We can ask the question: Is there any evidence that the pattern recognition processes embodied in artificial neural networks have *psychological reality*? Specifically, when humans learn to distinguish a standard geometric form from a set of distractors do they extract features and progressively assign more weight to the more discriminating features? To answer these questions it is necessary to compare closely the performance of artificial neural networks and human respondents during recognition of geometric forms. The essential experimental strategy is to train a neural network to discriminate a standard from comparison forms and compare its feature-weightings with those of participants trained to perform the same task. It is a simple matter to observe and record feature-weighting in a network, but one must find valid and reliable indicators of the features extracted and of the weights assigned to these features by the participants. The research reported here makes use of eye movement and fixation indices of human feature-extraction and feature-weighting processes.

Eye Movement and Fixation Indices of Form Perception Processes

The methods and assumptions involved in this approach to form perception have been set out in detail by Latimer (1988, 1990). In summary, a standard geometric form and a set of comparison forms that differ from the standard by varying degrees are created. Participants are instructed on each trial to inspect the standard form and then to judge whether a succeeding form is the same as or different from the standard. Succeeding forms are presented under conditions of high illumination and low contrast that produce a spotlight of clear vision within a radius of approximately 5 to 6 degrees around fixation. The effect, illustrated in Fig. 5.1, forces the respondent to scan the succeeding forms in order to judge their sameness or difference. In this way, fast feature-extraction and feature-weighting processes are slowed and, as such, become observable, measurable, and quantifiable. During serial inspection of the succeeding forms, fixations, fixation duration, and order of scan are recorded by electro-oculography (EOG).

Cumulative Fixation Time.   Cumulative fixation time (CFT) can be used as a measure of weight assigned to regions of forms. It is assumed that, with experience, respondents learn to attend to the more discriminating parts of the forms, and the resulting nonuniform distribution of attention, represented by fixation time, can be used as an indication of assigned weight.

Scanpath Order.   Another measure of weight assigned to features by participants is order of scan. Assume that while subjects continue to scan a form, they have not extracted sufficient information for its discrimination. Scanpath order can then be an indicator of weight if we assume that the most discriminating regions of the forms are scanned last in scanpaths. Weight is then measured as a function of inverse order of scan. This may

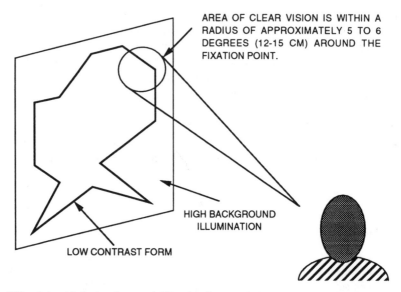

FIG. 5.1. High background illumination and low contrast restrict the participant's view of the large geometric forms to within a radius of approximately 5° - 6° (12-15 cm) around each fixation. From Latimer (1990). Reprinted by permission of Elsevier Science Publishers.

not be a valid assumption on any *one* trial, but, across many trials participants often come to terminate their scanpaths on the most discriminating regions and, in fact, some participants often discriminate on the basis of one fixation on the most discriminating region. The assumptions underlying the scanpath inverse order measure have been outlined in detail by Latimer (1990).

EXPERIMENT 1: FEATURE-WEIGHTING IN COMPLEX FORM PERCEPTION

Artificial Neural Network Simulation 1

To generate hypotheses for test in this experiment it was first necessary to train a neural network to discriminate a standard from a set of comparison forms. Figure 5.2 illustrates how the comparison forms were so constructed that they all differed from the standard in the top-right corner but were the same as the standard in the top-left corner. Two comparison forms were the same and five were different from the standard in the lower-left corner, whereas three comparison forms were the same and four were different in the lower-right corner. In this way, the top-right corner was established as

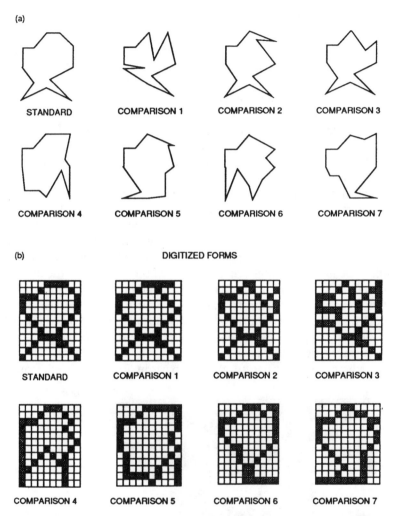

FIG. 5.2. (a) Standard and comparison geometric forms. (b) Digitized versions of forms in 10 × 12 matrices for presentation to the single-layer perceptron. From Latimer (1990). Reprinted by permission of Elsevier Science Publishers.

a region of maximum difference and the top-left corner a region of absolute sameness. The remaining two regions were intermediate regions of sameness and difference.

A single-layer network with 120 input units and one output unit was trained using MacBrain software and the digitized forms depicted in Fig. 5.2, to switch on the output unit when it received the standard pattern and to switch off the output unit when it received any one of the comparison patterns. A multilayer network is unnecessary for this task and a single-layer architecture, besides being more parsimonious, affords a much clearer interpretation of the weights between the input and output units. For a recent discussion of the merits of modeling learning processes with single-layer networks see Gluck and Bower (1988). The network was trained using the simple delta learning rule and the activation function for the output unit was the weighted sum of inputs minus the threshold, which was set to 0.5. The learning rate was 0.2 and the network was able to discriminate the standard from the comparison patterns after 500 cycles. The network architecture, with the input units arranged in the form of a 10 × 12 retinal array, together with formulae for activation function and learning rule are presented in Fig. 5.3. Additionally, in Fig. 5.3, the standard form has been clamped onto the input units and the output unit switched on.

Figure 5.4 is a three-dimensional representation of the final weights assigned to connections between the input units and the single output unit. The figure depicts the input array viewed from above the lower left-hand corner where column height indicates magnitude of weight. The higher the column, the more weight assigned to the connection between the input and the output unit, and white-topped columns signify positive weights whereas, black-topped columns indicate negative weights. It can be seen that the network has placed most weight on the most discriminating top-right region of the forms. It should also be noted that positive weight has been assigned to connections between the output unit and input units in the lower-left region where, in fact, five of the comparison forms differed from the

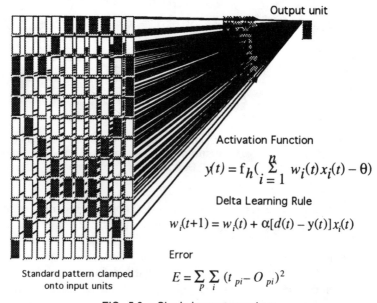

Output unit

Activation Function

$$y(t) = f_h(\sum_{i=1}^{n} w_i(t)x_i(t) - \theta)$$

Delta Learning Rule

$$w_i(t+1) = w_i(t) + \alpha[d(t) - y(t)]x_i(t)$$

Error

$$E = \sum_p \sum_i (t_{pi} - O_{pi})^2$$

Standard pattern clamped
onto input units

FIG. 5.3.   Single-layer perceptron.

FIG. 5.4. Three-dimensional representation of final weights assigned to connections between input and output units. The distribution of weights is viewed from the bottom-left-hand corner of the input array. Column height represents connection strength or weight: Black-topped columns indicate negative weight; white-topped columns indicate positive weight.

standard. However, by far the most weight has been assigned to connections between the output unit and the most discriminating top-right input units.

Hypotheses

Like the artificial neural network, participants, with practice at discriminating the standard from comparisons, should progressively assign more weight to the most discriminating region of the forms and, as a corollary, less weight to the less discriminating regions. Concomitantly, participants should require fewer fixations and less time to discriminate the standard from comparisons.

Method

Participants.   Participants were two postgraduate and two undergraduate students enrolled in psychology at the University of Sydney. Participants were between 21 and 25 years of age and had uncorrected and corrected 20/20 vision.

Apparatus.   A complete account of apparatus and procedure is provided in Latimer (1990). In summary, the forms measuring 104 cm high × 84 cm wide (40.22 degrees × 32.96 degrees) were back projected onto a large screen from a Kodak slide projector placed 1.44 meters behind the screen and viewed by the respondent from a distance of 1.42 meters. Comparison forms were presented under high illumination and low contrast, where contrast is measured by the formula *(Lmax − Lmin)/(Lmax + Lmin)* and where *Lmax* (maximum luminance) $= 64.9796$ cd/m^2 and where *Lmin* (minimum luminance) $= 64.6213$ cd/m^2. These luminance values produced a contrast of 0.0028 and retinal luminance of 734.53 trolands. Eye movements and fixations were recorded by EOG using a pair of DC amplifiers connected to a MacLab system and a Macintosh SE computer running chart-recorder emulation software.

Procedure.   After EOG preparation, participants sat at a table facing the large screen and, during trials, bit onto an adjustable bite-bar attached to a metal frame on the right of the table. Participants were calibrated before and after each trial to ensure accuracy of the electro-oculograms. On each trial, a calibration slide appeared and respondents moved their eyes through established horizontal and vertical angles. Next, the standard form appeared for a 5-second period and during this time background illumination was increased to the set high level. The standard form was then removed and the participant was presented with either the standard form again or one of the seven comparison forms. Within each block of 14 trials, an equal number of standard and comparison forms were presented in random order. After scanning the presented form, respondents signalled "same" or "different" by pressing a button switch on the table. Finally, another calibration slide was presented and the calibration procedure repeated. After 5 practice trials, participants were given six blocks of trials (a total of 84) over two or three experimental sessions in a period of 1 week. Respondents were given feedback on each trial.

Stimulus Rotation.   In order to control for possible effects of the location of the most discriminating region, standard and comparison forms were presented to each respondent in one of four positions of rotation and/or reflection. Figure 5.2 shows the forms as they were presented to the participant in the top-right condition, that is, all forms different top-right. For the participant in the top-left condition, the forms were reflected about the vertical axis locating the most discriminating region top-left. In a similar way, forms were rotated or reflected to give the remaining two conditions:

lower-right and lower-left. Figure 5.5 shows the superimposed standard and comparison forms in the four rotated/reflected conditions.

Results

Figure 5.6 provides evidence supporting the hypothesis that across experimental sessions, all participants required fewer fixations and overall fixation time to discriminate the standard from comparisons.

Cumulative Fixation Time.   Details of procedures for computing and displaying CFT in two and three dimensions are described by Latimer (1988). Figure 5.7 presents the two-dimensional CFT plots for all four participants, and, in the figure, participants' fixation times on screen locations have been accumulated across trials. In each of the four CFT plots the screen (104 cm high × 84 cm wide) has been reduced to a 26 rows × 21 columns matrix with the number border indexing the screen locations. Numbers within each CFT plot represent the cumulative fixation times of the respondent on particular screen locations. Circled CFT values in Fig. 5.7 mark the points of maximum fixation, and it can be seen that respondents have concentrated attention on particular regions of the screen.

CFT is represented in three dimensions in Fig. 5.8. In this figure, the 26 × 21 matrix in Fig. 5.7 has been reduced to one of 15 × 12. For each

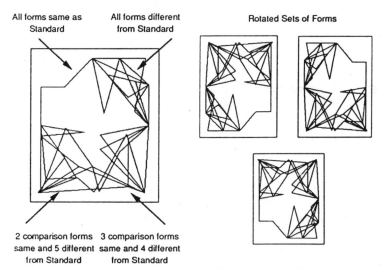

All forms same as Standard

All forms different from Standard

Rotated Sets of Forms

2 comparison forms same and 5 different from Standard

3 comparison forms same and 4 different from Standard

FIG. 5.5.   Standard and comparison forms superimposed to show regions of maximum, medium, and zero difference under the four conditions of reflection and rotation.

(a)

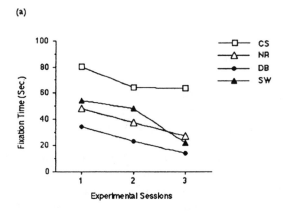

(b)

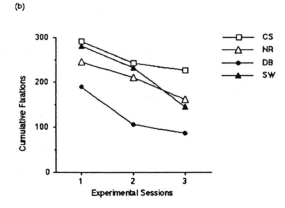

FIG. 5.6.   (a) Total fixation time per experimental session. (b) Cumulative fixations per experimental session.

participant the view of the three-dimensional representation is above the lower-left corner of the screen looking diagonally across to the top-right. The higher the columns, the greater the concentration of fixation time in that region. Taking each participant in turn, participant NR, whose CFT plots appear in the top left of Fig. 5.7 and 5.8, had her most discriminating region located top-left. It is clear that across trials she has come to concentrate her fixations not only on the top-left but also bottom-center region where she had a view of the next most discriminating regions. Participant CS whose CFT plots appear in the top-right of Figs, 5.7 and 5.8 had her most discriminating region located in the top-right. Across trials it is clear that she has come to concentrate her attention on the most discriminating region. Participants DB and SW, whose CFT plots appear in

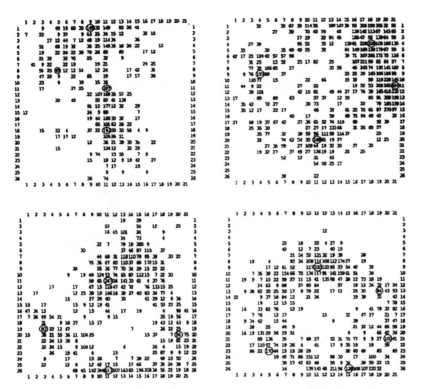

FIG. 5.7. Two dimensional representations of CFT for the four participants. Circled CFT values indicate points of maximum fixation duration. From Latimer (1990). Reprinted by permission of Elsevier Science Publishers.

the bottom-left and bottom-right respectively of Figs.5.7 and Figs 5.8, also had their most discriminating regions located bottom-left and bottom-right, respectively. Individual differences are again apparent: Participant SW has concentrated attention on the most discriminating region and on the top-center region of the screen, which gave him/her access to the next most discriminating regions; the highest concentration of fixation for participant DB lies on the border between the regions of absolute sameness and difference and he also has devoted attention to the top-center region.

K Means Cluster Analysis of Cumulative Fixation Time.   The division of CFT into regions using two-and three-dimensional representations of the distributions can involve a degree of subjectivity. A more objective and quantitative approach is through the use of the *k means* cluster analysis (MacQueen, 1967). The application of this procedure to CFT data is described in detail by Latimer (1988) and requires an initial estimate of the means of possible clusters. The objects to be clustered in this analysis are the CFT values and in the two-dimensional CFT distributions in Fig. 5.7,

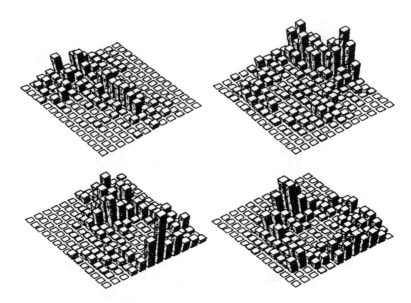

FIG. 5.8. Three dimensional representation of CFT for each participant.
View is from the bottom-left-hand corner of the screen and geometric forms.
From Latimer (1990). Reprinted by permission of Elsevier Science Publishers.

the highest CFT values described by their row and column coordinates
(circled in Fig. 5.7), were chosen as the initial means or centroids of the
possible clusters. The *k means* cluster analysis proceeds by selecting CFT
values at random, computing their Euclidean distances from the means,
assigning the CFT values to their closest clusters, and finally computing a
new position for the mean of the chosen cluster from the CFT values
already assigned to the cluster and the newly-assigned CFT value. During
this procedure the means of clusters wander within the distribution, but
MacQueen has proven that if, for example, the total CFT distribution in the
top-right of Fig. 5.8 is actually generated by four separate component
probability distributions, then the four initial mean estimates will asymp-
totically converge on the means of these four component distributions. In
other words, the final locations of the means of the clusters should not
diverge significantly from the locations of the initial mean estimates.

Figure 5.9 is a topographical representation of the cluster solutions for
the four CFT distributions depicted in Fig.5.7 and the final locations of the
cluster means are circled double stars. The values in the topographical
representations refer to the cluster membership of each CFT value. For
example, all entries labelled "1" are CFT values allocated to cluster 1, and
so on. It can be seen in Fig. 5.9 that the final locations of the clusters in each
CFT distribution have not diverged significantly from the initial mean
estimates in Fig.5.7. This suggests that respondents have indeed devoted

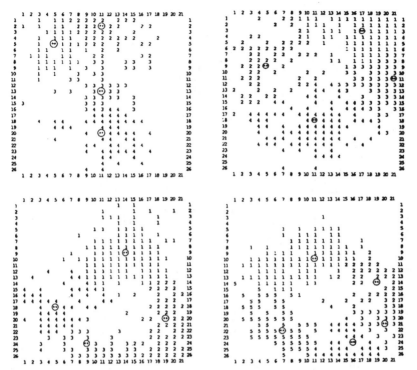

FIG. 5.9. Topographical representations of the cluster solutions for all four participants in Experiment 1. Numbers refer to the clusters to which CFT points have been assigned and double stars indicate the final positions of the mean or centroid of each cluster.

attention to and within the regions depicted by the clusters and supports the original partition of the distribution indicated by the two and three-dimensional representations of CFT.

Scanpath Order Measures. A second measure of weight assigned to regions by participants is order of scan. CFT *alone* may not necessarily be a valid measure of the weight assigned to areas of the forms by subjects. Some participants, even though instructed to respond quickly and accurately, continue to scan undifferentiating features of the forms before making a final same/different judgment. Additionally, some participants require many trials to discover the most and least differentiating features of the forms and develop an optimal set of feature weights. Because, in such cases, CFT alone may not be a sensitive measure of weight assignment, we have used scanpath-inverse-order (SCIO) theory as a supplementary measure of assigned weight. SCIO theory is described in detail in Latimer (1990), but a brief explanation given by example follows.

It is assumed that while a participant continues to scan a form, he or she has not extracted enough information to judge it same or different from the standard. Consequently, it is assumed that, over many trials, features scanned at the end of a scanpath carry more information than features scanned at the start. It follows that the weight assigned by participants to feature locations can, on each trial, be measured as a function of the inverse order of scan. Here the unit of weight measurement is fixation time and the first feature location scanned in a scanpath is given the fixation time spent on that location as a weight. The next location scanned is awarded the fixation time spent on it *plus* the fixation time spent on the previous location. In this way, feature locations accumulate the sum of their own fixation time and the fixation times of previously scanned locations. Thus, assigned weight is measured as an inverse function of scanpath order.

Using SCIO theory, weight assigned to locations by Participants CS and DB are graphed as examples in Fig. 5.10. Over time, Participant CS gradually assigns more weight to her most differentiating Regions 1 and 3, whereas Participant DB assigns more weight to his Region 1 (the area between his second most discriminating regions) suggesting that by the end of the experiment he had not developed an optimum set of weights. Like Participant DB, Participant SW assigned most weight to the area between his second most discriminating regions, whereas, although Participant NC assigned a lot of weight to her most discriminating regions, she did have a tendency to terminate her scanpaths on the noninformative central region.

Discussion

Of all the respondents in Experiment 1, Participant CS was the only one to show evidence of having an optimum set of weights and an efficient strategy for discriminating the standard from comparisons. Her assigned weights were closest to those predicted from the network simulation. The remaining respondents were able to discriminate the standard from comparisons but, unlike the neural network, gave evidence of assigning weight to regions that, although they discriminated the standard from comparisons, were not the most discriminating regions. Individual differences (Chantrey, 1977), and flexibility (Corcoran & Jackson, 1979) in the assignment of weight to features of objects and patterns have been observed, but the structure of the pattern set may have contributed to the individual differences in weight-assignment observed in this experiment. Because of the close proximity of the two second most discriminating regions, participants were able to scan both regions from an area midway between the two. Being able to conjoin both regions in this way may have allowed respondents to make correct decisions on the basis of these features rather than on the basis of the single

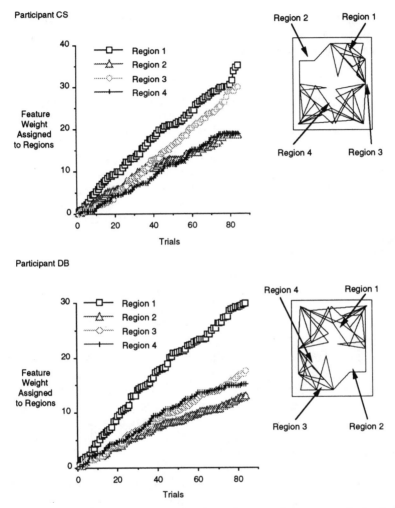

FIG. 5.10. Progressive assignment of weight to regions across trails for Participants CS and DB.

most discriminating feature. Consequently, most participants developed a strategy that resulted in correct decisions but that was not the most efficient strategy.

There are important differences here between the weights assigned by three of the respondents and the weights assigned by the neural network. A partial explanation of this may be that, in addition to the foregoing problem with the structure of the geometric forms, the level of complexity of the forms may have precluded the development of an optimal strategy within the 84 experimental trials. With simpler forms and/or more trials would respondents have developed efficient and optimal feature-weighting strategies? Experiment 2 investigates this question.

EXPERIMENT 2: FEATURE WEIGHTING IN SIMPLE FORM PERCEPTION

Experiment 2 investigated the possibility that with simpler forms to discriminate, respondents may more readily develop optimal feature weights. Accordingly, a new standard and set of four comparison forms were generated — see Fig. 5.11. It can be seen that the forms are all the same as the standard in the top-right region but are all different in the bottom-left region. Two forms differ and two are the same as the standard in the bottom-right and top-left regions.

Artificial Neural Network Simulation 2

As in the previous simulation, a single-layer network was trained to discriminate the digitized versions of the comparison forms in Fig.5.11 from the standard, and in line with these forms, the network had 24 input units in a 6 × 4 array and one output unit. The former learning rule, learning rate, and activation function (Fig.5.3) were used, and the network was able to discriminate the standard from the comparisons after 96 cycles. A three-dimensional representation of the final network weights is presented in Fig. 5.12 where, as expected, the highest negative weight has been assigned to the most discriminating bottom-left input unit. However, it should be noted that negative weight has also been assigned to the bottom-right and top-left regions, which do have some discriminatory value. These weights were then taken as the basis for hypotheses about how respondents would optimize their feature weightings when confronted with the same discrimination task.

Hypotheses

With practice at discriminating the standard from comparisons, participants should progressively assign more weight to the bottom-left region of the forms and, as a corollary, less weight to the other less discriminating regions. Again, with practice, participants should require fewer fixations and less time to discriminate the standard from comparisons.

NORMAL ORIENTATION

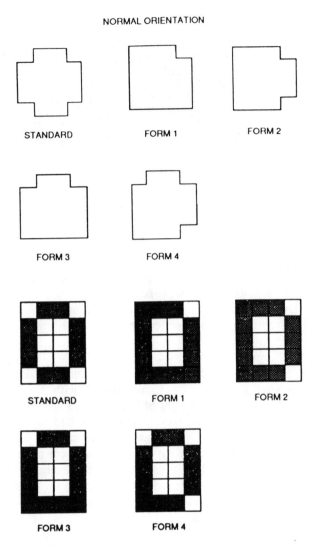

FIG. 5.11. Geometric forms used in Experiment 2 and their digitized versions for presentation to the single-layer perceptron.

Method

Participants.   Participants were two staff members of the Department of Psychology at the University who were between 20 and 30 years old, had uncorrected 20/20 vision, and were naive as to the nature and purpose of the experiment.

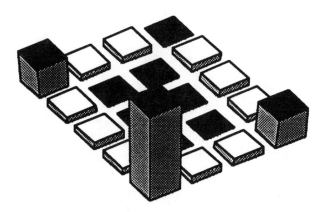

FIG. 5.12. Three-dimensional representation of network weights. Experiment 2: Highest negative weight has been assigned to the most discriminating bottom-left input unit.

Stimuli and Apparatus.   The stimulus forms were those in Fig.5.11 and were presented at exactly the same size, viewing distance, visual angles, and contrast levels as those in Experiment 1. The stimulus presentation and eye-movement recording apparatus described for Experiment 1 was again employed.

Procedure.   Participants served in two experimental sessions, and the procedure was that described for Experiment 1 with three important changes. First, the rotation conditions of Experiment 1 were not employed. Second, both participants were trained until they had achieved perfect discrimination performance. Third, when Participant NK had achieved fast, errorless performance, his comparison forms were rotated through 180° so that, unbeknownst to him, his most and least discriminating regions exchanged locations. This was done to test whether or not he could adjust his scanning and weighting strategy to suit the new locations of the most and least discriminating regions.

Results

Participant NK achieved errorless performance within 60 trials and Participant FH within 90 trials. Fig. 5.13 demonstrates that both participants gave evidence of learning by making fewer fixations and requiring less fixation time across trials. As mentioned in the account of the procedure earlier, when Participant NK had achieved fast errorless performance, his comparison forms were rotated through 180°, and Fig. 5.13 shows how his fixation frequency and fixation time increased as he was forced to change his

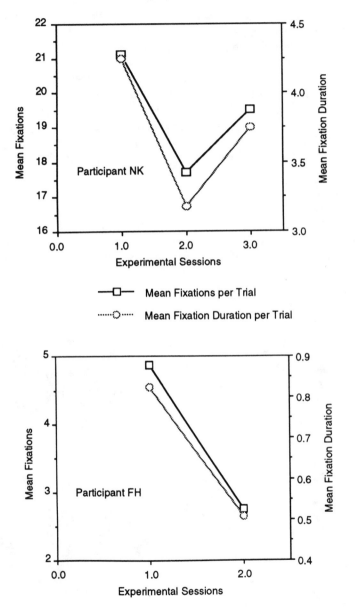

FIG. 5.13. Mean number of fixations and mean fixation duration across sessions for Participants NK and FH in Experiment 2.

scanning strategy to cope with the new region locations. However, with the benefit of his former experience, he quickly located the new position of the most discriminating region and, within a few trials, adjusted his scanning (and weighting) strategies accordingly. Fig. 5.14 and 5.15 depict the two- and three-dimensional representations of cumulative fixation time for both participants and their respective *k means* cluster solutions. Participant NK concentrated his attention on the center and most discriminating, bottom-left regions. Participant FH distributed her attention fairly evenly across the four corner regions of difference. However, as Fig. 5.16 demonstrates, the scanpath order measure of weight suggests that, across trials, both participants gradually came to terminate their scanpaths on (and assign more weight to) the most discriminating bottom-left region of the forms.

Discussion

The results of Experiment 2 indicate that, with simpler forms, the two respondents were able to develop efficient scanning strategies and adopt optimal weightings of features in a relatively short space of time. Further-

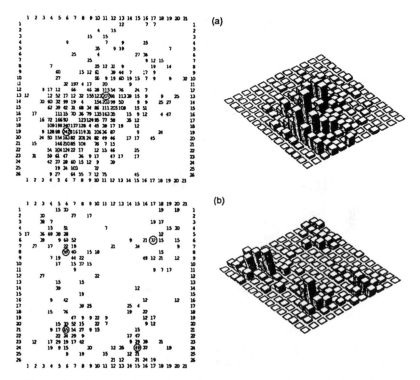

FIG. 5.14. Two-and three-dimensional representations of CFT for (a) Participant NK and (b) Participant FH in Experiment 2.

(a)

(b)

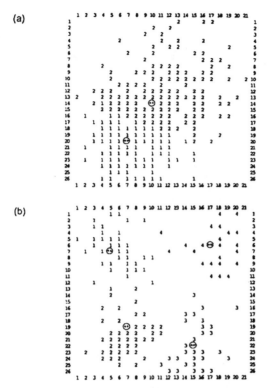

FIG. 5.15 Cluster solutions for Participants NK (a) and FH (b) in Experiment 2. Numbers refer to cluster membership and double stars indicate the final positions of the cluster means or centroids.

more, Participant NK was able to adjust his scanning and weightings to suit the rotated comparison forms in a small number of trials. Nonetheless, the results of Experiments 1 and 2 remain tied to the spotlight viewing method, which denies participants the use of global properties and forces the adoption of serial scanning of local features. By slowing down the recognition of geometric forms, this method provides a way of investigating possible feature-extraction and weighting processes. The question may still be asked: "Do the processes that seem to be operating in the spotlight viewing conditions still operate in a normal situation when participants are not so constrained and can view an entire form in a glance?" Experiment 3 attempts to answer this question.

Experiment 3: Local Versus Global Processes in Form Perception

As mentioned earlier, one problem with the spotlight method of presentation is that it eliminates the possibility of participants using global

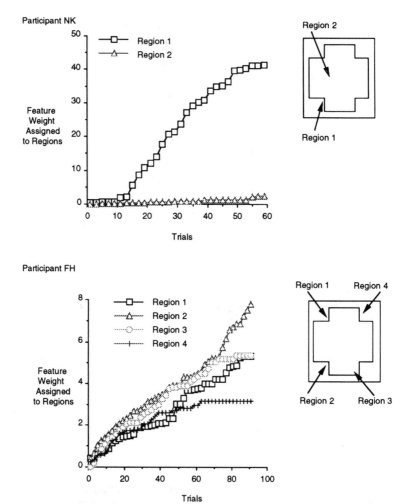

FIG. 5.16. Progressive assignment of weight to regions across trials for Participant NK and Participant FH in Experiment 2.

properties to discriminate the patterns. For example, it is possible to discriminate the standard and comparison forms from Experiment 2 (Fig. 5.11) on the basis of the global property of *symmetry*; the standard has bilateral symmetry but comparisons do not. To control for this possibility, it is necessary to test participants where they are not restricted to spotlight viewing conditions. In this controlled experiment, the stimulus sequence was the same as in the previous two experiments: Participants were presented with a standard pattern followed by a comparison pattern or the standard and were required to judge whether or not the second pattern was the same as or different from the standard. The major difference in the controlled experiment was that although the geometric forms were those from Experiment 2 (Fig. 5.11) they subtended small visual angles of $4 \times 5°$ so that participants did not have to move their eyes to discriminate the standard from comparison forms.

Participants were randomly assigned to three experimental conditions: Top-Right (TR)—all comparisons were different from the standard in the bottom-left corner and same in the top-right; Bottom-Left (BL)—all comparisons were different from the standard in the top-right corner and same in the bottom-left; Control: Top-Right/Bottom-Left (TRBL)—all comparisons were equally same and different in all corners. After a period of training in discriminating the standard from comparisons, the respondents in the TR and BL groups had, without warning, *their comparisons rotated through 180°*. In other words, the most discriminating and least discriminating regions in the TR and BL groups were exchanged and the control TRBL group continued to receive forms that were equally same and different in all corners.

Hypothesis

If respondents are making use of the reliable local differences in the standard and comparison forms, the changeover in locations of these differences will be reflected in significantly longer discrimination times just after the changeover point. The TRBL Control group, not having had the benefit of a reliable region of difference, will show no difference in response time at the changeover point. Figure 5.17 illustrates the predicted response-time curves from a theory that assumes that participants are responding to local differences in the standard and comparisons. However, if participants are responding to global properties such as symmetry/asymmetry, manipulations of local properties of the shapes that do not destroy the symmetry of the standard or the asymmetry of the comparisons should have no effect, and there should be no difference in response time after the changeover point.

Method

Participants. Forty-eight male and female respondents participated in the experiment as partial fulfilment of the requirements for Psychology I at the University of Sydney; their ages ranged between 18 and 24 years.

Stimuli & Apparatus. The stimulus forms were small versions of those presented in Experiment 2 and measured 5.5 cm high $\times$ 4 cm wide. Viewed at a distance of 75 cm they subtended the visual angles 3.06° horizontal by

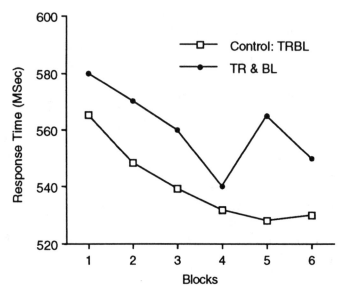

FIG. 5.17. Predicted response time functions for the conditions in Experiment 3.

4.2° vertical. The forms, composed of black lines measuring 2 pixels in width, were presented by a Macintosh LC computer centered on an Apple 12 inch color monitor. Participants' responses, recorded by way of a voice key, which replaced the Macintosh mouse (Algarabel, Sanmartin, & Ahuir, 1989), were stored on disk.

Procedure. Participants were informed that the experiment would involve learning to discriminate a standard geometric form from a group of comparison forms and that the aim of the experiment was to test how quickly discriminations could be made. Prior to testing, respondents were given a six-trial demonstration of the stimulus sequence and practiced responding by using the voice key. Participants were encouraged to respond "same" or "different" as quickly and as accurately as possible. The stimulus sequence was as follows: Participants were warned of stimulus onset by a tone; after a 1-second delay the standard was drawn center screen and remained for 1 second before disappearing; 2 seconds later either the standard or comparison form was drawn center screen; when drawing of the second form had been completed the timer started and was stopped by the participant's voice-key response; after the participant's response, the second form disappeared and there was a 3-second interval before the warning tone and the start of the next trial. Standard and comparison forms had an average screen drawing time of 63 milliseconds.

Respondents were given six blocks of 16 trials in all. Blocks one to four each contained a randomized sequence of 8 standards and 8 comparison forms. Within each block, the 8 comparison trials consisted of 2 trials each of the 4 comparison forms (Fig. 5.11). Block 5 was the first block in the changeover that involved the rotation of comparison forms in the TR and BL conditions. The TR group, whose comparison forms differed from the standard consistently in the bottom-left corner, were now given two blocks of trials in which the comparison forms differed consistently in the top-right corner. Similarly, the BL group, whose comparison forms had differed consistently in the top-right corner, were now given two blocks of trials in which the comparison forms differed consistently in the bottom-left corner. The TRBL or Control group was not subject to the changeover but was given six blocks of trials containing a mixture of the TR and BL forms in which there were no consistent regions of difference between the standard and comparison forms. Participants were given a 30-second rest period between Blocks 3 and 4. Order of presentation of forms was counterbalanced within conditions and the experiment lasted 25 minutes.

Results

Data were analysed by a three-way analysis of variance (condition (3) × block (6) × form (5)) with repeated measures on the latter two factors. There was a significant main effect of experimental condition, $F(2,45) = 3.759, p < .05$; a significant effect of blocks, $F(5, 225) = 8.995, p < .05$; and a significant effect of forms, $F(4, 180) = 6.008, p < .05$. Figure 5.18 shows the mean response times across blocks for each experimental condition. In line with the hypothesis, there was a significant interaction between experimental condition and blocks, $F(10, 225) = 2.180, p < .05$. Planned comparisons revealed that the difference between the mean response times in Blocks 4 and 5 in the TRBL control condition (1.51 msec) was not significant. However, in the BL condition, respondents were significantly slower on the rotated patterns of Block 5 (28.45 msec), $F(1,225) = 5.856, p < .05$. In the TR group respondents took an average 15.77 msec longer in Block 5 but this difference was not significant $F(1, 225) = 1.79, p > .05$. Significance levels of contrasts between means of within-participant variables were maintained after Epsilon correction (Geisser & Greenhouse, 1958).

Discussion

Experiment 3 was carried out as an investigation of possible artifacts of the spotlight viewing methods used in Experiments 1 and 2. Such methods deny participants the use of global properties of forms, and the nonuniform

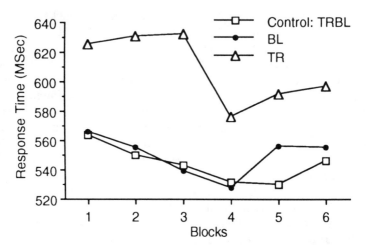

FIG. 5.18. Obtained response time functions for the conditions in Experiment 3 showing response time as a function of condition and blocks of trials.

distributions of fixations on local features may be the result of forcing participants to scan forms in a serial manner. In Experiment 3 respondents were able to see the forms in their entirety and were able to extract both local and global properties without the need for eye movements. In line with the hypothesis, the results suggest that even when the entire form can be viewed in one glance, participants' same/different judgments are influenced by manipulations of local, differentiating regions. For example, in the BL condition relocation of the region of reliable difference in Block 5 resulted in significantly slower response times. Relocation of the most discriminating region in the TR condition, although it slowed participants' responses in Block 5, it did not do so significantly. In comparison, it should be noted that response times in the control group remained unchanged between Blocks 4 and 5. It is difficult to see how a global theory could explain the results of the effects of these manipulations on local regions of differentiation. For example, if participants were making discriminations on the basis of the symmetrical standard and the asymmetrical comparisons there should be no difference between Blocks 4 and 5 in both TR and BL groups.

A finding to be explained however, is the significant difference in response time between the TR and BL groups; on average respondents in the TR group took 59 ms longer to make their judgments. One possible explanation of this is in terms of the well-documented propensity for respondents to allocate initial attention to the upper rather than the lower regions of stimuli (Brandt, 1940, 1941; Ford, White, & Lichtenstein, 1959; Levy-Schoen, 1973). If respondents in Experiment 3 adopted a serial attentive strategy and initially attended to the top of the forms rather than the bottom during the first four blocks of trials, then the location of the region of reliable difference at the top of the forms in the BL group would have facilitated fast response times in comparison with the TR group, whose region of reliable difference was located at the bottom of the forms. Furthermore, in the TRBL group, although they had no reliable region of difference, it would still have been possible to discriminate the standard from the comparisons on the basis of the top regions on 75% of the trials. This may explain their fast response times in comparison to the TR group, who could have distinguished the forms on the basis of top regions on only 50% of the trials. Additionally, it can be seen from Fig. 5.18 that the TR group show very little reduction in response time over the first three blocks and a significant improvement on Block 4. This may indicate that with initial attention being given to the top regions of forms it took longer for this group to learn that the bottom-left of the forms was in fact a reliable region of difference. The assumption of this local feature-analytic strategy with bias towards the topmost regions may also explain the significant effects of rotation on the BL but not the TR group. The relocation of the region of reliable difference to the bottom of the forms in Blocks 5 and 6 for the BL group may have had a more disruptive effect than the relocation of the most reliable region of difference to the top of the forms for the TR group.

Clearly, further experimentation is required to determine the factors responsible for the significant differences in response time between the TR and BL groups. Notwithstanding, the results of Experiment 3 suggest that even when the forms are presented at small visual angles and are available in their entirety, participants' responses are influenced by manipulations of the differentiating capacity and location of local elements of the form just as they were in Experiments 1 and 2. Such results suggest that the findings of Experiment 1 and 2 are not mere artifacts of the spotlight viewing conditions but may be further evidence that geometric form perception is mediated by the extraction and differential weighting of local features.

GENERAL DISCUSSION AND CONCLUSIONS

Connectionist models of form perception have received some support from the results reported here. There is evidence that in the discrimination of geometric forms, respondents can learn to assign weight differentially to the component parts of the forms. Furthermore, there are definite indications that well-trained participants and the neural networks tested here are assigning weight to the same regions of the forms. In Experiment 1, which used relatively complex forms, there was evidence of individual differences in weight assignment and in some cases respondents did not develop optimal weightings for efficient recognition strategies. However, in Experiment 2, with simpler forms and a thorough training schedule, results indicated that both respondents assigned most weight to the most discriminating parts of the forms. Experiment 3 provided the necessary control for the spotlight viewing methods adopted in Experiments 1 and 2, and revealed that, even when global properties of forms are accessible and forms can be seen in their entirety without eye movements, manipulations of the differentiating capacity of local features still has significant effect on response time. Experiment 3 also raised the problem of positional bias; it may be the case that respondents initially attend to the upper regions of patterns in preference to lower regions. Further experimentation, where the location of the reliable region of difference is systematically varied (as in Experiment 1), will be necessary for a complete investigation of this phenomenon. Additionally, the effects of further reduction in the size of the forms will also need to be investigated. It may be that with very small patterns the positional bias effect disappears.

The connectionist models employed in the present study were single-layer perceptions with simple learning rules and activation functions, and the assumption in these models is that features are extracted in parallel. Results reported here suggest the possibility that some feature-extraction processes in form recognition may be serial rather than parallel. One way of thinking about processes underlying the results would be in terms of a model of systems of processes in cascade (McClelland, 1979; see also: Cohen, Dunbar, & McClelland, 1990). In this model, patterns of input are represented by the activation of units in a multilevel feed-forward network. Patterns of activation of the lowest level units are gradually propagated forward and units at each level have their activations updated on the basis of inputs received from lower levels. Over time, a pattern of activation emerges across units at the topmost level and a response is generated. Cohen et al. (1990) demonstrated how a revision of McClelland's original model (which incorporates nonlinear relations between input and output and a learning mechanism and which is given a greater amount of practice with word reading than with color naming) can explain the attentional and reaction time differences that led to the Stroop effect. A similar explanation may be found for the observed attentional and response-time differences in experiments reported here. With training, respondents learn to attend to and assign more weight to the more discriminating features of geometric forms in preference to less discriminating features. Consider a cascade model that, like the models considered in this chapter, has only one output unit, which fires when the standard pattern in Fig. 5.11 is presented and remains inactive when nonstandard patterns are presented. In terms of this model, when a nonstandard pattern is presented to trained participants who immediately attend to the most discriminating region, the greater strength of negative connection between the input unit responsible for this region and upper layers of units would result in a rapid decrease of activation in the output unit. On the other hand, when a standard pattern is presented, the input unit in the most discriminating region remains off and does not propagate its high negative signal to the output unit. In consequence, the output unit is more likely to fire. In the case of untrained participants, who neither attend to nor weight heavily the most discriminating regions, the buildup and reduction of activity in the output unit is not so rapid.

One final connectionist approach to the explanation of the current results is a model of attentional learning containing a sequentially allocatable spotlight of attention mechanism (Schreter & Latimer, 1992). This model, like the respondents in the present experiments, learns to focus its attentional spotlight on the most discriminating parts of the input field. After learning is finished the network starts scanning the input pattern at the most discriminative features and tends to limit scanning to those features that are necessary and sufficient to discriminate the patterns from each other. As such, the model displays many of the characteristics observed in the recognition of geometric forms by human participants.

ACKNOWLEDGMENTS

This research was supported by University of Sydney Research Grants to the first author and an Australian Commonwealth Postgraduate Award to the second author. MacBrain is a trademark of Neurix, Boston, Massachusetts. MacLab is a trademark of ADInstruments, Dunedin, New Zealand.

REFERENCES

Algarabel, S., Sanmartin, J., & Ahuir, F. (1989). A voice-activated key for the Apple Macintosh computer. *Behavior Research Methods, Instruments, & Computers, 21*, 67–72.

Baker, M. A., & Loeb, M. (1973). Implications of measurement of eye fixations for a psychophysics of form perception. *Perception & Psychophysics, 13*, 185–192.

Barlow, D. H., & Hersen, M. (1984). *Single case experimental designs.* Oxford: Pergamon.

Bechtel, W., & Abrahamsen, A. (1991). *Connectionism and the mind: An introduction to parallel processing in networks.* Oxford: Blackwell.

Bozkov, V., Bohdanecky, Z., & Radil-Weiss, T. (1987). Toward the problem of physical and semantic component of the form during eye scanning. *Acta Neurobiologiae Experimentalis, 47*, 93–101.

Bozkov, V., Bohdanecky, Z., Radil-Weiss, T., Mitrani, L., & Yakimoff, N. (1982). Scanning open and closed polygons. *Vision Research, 22*, 721–725.

Brandt, H. F. (1940). Ocular patterns and their psychological implications. *American Journal of Psychology, 53*, 260–268.

Brandt, H. F. (1941). Ocular patterns in visual learning. *American Journal of Psychology, 54*, 528–535.

Bush, R. R. (1963). Estimation and evaluation. In R. D. Luce, R. R. Bush, & E. Galanter (Eds.), *Handbook of mathematical psychology: Vol. 1* (pp. 429–469). New York: Wiley.

Chantrey, D. F. (1977). Individual differences in the selection and use of features for classifying visual stimuli. *Perception, 6*, 271–280.

Cohen, J. D., Dunbar, K., & McClelland, J. L. (1990). On the control of automatic processes: A parallel distributed processing account of the Stroop effect. *Psychological Review, 97*, 332–361.

Corcoran, D. W. J., & Jackson, A. (1979). Flexibility in the choice of distinctive features in visual serach with blocked and random designs. *Perception, 8*, 629–634.

Findlay, J. M. (1985). Saccadic eye movements and visual cognition. *Annee Psychologique, 85*, 101–136.

Ford, A., White C. T., & Lichtenstein, M. (1959). Analysis of eye movements during free search. *Journal of the Optical Society of America, 49*, 287–292.

Geisser, S., & Greenhouse, S. (1958). An extension of Box's results on the use of the F distribution in multivariate analysis. *Annals of Mathematical Statistics, 29*, 885–891.

Gluck, M. A., & Bower, G. M. (1988). Evaluating an adaptive network model of human learning. *Journal of Memory & Language, 27*, 166–195.

Hinton, G. E. (1981). A parallel computation that assigns canonical object-based frames of reference. In *Proceedings of the Seventh International Joint Conference on Artificial Intelligence* (pp. 683–685). Los Altos, CA: International Joint Conference on Artificial Intelligence.

Hrechanyk, L. M., & Ballard, D. H. (1982). A connectionist model of form perception. *Proceedings of the IEEE workshop on computer vision: Representation and control* (pp. 44–52).

Just, M. A., & Carpenter, P. A. (1976). Eye fixations and cognitive processes. *Cognitive Psychology, 8*, 441–480.

Latimer, C. R. (1988). Eye-movement data: Cumulative fixation time and cluster analysis. *Behavior Research Methods, Instruments, & Computers, 20*, 437–470.

Latimer, C. R. (1990). Eye-movement indices of form perception: Some methods and preliminary results. In R. Groner, G. d'Ydewalle, & R. Parham (Eds.), *From eye to mind: Information acquisition in perception* (pp.41–57). North-Holland: Elsevier Science Publishers.

Levy-Schoen, A. (1973). Position of stimuli within a pattern, as determinants of the fixation response. In V. Zikmund (Ed.), *The oculomotor system and brain functions* (pp. 243–255). London, Butterworths.

MacQueen, J. (1967). Some methods for classification and analysis of multivariate observations. In *Proceedings of the 5th Berkeley Symposium on Statistics and Probability* (pp. 281–297). Berkeley, California: University of California Press.

McClelland, J. L. (1979). On the time-relations of mental processes: An examination of systems of processes in cascade. *Pychological Review, 86*, 287–330.

McClelland, J. L., & Rumelhart, D. E. (1986). *Parallel distributed processing: Explorations in the microstructure of cognition* (Vols. I and II). Cambridge, MA: MIT Press.

Newell, A. (1973). You can't play 20 questions with nature and win. In W. G. Chase (Ed.), *Visual information processing* (pp. 283–308). New York: Academic Press.

Pasnak, R. (1971). Pattern complexity and response to distinctive features. *American Journal of Psychology, 84*, 235–245.

Pasnak, R., & Tyer, Z. E. (1985). Distinctive local features of visual patterns. *Bulletin of the Psychonomic Society, 23*, 113–115.

Pasnak, R., & Tyer, Z. E. (1986). Complex local features as determinants of pattern discrimination. *Bulletin of the Psychonomic Society, 24*, 41–43.

Pomerantz, J. R. (1986). Visual form perception. In E. C. Schwab & H. C. Nusbaum (Eds.), *Pattern recognition by humans and machines. Vol. 2: Visual perception* (pp. 1-30). Orlando: Academic Press.

Quinlan, P. (1991a). *Connectionism and psychology: A psychological perspective on new connectionist research*, Chicago: University of Chicago Press.

Quinlan, P. (1991b) Differing approaches to two-dimensional shape recognition. *Psychological Bulletin, 109*, 224-241.

Schreter, Z., & Latimer, C. (1992). A connectionist model of attentional learning using a sequentially allocatable "spotlight of attention." In *Proceedings of the Third Australian Conference on Neural Networks*, (pp. 143-146) Sydney: Sydney University Electrical Engineering.

Smith, L. B., & Evans, P. (1989). Similarity, identity, and dimensions: Perceptual classification in children and adults. In B. E. Shepp & S. Ballesteros (Eds.), *Object perception: Structure and process* (pp. 325-356). Hillsdale, NJ: Lawrence Erlbaum Associates.

Sutherland, N. S. (1968). Outlines of a theory of pattern recognition in animals and man. *Proceedings of the Royal Society of London*, (Series B), *171*, 297-317.

Treisman, A. (1986). Properties, parts and objects. In K. B. Boff, L. Kaufman, & J. P. Thomas (Eds.), *Handbook of perception and human performance, Vol 2, Cognitive processes and performance* (pp. 35:1-35:70). New York: Wiley.

Uhr, L., & Vossler, C. (1963). A pattern recognition program that generates, evaluates and adjusts its operators. In E. A. Feigenbaum & J. Feldman (Eds.), *Computers and thought* (pp. 251-268). New York: McGraw-Hill.

Zusne, L. (1970). *Visual perception of form*. New York: Academic Press.

6 Interference Effects in Perceptual Organization

James R. Pomerantz
Cathy E. Carson*
Evan M. Feldman
Rice University, Houston, Texas

The cognitive approach to human perception differs from others, such as the psychophysical approach, in the methods and measurements it uses. The cognitive approach usually distinguishes itself through the use of *performance tasks* in which observers participate. These information processing tasks entail responses that are scored either as correct or incorrect, and variations in the speed and accuracy of responding are used to make inferences about what observers must be seeing.

Our focus in this chapter is on the use of such performance tasks in studying the phenomenon of perceptual grouping, a problem as old as Gestalt psychology itself and that until recently was studied at best through psychophysical methods and more typically through mere demonstrations rather than through actual experiments. To appreciate the contrast, consider the grouping effect demonstrated in the panels of Fig. 6.1. They show two separate fields of dots that, when superimposed, yield a single, homogeneous field whose density of dots is doubled. When the two fields are shifted slightly, they yield clear clusterings, sometimes called elongated blobs, that constitute a textbook demonstration of grouping by proximity. When the two fields of dots are then rotated slightly with respect to each other, these elongated blobs form a higher order structure of circular swirls. These effects are so compelling and universal that one might wonder whether we would gain much new understanding from conducting a proper laboratory experiment, using measurement procedures more objective than a subject's incontestable verbal report. One might also wonder how to

*Cathy Carson is now at AT&T Bell Laboratories, Holmdel, New Jersey

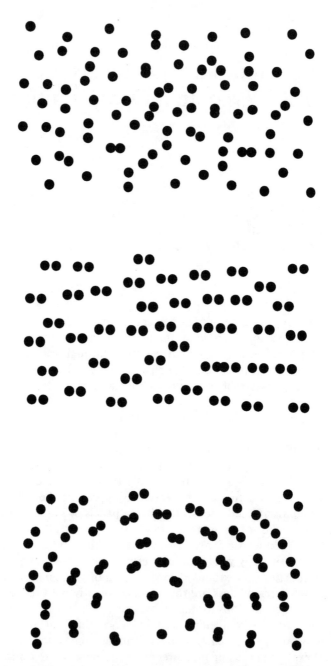

FIG. 6.1. Demonstration of grouping. (A) Two superimposed sheets of dots. (B) The same two sheets shifted slightly, revealing a grouping structure based on proximity. (C) The same two sheets then rotated slightly to reveal another grouping structure.

124

capture the grouping that is so compelling and obvious in Fig. 6.1 with a performance task.

The approach we pursue here has its roots in earlier work both in our lab (e.g., Pomerantz & Garner, 1973; Pomerantz, Pristach, & Carson, 1989) and in those of others (Kahneman & Henik, 1981; Neisser, 1967). At the root of this approach is the idea that when two elements (such as two dots in Fig 6.1) combine to form a perceptual group (such as the elongated blobs or circular swirls in Fig. 6.1), the newly formed group becomes an effective unit of attention for the perceiver. The logic runs as follows: When dots do not group, selective attention to an individual dot should be easy, whereas divided attention across two or more dots should be difficult. By contrast, when two dots do group, selective attention to an individual dot should be difficult whereas divided attention across a group of dots should be easy. In this fashion, performance on selective and divided attention tasks can provide an objective diagnostic indicator for grouping.

For the purposes of this chapter, we confine ourselves to a restricted type of information processing task with a restricted set of stimuli. Specifically, we ask subjects to do the following. In one part of a video display screen, one of two possible visual forms appears. To be concrete, the form might be a square or a circle. The subject's task is to indicate, as quickly and accurately as possible, which of the two forms actually appears by pressing one of two response buttons laid out below the screen. Immediately adjacent to the place on the screen where the circle or square may appear is a second location. Here one of the same two alternative forms appears, but its identity (indeed even its presence) is irrelevant to the decision the subject must make. In our experiments, we measure the extent to which the form presented at the irrelevant location affects the speed and accuracy of subjects' responses to the form presented at the relevant location. When the form at the irrelevant location produces an effect, we conclude that selective attention to the relevant location did not occur. Instead we conclude that the visual information presented there has grouped with the information at the relevant location to form a single, larger unit of attention.

OVERVIEW OF MAIN FINDINGS

The major results we summarize in this chapter are twofold. First, whether selective attention to the relevant location succeeds or fails depends in part on how selective attention has been measured. In our experiments, we measure selective attention in two logically independent ways, and these two methods give us different results (Pomerantz, Pristach, & Carson, 1989). Second, whether selective attention to the relevant location succeeds also depends on what stimuli are used. Even with the restricted stimuli we report on here (two adjacent locations each containing one of the same two alternative forms), the stimulus matters. This result underscores the basic point made by Garner years ago that the nature of the stimulus is significant for human information processing (Garner, 1970, 1974; Garner & Felfoldy, 1970).

In the remainder of this chapter we first describe the general methods we use in our experiments, followed by the stimuli we have tested, and the results they have yielded. After reviewing these results we discuss their implications for our understanding both of perceptual grouping and of the methods underlying this cognitive approach to perception.

Methods

The methods we used in the experiments to be summarized here have been outlined elsewhere (Pomerantz, 1983; Pomerantz, Pristach, & Carson, 1989), but we review them here briefly because our measurement procedures are themselves one focus of interest and not merely a means to an end. As we noted earlier, in all these experiments subjects are presented a visual form in one location on a screen, a form that is selected from just two alternatives such as a circle and a square, as shown in Fig. 6.2. At the same time a second, nominally irrelevant form selected from the same two alternatives appears to the immediate left (or right) of the relevant form. Thus, in this example there are four possible left–right combinations that can appear on the screen: square-square, square-circle, circle-square and circle-circle. The subject's task is to press one of two response keys if the form in the relevant location is a circle and to press the other key if it is a square. We measure the average speed and accuracy of these responses through a series of trials (i.e., stimulus exposures).

Stroop and Garner Interference.   The success of selective attention is gauged through calculating for each trial the effects of the irrelevant dimension (here represented by a form) on performance for the relevant dimension. These effects appear in two different manifestations:

- In the *control* condition, the irrelevant form remains the same throughout a series of trials, whereas in the *filtering* condition, the irrelevant form varies randomly from trial to trial orthogonally to (not correlated with) the relevant form. This irrelevant variation often disrupts performance, generating what is called *Garner interference*. This measure is computed by subtracting the mean reaction time (RT) or error rate in the control condition from that in the filtering condition.
- For both these conditions, in half of the stimulus combinations the

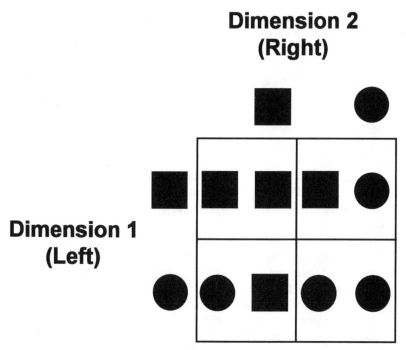

FIG. 6.2. One of the stimulus sets tested in the present experiments. Each set contains exactly four stimuli, each of which consists of two side-by-side forms. In this set, the form on the left can be either a square or a circle; the same is true for the form on the right. On a particular trial, the subject would see just one pair (e.g., a circle on the left and a square on the right) positioned at a random position outside the fovea. The subject's task is to indicate which shape appears in the relevant location (either the left or the right position) as quickly and accurately as possible.

irrelevant form is identical to the relevant form and so would call for the same response, whereas in the other half the relevant and irrelevant forms are different and thus would call for different responses. This incongruity often disrupts performance as well, generating what is called, generically, *Stroop interference*[1]. This measure is computed by subtracting the mean RT or error rate on congruous (same form) trials from that on incongruous trials.

---

[1]By generic Stroop interference, we mean interference that arises when subjects are presented with a second, irrelevant source of information that would call for a different response than does the relevant information. We do not believe that the interference we observe in the experiments we report here is identical or even necessarily similar to that observed in the original Stroop color–word interference effect. In fact our experiments indicate that generic Stroop effects assume many different forms and probably do not have a common origin.

Garner interference reflects the deleterious effect of the variation on the irrelevant location from trial to trial, whereas Stroop interference reflects the deleterious effects of the content of the irrelevant location within a trial. Both effects assess the effectiveness of selective attention because if subjects confined their processing exclusively to the relevant location, neither Stroop nor Garner would arise. Note that we compute both forms of effect from the same set of data, using orthogonal contrasts. In this fashion we avoid possible confounds that could arise if Stroop and Garner interference were assessed in separate tasks, including strategy shifts between tasks that make direct comparisons difficult.

In a large number of experiments measuring Stroop and Garner effects concurrently with a wide variety of stimuli (not only the same shapes side by side as reported here), we have established five basic findings about these two phenomena:

1. First, some stimulus pairs show neither Stroop nor Garner interference. These are prototypical examples of *separable* stimuli (Garner, 1970; Lockhead, 1966; Shepard, 1964, 1991).

2. Many stimulus sets, including side-by-side forms emphasized in this chapter, show high levels of Garner interference. The range of Garner interference runs from a few hundred milliseconds to zero, but it seems never to go negative. That is, we have not yet witnessed a case of Garner *facilitation*.

3. Many stimulus sets also show Stroop interference. Generally Stroop interference (at least as we measure it) is smaller in its maximum levels than Garner interference. In addition, Stroop interference is significantly negative for some stimuli. That is, we have observed several cases of Stroop *facilitation*. Note that whether facilitation or interference is found, the implication remains that attention must have been paid to the irrelevant location.

4. We have uncovered several stimulus sets that show Garner interference but not Stroop. Despite many efforts, however, we have yet to find and replicate a case of Stroop interference without Garner. As shown across dozens of experiments summarized in Fig. 6.3, Stroop and Garner interference show no significant correlation. This means that although Stroop and Garner both tap into selective attention, they do so in ways that are not simply related to each other.

5. Both Stroop and Garner interference sometimes show significant asymmetries between the pairs of locations or other dimensions out of which the stimuli are composed. That is, the amount of interference emanating from the first dimension when the second dimension is relevant is not always matched by an equivalent

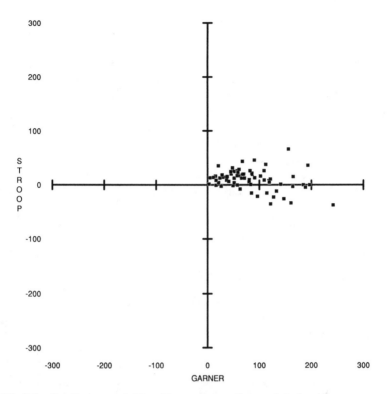

FIG. 6.3. Scattergram plotting Stroop versus Garner interference across a number of experiments in our lab. Each point shows the two levels of interference (expressed in milliseconds) measured concurrently for a single stimulus set. As this figure reveals, Stroop and Garner interference are not correlated across stimulus sets, indicating that they do not tap failures of selective attention in the same fashion.

amount of interference emanating from the second dimension when the first dimension is relevant. In addition, the asymmetry shown for Garner interference is not always identical to the asymmetry shown by Stroop. Indeed, we have observed one case of stimuli that show significant Stroop and Garner asymmetries but where these two asymmetries run in opposite directions (Pomerantz, 1983).

In previous work, we sketched a model to account for the similarities and differences between Stroop and Garner interference as well as to explain the origins of each. In an effort to test this model, however, we have concentrated on examining new and potentially interesting stimulus sets to test in the laboratory. We will now examine a few of these sets that have been described earlier, followed by some results with stimuli that have been tested only recently and have not previously been reported.

Stimulus Sets

The experiments we are about to discuss all use the same procedure described above. They differ only in the stimuli used. As noted earlier, these stimuli were all constructed by placing two visual forms side by side, with each of the two forms having been selected from the same two alternatives, such as a square and a circle as shown in Fig.6.2. Many of these form pairs have been shown to be perceived as *configural* (as opposed to *separable* or *integral*) in that they produce Garner interference, they manifest virtually no redundancy gains, and on divided attention tasks they yield performance as good as or superior to that on selective attention (filtering) tasks (see Pomerantz, 1981).

The rationale for focusing on this restricted set is as follows. First, because the two alternatives are the same for the two side-by-side forms, they allow the possibility of Stroop interference. (If the two alternative forms on the left were circle and square while the two on the right were triangle and oval, no Stroop interference would be expected because no pairings would be regarded, a priori, as congruous or incongruous). Second, placing identical forms side by side generates important emergent features, such as symmetry, that should have significant effects on perceptual organization. Third, given the extreme diversity of results we have obtained in the past using a wide range of stimuli, it is important to restrict the range of stimuli used to attempt to bring some order to the situation and better understand what stimulus factors are responsible for Stroop and Garner interference. Perhaps if we can understand how identical, side-by-side forms group perceptually, we will stand a better chance of learning how other, more complex stimulus configurations group.

We lead off by discussing a few stimulus sets that have been reported on previously: parentheses and letter pairs. We then present results on several newly tested sets.

Stimulus Set 1: Parentheses

The four configurations that result from placing left- or right-oriented parentheses side by side are shown in Fig. 6.4. Parenthesis pairs were shown long ago to produce significant Garner interference, often 300 ms or more in magnitude (Pomerantz & Garner, 1973). That is, judgments of the orientation of the left parenthesis are disrupted by irrelevant variation of the right parenthesis, and vice versa. At the same time, these stimuli produce no Stroop interference. That is, judgments of the orientation of the left parenthesis are made no more slowly or less accurately when the right parenthesis has the opposite orientation, or vice versa. Data from a typical

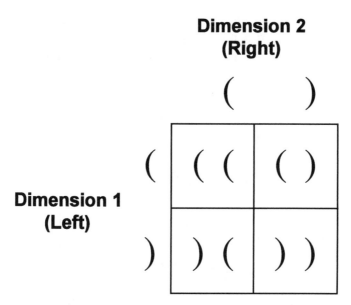

FIG. 6.4.   The parenthesis pair stimulus set, which yields large Garner but no Stroop interference and which shows perfect left-right symmetry.

experiment with parentheses are shown in Table 6.1. Because this table presents a 2 × 2 × 2 design, it may be difficult to follow. We will discuss this table in some detail, because once it is understood, the tables that come later will be easy to follow.

The data in the left side of Table 6.1 are reaction times (RTs) from trials where the parenthesis on the left side was relevant; the data on the right are RTs when the right parenthesis was relevant. Starting with the left, a 2 × 2 table is shown that presents RTs from the control and filtering tasks for both congruous and incongruous (Stroop) stimuli. Also shown on the left are the mean levels of Garner interference (computed by subtracting RTs on the control task from RTs on the filtering task), as well as mean levels of Stroop interference (computed by subtracting RTs for congruous parenthesis pairs from RTs for incongruous pairs). As these means reveal, Garner interference averaged 184 ms per response, whereas Stroop interference averaged -8 ms (for a slight and insignificant Stroop *facilitation* effect). The right side of Table 6.1 shows the corresponding data for trials where the right hand parenthesis was relevant. Here, Garner averaged 192 ms whereas Stroop averaged -1 ms. Combining data from the left and right halves of this table, Garner averaged 188 ms and Stroop -5 ms. These data are representative of results we have obtained from several replications of this experiment.

TABLE 6.1
Stimuli: Parentheses

	Left Relevant				Right Relevant				Grand Mean
	Cntl	Filt	Garner	Mean	Cntl	Filt	Garner	Mean	
Congruous	561 (2.13)	770 (7.59)	209 (5.46)		565 (2.04)	756 (2.96)	191 (0.92)		
				184 (3.10)				192 (1.48)	188 (2.29)
Incongruous	578 (3.52)	737 (4.26)	159 (0.74)		563 (2.04)	756 (4.07)	193 (2.03)		
Stroop	17 (1.39)	−33 −(3.33)			−2 (0.00)	0 (1.11)			
Mean	−8 −(0.97)				−1 (0.56)				
Grand Mean									−5 −(0.21)

Note: Table shows mean response time (in milliseconds) and mean error rate (in percentages, shown below RT's in parentheses) for the various conditions of experiment along with calculations of mean Stroop and Garner interference levels.

Interpretation. These parenthesis pairs form a prototypical pattern of results that we have observed for other stimuli as well: They show large Garner interference, no Stroop interference, and complete symmetry. By symmetry, we mean that whatever interference (or facilitation) the item on the left produces toward the item on the right is mirrored by equivalent interference back from the right to the left. We interpret the sizable Garner interference as resulting from subjects' attending to emergent features of the parenthesis pairs, such as symmetry about the vertical axis or closure (see Pomerantz & Pristach, 1989, for elaboration and further evidence). For example, when the task is to discriminate between ( ) and ((, subjects appear not to attend to the orientation of the right parenthesis, even though this is in one sense the only difference between the pairs. Instead they pay attention to the fact that one of these pairs is bilaterally symmetric (or that one involves two parallel contours). These strategies work effectively and quickly in the control conditions. In the filtering conditions, however, they do not work at all. For example, if the task requires one response to the stimuli ( ) and)), and another response to the stimuli ((and) (, then attending to the emergent feature of bilateral symmetry is of no use whatsoever. Instead, subjects are forced to attend to the orientation of individual parentheses in the filtering condition. Because this feature is not as salient as the emergent feature of symmetry or parallelism, the filtering task is performed more slowly than the control task, and the result is Garner interference.

Stroop interference does not arise with these parenthesis pairs for the simple reasons that these stimuli are indeed seen as pairs. For Stroop conflict to arise, one must perceive these configurations as two stimuli that either agree or disagree in orientation. When they are perceived instead as a single unit, no conflict can arise. Finally, the interference observed is symmetric for the same reason, namely that the two parentheses are seen as a single unit rather than as two units that are scanned from left to right, for example.

Stimulus Set 2: Modified Parentheses ("Yo-Yos")

Two more previously reported experiments may help clarify the results observed with parenthesis pairs. The first of these used the modified parentheses that are shown in Fig. 6.5. Here a vertical line segment has been added to each parenthesis to make it into a closed figure. Our logic was as follows: If the parentheses' pattern of large, symmetric Garner interference accompanied by zero Stroop interference results from subjects' perceiving two parentheses as a single unit, then adding these vertical segments should allow each parenthesis to stand as a separate unit on its own. This logic led us to predict that Stroop might vary reciprocally with Garner as grouping

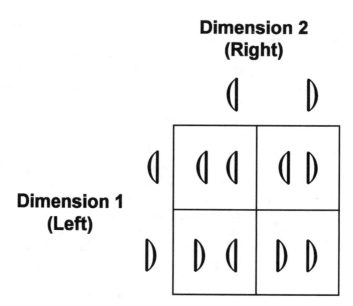

FIG. 6.5.   The modified parenthesis pairs ("Yo-yos"), which produce results similar to those for the original parentheses in Fig. 6.4.

strength varies. Specifically, we expected that compared with the original parentheses, these modified parentheses would show increased Stroop interference but reduced Garner interference. We also were prepared to find left-to-right asymmetries in interference levels if the elements were processed sequentially, as the letter pairs discussed following appear to be. The data shown in Table 6.2 suggested slight movement of the results in the predicted direction: Compared with the original parenthesis data in Table 6.1, Garner interference with the modified parentheses was reduced and Stroop was increased, albeit not to significant levels. Our conclusion, however, is that the addition of the vertical segments did not achieve its full, desired effect of breaking the parenthesis pairs into two separate entities. Subjects continued to perceive each pair as a single unit, and some subject volunteered that the pairs looked like yo-yo's, that is like single, nameable objects.

The last experiment in this set, which used the original unmodified parentheses of Fig. 6.4, was reported by Pomerantz (1991). With the conventional instructions we use in our experiments, subjects are not told how to deploy their attention across the stimulus elements. In fact, they are not even told which element is relevant; they are left to figure that out for themselves. In the present experiment, we altered these instructions by telling subjects to attend just to the left parenthesis (or right parenthesis, as

TABLE 6.2
Stimuli: Modified Parentheses ("Yo-Yos")

	Left Relevant				Right Relevant				Grand
	Cntl	Filt	Garner	Mean	Cntl	Filt	Garner	Mean	Mean
Congruous	559 (4.82)	691 (9.26)	132 (4.44)		555 (4.35)	642 (7.04)	87 (2.69)		
				125 (2.08)				98 (1.25)	111 (1.67)
Incongruous	565 (4.35)	683 (4.07)	118 −(0.28)		563 (4.44)	671 (4.26)	108 −(0.19)		
Stroop	6 −(0.46)	−8 −(5.19)			8 (0.09)	29 −(2.78)			
Mean				−1 −(2.82)				19 −(1.34)	
Grand Mean								9 −(2.08)	

Note: Table shows mean response time (in milliseconds) and mean error rate (in percentages, shown below RTs in parentheses) for the various conditions of experiment along with calculations of mean Stroop and Garner interference levels.

appropriate) in performing the tasks. The results, displayed in Table 6.3, showed that the new instructions produced the very effect that the vertical line segments in the previous experiment failed to yield: Garner interference was reduced to one-third its original magnitude (down to 62 ms), whereas Stroop climbed to now-significant levels (29 ms). Thus, instructions to focus attention effectively broke up the parenthesis pairs from single perceptual units into two separate parentheses located side by side.

Interpretation.   These results provide evidence for our hypothesis that Stroop and Garner might behave reciprocally as subjects' allocation of attention changes. Specifically, when two objects are perceived as a unitary group, we should expect Garner interference (because subjects are attending to emergent features rather than to the individual objects), but we should not expect Stroop (because Stroop depends on conflict between two objects, conflict that might not arise if subjects are perceiving just a single object). We assume here that emergent features are more likely to arise within than between objects, and that conflict requires for its very existence the presence of two or more entities.

Stimulus Set 3: Letter Pairs As and Ns

Our third stimulus set is constructed by substituting the letters A and N for the left and right parentheses respectively. The resulting four letter pairs are shown in Fig.6.6. Despite their many physical similarities with the parenthesis pairs, the results from the letters pairs are quite different, as shown in Table 6.4.

Collapsing the left and right halves of Table 6.4, we see that these letter pairs yielded 111 ms of Garner compared with 38 ms of Stroop interference, both of which are significantly greater than zero. Looking separately at the two halves of this table, we see a very different picture. Although the levels of Stroop interference were comparable between the two halves (28 ms vs. 48 ms), the levels of Garner were not: Garner interference from the right letter to the left (i.e., when the left letter was relevant) was quite small (24 ms) compared with Garner interference in the reverse direction (199 ms from left to right when the right letter was relevant).

Interpretation.   These data from letter pairs differ from the results with parenthesis pairs both because the letter pairs show Stroop interference and because the Garner interference they demonstrate is highly asymmetric, running nearly 10 times as strong from left to right as from right to left. Our interpretation is as follows. Following the logic described earlier for the parenthesis pairs, the presence of Stroop interference indicates the letter pairs are seen as two separate elements that are congruous or incongruous,

TABLE 6.3
Stimuli: Parentheses With Instructions to Attend to Individual Elements

	Left Relevant				Right Relevant				Grand Mean
	Cntl	Filt	Garner	Mean	Cntl	Filt	Garner	Mean	
Congruous	503 (3.52)	552 (5.85)	49 (2.33)	71 (2.22)	508 (3.79)	538 (3.25)	30 −(0.54)	53 −(0.45)	62 (0.88)
Incongruous	506 (4.60)	599 (6.70)	93 (2.11)		518 (4.67)	593 (4.31)	75 −(0.36)		
Stroop	3 (1.07)	47 (0.85)			10 (0.88)	55 (1.07)			
Mean	25 (0.96)				33 (0.97)				
Grand Mean				29 (0.97)					

Note: Table shows mean response time (in milliseconds) and mean error rate (in percentages, shown below RTs in parentheses) for the various conditions of experiment along with calculations of mean Stroop and Garner interference levels.

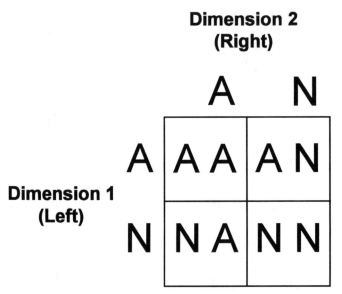

FIG. 6.6. The letter-pair stimulus set using As and Ns, which shows large Garner asymmetries.

not as a single unit. The asymmetric Garner interference indicates that the two letters must be accessed in a left-to-right fashion associated with normal reading order.[2] The left letter virtually escapes Garner interference from the right because the left letter can be processed first and responded to before significant processing has been performed on the right letter. The puzzle in these data is that the Stroop interference is hardly asymmetric at all. At a minimum, this result indicates that Stroop and Garner interference tap into different levels of processing. A variety of variations on these As and Ns have been tested and reported on elsewhere (Pomerantz, Pristach, & Carson, 1989). Although these variations, which include altering the spacing, brightness, and font of the two letters, affect the magnitude of Stroop and Garner interference, the basic results shown in Table 6.4 remain.

Let us now proceed to several newly conducted experiments that were intended to clarify the origin of Stroop and Garner interference with identical, side-by-side forms.

---

[2]Feldman (1991) confirmed that reading order is the factor responsible for the left-to-right asymmetry seen with these stimuli. He showed that when Hebrew-speaking subjects are tested with letters drawn from the Hebrew alphabet, Garner interference now runs in the opposite direction, with the right letter generating more interference on the left than vice versa.

TABLE 6.4
Stimuli: Letter Pairs As and Ns

	Left Relevant				Right Relevant				Grand Mean
	Cntl	Filt	Garner	Mean	Cntl	Filt	Garner	Mean	
Congruous	480 (2.32)	490 (1.85)	10 -(0.46)		484 (2.59)	665 (3.52)	181 (0.93)		
				23 -(0.56)				199 (0.19)	111 -(0.19)
Incongruous	495 (3.43)	531 (2.78)	36 -(0.65)		514 (4.26)	730 (3.70)	216 -(0.56)		
Stroop	15 (1.11)	41 (0.93)			30 (1.67)	65 (0.19)			
Mean	28 (1.02)				48 (0.93)				
Grand Mean				38 (0.97)					

Note: Table shows mean response time (in milliseconds) and mean error rate (in percentages, shown below RTs in parentheses) for the various conditions of experiment along with calculations of mean Stroop and Garner interference levels.

Stimulus Set 4: Letter Pairs Qs and Fs

We have conducted several studies examining side-by-side letter pairs to determine the generality of the asymmetries we found with the pairs composed with As and Ns and with the Hebrew letters tested by Feldman (1991). One set we studied extensively employed the letters Q and F but otherwise was identical to the study with As and Ns.[3] One reason for studying Qs and Fs is that these two letters are less similar than are As and Ns at the level of featural similarity: Qs are curvilinear and closed whereas Fs are rectilinear and open. In addition, Qs and Fs rarely co-occur in either order in English words, either contiguously or in separated letter positions. The data for Qs and Fs are shown in Table 6.5. Compared with the As and Ns, the Qs and Fs showed far less overall Garner interference, and what Garner they showed is fairly symmetric. The Qs and Fs manifested small but significant Stroop, but this Stroop too was not significantly asymmetric. To determine the extent to which practice might affect this result, we tested one subject repeatedly in this experiment for a total of 21 sessions rather than the usual, single session. The data for this subject are shown in Table 6.6. These data reflect means across all 21 sessions, but they are representative of her performance throughout all these sessions, because there were no significant trends in the pattern of her results with practice. Again, the magnitude of overall Garner interference was smaller than with the As and Ns, and the Garner asymmetry was somewhat less pronounced, although both these effects were stronger with this highly practiced subject than with the less experienced subjects in Table 6.5. Note that the Stroop asymmetry suggested in Table 6.5 is virtually absent from Table 6.6.

Interpretation. We interpret these results for Qs and Fs, which are attenuated by comparison with those for As and Ns, to imply that overall levels of Garner interference and Garner asymmetry are partly determined by the degree to which the letters tested are associated either through featural similarities or through previous experience. Further experiments will be needed to determine whether only one or both of these factors are at work. The fact that extensive practice at the task did not alter the results with Qs and Fs shows us that these effects are fairly stable over time and that moderately heavy doses of practice do not allow subjects to escape from Garner interference.

Stimulus Set 5: Red and Green Squares

The next experiment used two squares side by side, either of which could be red or green as depicted in Fig. 6.7. Unlike all the other experiments

---

[3]This experiment was initiated with the assistance of Mei Ling Chen.

TABLE 6.5
Stimuli: Letter Pairs Qs and Fs

	Left Relevant				Right Relevant				Grand Mean
	Cntl	Filt	Garner	Mean	Cntl	Filt	Garner	Mean	
Congruous	459 (2.62)	513 (2.47)	54 -(0.15)	40 -(0.02)	445 (1.59)	495 (0.89)	50 -(0.70)	61 -(0.30)	50 -(0.16)
Incongruous	484 (3.28)	509 (3.40)	25 (0.12)		478 (1.56)	550 (1.67)	72 (0.11)		
Stroop	25 (0.66)	-4 (0.93)			33 -(0.04)	55 (0.78)			
Mean		11 (0.79)				44 (0.37)			
Grand Mean				27 (0.58)					

Note: Table shows mean response time (in milliseconds) and mean error rate (in percentages, shown below RTs in parentheses) for the various conditions of experiment along with calculations of mean Stroop and Garner interference levels.

TABLE 6.6

Stimuli: Letter Pairs Qs and Fs Long-Term Subject (21 Sessions)

	Left Relevant				Right Relevant				Grand Mean
	Cntl	Filt	Garner	Mean	Cntl	Filt	Garner	Mean	
Congruous	401 (6.26)	420 (6.29)	19 (0.03)		418 (6.27)	558 (6.10)	140 -(0.17)		
				25 (0.02)				144 -(0.11)	84 -(0.05)
Incongruous	416 (6.46)	446 (6.46)	30 (0.00)		434 (6.37)	582 (6.32)	148 -(0.05)		
Stroop	15 (0.20)	26 (0.16)			16 (0.10)	24 (0.23)			
Mean		21 (0.18)				20 (0.16)			
Grand Mean						20 (0.17)			

Note: Table shows mean response time (in milliseconds) and mean error rate (in percentages, shown below RTs in parentheses) for the various conditions of experiment along with calculations of mean Stroop and Garner interference levels.

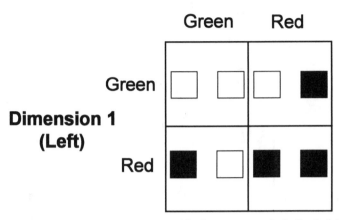

FIG. 6.7.   Red and green squares. In this figure, green is indicated by an empty or white square, and red is indicated by a shaded square.

described so far, the two side-by-side elements here do not differ in form; they differ only in color. Whereas differing forms placed side by side can yield geometric emergent features such as parallelism and collinearity, side-by-side color patches generally yield no readily named emergent features, with the possible exception of color identity or color symmetry. The results with this set are shown in Table 6.7. The pattern of results is virtually identical to those with the original parenthesis pairs: large, symmetric Garner interference but no Stroop interference.

Interpretation.   Because the red and green squares act indistinguishably from the original parentheses in producing Garner interference, these side-by-side color patches must generate an emergent feature that is comparable in its effects to that generated by the parentheses. The fact that the colored squares produced no significant Stroop interference implies that the red and green pairs of squares were, like the parentheses, seen as single objects rather than as two objects side by side. This result stands in sharp contrast with the results from our letter pairs as well as with the large literature on flanker effects coming from the work of Eriksen and his coworkers (Eriksen & Eriksen, 1974; St. James & Eriksen, 1991), of Flowers (Flowers & Wilcox, 1982), and of others.

Two aspects of these conclusions are noteworthy. First, one might have expected some Stroop effects to arise if only from the effects of color

TABLE 6.7
Stimuli: Red and Green Squares

	Left Relevant				Right Relevant				Grand Mean
	Cntl	Filt	Garner	Mean	Cntl	Filt	Garner	Mean	
Congruous	419 (1.77)	535 (2.78)	116 (1.00)	112 (0.83)	404 (1.07)	511 (1.44)	107 (0.37)	109 −(0.07)	111 (0.38)
Incongruous	412 (2.51)	520 (3.16)	108 (0.66)		417 (1.22)	528 (0.70)	111 −(0.52)		
Stroop	−7 (0.73)	−15 (0.39)			13 (0.15)	17 −(0.74)			
Mean	−11 (0.56)				15 −(0.30)				
Grand Mean				2 (0.13)					

Note: Table shows mean response time (in milliseconds) and mean error rate (in percentages, shown below RTs in parentheses) for the various conditions of experiment along with calculations of mean Stroop and Garner interference levels.

adjacency: If the squares had experienced color assimilation, that could have yielded Stroop interference, whereas if they had experienced color contrast, that could have yielded Stroop facilitation. To grasp the latter point, consider that if a flanking green square had made a red square seem even more red than it would otherwise appear, then the presence of the conflicting colored green square would have facilitated performance rather than interfered with it. The fact that no Stroop interference or facilitation was observed indicates that, at least with the colors and spacings tested, no sensory color interactions seem to have occurred.

Second, one possible emergent feature these colored squares could have produced is the simple property of sameness versus difference. That is, in discriminating between the left-right pairs RED-RED and RED-GREEN, subjects could have coded the first simply as "same" and the second as "different" without regard for what colors were present or what positions those colors held. We maintain that this is not an adequate explanation for the present data for the simple reason that *all* of the present experiments, by using side-by-side elements drawn from the same two alternatives such as red and green, possess this ostensible emergent feature. Yet as we have seen, some stimulus sets we have tested yield Stroop and others do not, and the magnitudes of Garner interference they manifest is extremely wide ranging, from zero for some forms up over 300 ms for others. Because all stimulus sets have the same–different emergent feature, this property does not help explain differences in how the stimuli are perceived and processed. However a more specific distinguishing feature, such as color sameness versus color difference, might explain the present results.

Stimulus Set 6: Circles and Squares

This penultimate experiment used the circles and squares shown previously in Fig. 6.2. In some respects these stimuli mimic the parentheses, except that the circles and squares are closed forms that, unlike the yo-yos, are not mirror images of one another. In other respects the circles and squares are like letter pairs, except that they are not letters. (The circle could have been interpreted as the letter "O," but the square could not be interpreted as any letter.)

The results, shown in Table 6.8, reveal moderate, symmetric levels of Garner interference, averaging 88 ms, accompanied by modest (23 ms but statistically significant), fairly symmetric Stroop. The presence of significant Stroop interference makes it clear that these circles and squares are not perceived like either the parentheses or the red and green squares, neither of which showed any Stroop whatsoever. The symmetry of interference effects shows that the circles and squares were not perceived like the letter pairs in a left-to-right sequence. Finally, the moderate levels of Garner interference

TABLE 6.8
Stimuli: Circles and Squares

	Left Relevant				Right Relevant				Grand Mean
	Cntl	Filt	Garner	Mean	Cntl	Filt	Garner	Mean	
Congruous	411 (2.31)	495 (2.70)	84 (0.39)	80 −(0.13)	417 (2.74)	515 (3.55)	98 (0.81)	96 −(0.17)	88 −(0.15)
Incongruous	433 (3.97)	509 (3.32)	76 −(0.65)		447 (3.94)	540 (2.78)	93 −(1.16)		
Stroop	22 (1.66)	14 (0.62)			30 (1.20)	25 −(0.77)			
Mean	18 (1.14)				28 (0.21)				
Grand Mean				23 (0.68)					

Note: Table shows mean response time (in millisecond.) and mean error rate (in percentages, shown below RTs in parentheses) for the various conditions of experiment along with calculations of mean Stroop and Garner interference levels.

146

suggest the presence of an emergent feature.[4] Overall, the data from this stimulus set most closely resemble those from the parentheses under instructions to focus attention.

Interpretation.   These stimuli present a paradox. On the one hand, the subjects appear to be attending to an emergent feature with these stimuli, rather than attending to the individual circles and squares in the two side-by-side positions. On the other hand, if subjects are attending to an emergent feature, why did we observe significant Stroop interference with these stimuli? We have argued that Stroop arises when the pairs are seen as two objects side-by-side, rather than as a single perceptual object containing an emergent feature. The explanation we offer is that these results represent a hybrid between two different types of perceptual processing. Perhaps there exists a continuum of processing side-by-side objects, ranging from treating them as separate and potentially conflicting objects to treating them as a single object. These circles and squares lie somewhere along the middle of this continuum, occupying a position similar to that of the parenthesis pairs when subjects are instructed to focus their attention on just one parenthesis.

Stimulus Set 7: Open and Closed Circles

The final stimulus set we will consider here is shown in Fig. 6.8. One of the two forms is a circle; the other is the same circle but left open at the top. The resulting two forms are thus similar in some respects (e.g., in template overlap, curvilinearity, etc.) and different in others (closure, presence of terminators). In addition, these shapes can be interpreted either as geometric forms or as the letters "O" and "U." Following our customary procedure, our instructions to subjects did not name or describe the stimuli; instead we simply directed subjects to look at example stimuli printed on the page of instructions and on cards they placed next to the response keys.

The results from this stimulus set are shown in Table 6.9. In brief, the pattern of results corresponds most closely to that for the letter pairs: moderate asymmetric Garner accompanied by minor and slightly asymmetric Stroop.

---

[4]This conclusion is further supported by data from another condition of the present experiment not reported here, specifically a divided-attention task requiring responses based on both the left and right elements. As we have shown in previous papers, stimuli such as the parentheses pairs show fast and accurate performance on this task, faster in fact than on the selective-attention (i.e., filtering) task that requires responses based on just the left or just the right element. The circle and square stimuli show this same superior performance on the divided-attention task, providing converging evidence that these stimuli possess an emergent feature.

**Dimension 2
(Right)**

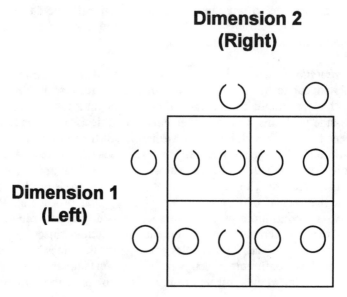

**Dimension 1
(Left)**

FIG. 6.8.   Open-and closed-circle stimulus set.

Interpretation.   Garner interference was three times as great in the left to right direction as in the right to left (83 ms vs. 29 ms). Although this lopsidedness is not as pronounced as it was for the As and Ns (where it reached almost a 10 to 1 ratio) or for the extended-practice subject processing Qs and Fs (where it reached almost 6 to 1), it is still more pronounced than for the Qs and Fs tested with regular, unpracticed subjects. Our interpretation is that subjects perceived these open and closed circles not as forms but as letters, and scanned them in a left-to-right fashion accordingly. Unlike with some of the other letter pairs tested, these stimuli showed an asymmetry of Stroop interference that, at over 4 to 1, was almost as pronounced as the Garner asymmetry. Given that the overall levels of Stroop interference were quite low (averaging just 19 ms), we need to pursue this effect more closely before attempting to explain it.

CONCLUSIONS

Our goals in these experiments were, first, to examine the kinds of perceptual organization that take place when two visual forms are placed side by side; and second, to learn how failures of selective attention to just one of these forms, as manifested in Garner and Stroop interference, can illuminate these organizational processes.

TABLE 6.9
Stimuli: Open and Closed Circles

	Left Relevant				Right Relevant				Grand Mean
	Cntl	Filt	Garner	Mean	Cntl	Filt	Garner	Mean	
Congruous	414 (1.11)	457 (1.30)	43 (0.19)	29 −(0.06)	416 (1.31)	496 (1.70)	80 (0.39)	83 −(0.08)	56 −(0.07)
Incongruous	435 (1.91)	449 (1.59)	14 −(0.31)		444 (1.89)	530 (1.33)	86 −(0.56)		
Stroop	21 (0.80)	−8 (0.30)			28 (0.57)	34 −(0.37)			
Mean	7 (0.55)				31 (0.10)				
Grand Mean									19 (0.32)

Note: Table shows mean response time (in milliseconds) and mean error rate (in percentages, shown below RTs in parentheses) for the various conditions of experiment along with calculations of mean Stroop and Garner interference levels.

149

Our results lead us to claim that even with the highly restricted set of configural stimuli considered here, more than one form of perceptual organization manifests itself. That is, when we consider only pairs of side-by-side elements, each drawn from the same set of just two alternatives, the two elements can and do interact differently in different pairs. Specifically, we find three types of perceptual organizations:

1. *Full fusions into single objects.* This category is exemplified by the parenthesis pairs, the modified "yo-yo" parentheses, and the red and green squares. These pairs show large amounts of Garner interference, virtually zero Stroop, and full left–right symmetry. These pairs seem to be perceived not as two elements side by side but as a single element possessing a salient emergent feature to which subjects attend whenever possible. Because the two elements are seen as one, there are no asymmetries (because there is no scanning order), and no Stroop interference arises (because that would require two elements that agree or conflict). Garner interference itself arises from one of two causes (Pomerantz, Pristach, & Carson, 1989): because subjects can base their responses in the control conditions on the salient emergent feature but must attend to the less salient individual elements (e.g., the direction of curvature of the left parenthesis) in the filtering condition; or because the filtering condition involves responding to four alternative stimuli, which is more difficult than just the two stimuli involved in the control conditions.

2. *Sequentially processed pairs of objects.* This category is represented by the letter pairs and by the open and closed circles, which seem to be perceived as letter pairs. These pairs show asymmetric Garner interference in a direction consistent with reading order. They also show Stroop interference, which also shows occasional asymmetries, albeit smaller than the Garner asymmetries. Our interpretation of the Stroop interference is that these pairs, unlike the parentheses, are seen as two elements side by side that can either agree or conflict. Our interpretation of the Garner interference these pairs show rests not on emergent features but on the larger number of stimuli in the filtering than in the control condition. The asymmetry present in the Garner means that this increase in the number of effective stimuli was more pronounced when the right letter was relevant (and thus the irrelevant left letter was mandatorily processed before the right letter) than when the left letter was relevant. The only puzzle with these stimuli is why the Stroop interference is not as asymmetric as the Garner interference. In any case, the organization these sequentially processed pairs manifest is

clearly more conceptual than perception in nature, compared with the pairs showing full fusion into single objects.

3. *Weakly fused pairs.* This final category is represented here by the parenthesis pairs under instructions to focus attention, and by the circle and square pairs. These stimuli show results similar to those for the fully fused pairs except that Garner interference is reduced whereas Stroop is increased from zero to significant levels. As with the fully fused pairs, they show full symmetry. Our interpretation of these weakly fused pairs is that an emergent feature is present but is weak in salience, either because of the stimuli or the attentional strategy in use. As a result, subjects operate on the margin between attending to the emergent feature (and thus showing Garner interference) or attending to the isolated elements (and thus showing Stroop). In the latter case, subjects appear to be able to focus on either the left or right element at will, as opposed to the situation with letter pairs where left-to-right scanning is generally mandatory.

These results contribute to our understanding both of the nature of perceptual interactions in vision and of how these interactions can be diagnosed by performance on information processing tasks. Through analyzing performance on these tasks and others, including similarity judgments and free classification, a number of researchers have identified and distinguished among separable, integral, and configural stimulus dimensions, the latter two in both their symmetric and asymmetric forms. The present results show us that seemingly similar sets of side-by-side forms can differ significantly in how they are perceived. They also show how two indices of selective attention—Stroop and Garner interference—appear to behave reciprocally as subjects' attentional allocation narrows from wholes to individual elements.

ACKNOWLEDGMENTS

The authors thank Susan Jerger and Henry Lew for their helpful comments and advice on this work.

REFERENCES

Eriksen, B. A., & Eriksen, C. W. (1974). Effects of noise letters upon the identification of a target letter in a nonsearch task. *Perception & Psychophysics, 16*, 143–149.
Feldman, E. M. (1991). Asymmetric Garner interference: Is it the same for both the English

and the Hebrew languages? Unpublished manuscript Rice University, Department of Psychology, Houston, TX.

Flowers, J. H., & Wilcox, N. (1982). The effect of flanking context on visual classification: The joint contribution of interactions at different processing levels. *Perception & Psychophysics*, *32*, 581–591.

Garner, W. R. (1970). The stimulus in information processing. *American Psychologist*, *25*, 350–358.

Garner, W. R. (1974). *The processing of information and structure*. Hillsdale, NJ: Lawrence Erlbaum Associates.

Garner, W. R., & Felfoldy, G. (1970). Integrality of stimulus dimensions in various types of information processing. *Cognitive Psychology*, *1*, 225–241.

Kahneman, D., & Henik, A. (1981). Perceptual organization and attention. In M. Kubovy, & J. R. Pomerantz (Eds.), *Perceptual Organization* (pp. 181–212). Hillsdale, NJ: Lawrence Erlbaum Associates.

Lockhead, G. R. (1966). Effects of dimensional redundancy on visual discrimination. *Journal of Experimental Psychology*, *72*, 95–104.

Neisser, U. (1967). *Cognitive psychology*. New York: Appleton-Century-Crofts.

Pomerantz, J. R. (1981). Perceptual organization in information processing. In M. Kubovy, & J. R. Pomerantz (Eds.), *Perceptual Organization* (pp. 141–180). Hillsdale, NJ: Lawrence Erlbaum Associates.

Pomerantz, J. R. (1983). Global and local precedence: Selective attention in form and motion perception. *Journal of Experimental Psychology: General*, *112*, 516–540.

Pomerantz, J. R. (1991). The structure of visual configurations: Stimulus versus subject contributions. In G. R. Lockhead & J. R. Pomerantz (Eds.), *The perception of structure* (pp. 195–210). Washington, DC: American Psychological Association.

Pomerantz, J. R., & Garner, W. R. (1973). Stimulus configuration in selective attention tasks. *Perception & Psychophysics*, *14*, 565–569.

Pomerantz, J. R., & Pristach, E. A. (1989). Emergent features, attention and perceptual glue. *Journal of Experimental Psychology: Human Perception & Performance*, *15*, 635–649.

Pomerantz, J. R., Pristach, E. A., & Carson, C. E. (1989). Attention and object perception. In B. Shepp & S. Ballesteros (Eds.), *Object perception: Structure and process* (pp. 53–89). Hillsdale, NJ: Lawrence Erlbaum Associates.

Shepard, R. N. (1964). Attention and the metric structure of the stimulus space. *Journal of Mathematical Psychology*, *1*, 54–87.

Shepard, R. N. (1991). Integrality versus separability of stimulus dimensions. In G. R. Lockhead & J. R. Pomerantz (Eds.), *The perception of structure* (pp. 53–71). Washington, DC: American Psychological Association.

St. James, J. D., & Eriksen, C. W. (1991). Response competition produces a "fast same effect" in same-different judgments. In G. R. Lockhead & J. R. Pomerantz (Eds.), *The perception of structure* (pp. 157–168). Washington, DC: American Psychological Association.

III MENTAL REPRESENTATION OF PICTURES, WORDS, AND OBJECTS

7 Facilitation and Interference Effects in Word and Picture Processing

Juan Mayor & Javier González-Marqués
Universidad Complutense, Madrid, Spain

One of the procedures most systematically used for the investigation of the nature and mechanism of word (W) and picture (P) processing is to construct experimental designs that permit the obtaining of differential reaction times that are conceived as facilitation and interference effects produced by the different variables that intervene in the processing: the data thus obtained have served to confirm or reject the different hypotheses, theories, and models.

In this chapter we carry out an analysis of the facilitation and interference effects obtained in the processing of words and pictures in an attempt to: (a) describe conceptually and operationally the nature and extent of these effects, (b) isolate and evaluate some of the more important variables that are responsible for them, and (c) propose and test a model for word and picture processing that explains these effects in terms of these variables.

THEORETICAL AND METHODOLOGICAL CONSIDERATIONS

Facilitation and Interference Effects

They are defined operationally in terms of the shorter or longer reaction times (RTs) obtained in a given experimental condition with respect to another that is considered to be neutral or controlled.

A certain confusion has arisen in the scientific literature due to the frequent use of facilitation and interference effects as absolute data, it being forgotten that they are only truly significant in relation to the neutral condition, while at the same time there being no general agreement on what is the most suitable neutral condition, nor is it made sufficiently clear on many occasions which is the neutral condition that is being used; as the neutral conditions are very diverse, it sometimes occurs that there is argument about the data of facilitation and interference as if these were objective, univocal, and independent of the conditions in which they were obtained, whereas in fact, one is referring to very different realities.

To clarify this question we distinguish different types of facilitation and interference effects in word and picture processing in terms of the neutral condition that serves as baseline.

On some occasions (few), two variables (x, y), or two values of the same variable $(x1, x2)$ are directly compared and it is said that (x) or $(x1)$ facilitates the processing in relation to (y) or $(x2)$ if the RTs attributed to the former are greater than those attributed to the latter; in this same sense, but reserved, it is said that (y) or $(x2)$ produces more interference than (x) or $(x1)$. Conceptually, this way of understanding facilitation and interference effects is useless and confusing, because it does no more than indicate (metaphorically) the direction of the differences between the RTs corresponding to two variables (or values of one variable). It would be sufficient therefore (and this is what is usually done, though not always) to say that significantly longer or shorter RTs correspond to the variable (x) than to (y) or that the variable (x) is critical for the processing of W or P, because for the value $(x1)$ of this variable shorter or longer RTs are obtained than are obtained for the value $(x2)$.

On many occasions, perhaps the majority, the neutral condition is defined by the nonexistence of relation between two stimuli that are presented together (between the irrelevant stimulus — prime or distractor — and the relevant — target); the no relation can be semantic, associative, orthographic, and phonemic, and so on. The facilitation and interference effects appear when the processing time of another two paired stimuli that have between them (between prime or distractor and target) some type of relation is shorter or longer than that of the neutral condition. This relation can be, as in the case of no relation, semantic, associative, orthographic, phonemic, and so on. The majority of the investigations on priming use this neutral condition (from Meyer & Schvaneveldt, 1976, to Tipper & Driver, 1988, or Biggs & Marmurek, 1990).

A further step can be taken to conceive the neutral condition as that stimular configuration in which the irrelevant stimulus is without meaning (or conventionally codified structure) and, thus, has no semantic relation (nor structurally codified relation) with the relevant stimulus; thus, for example, pseudowords or series of letters (often a series of xxxx is used) are used as primes or distractors if the target is a word table, dog, etc.), or dotted lines with no definitive meaning or form, series of asterisks or a kind of open frame if the target is a drawing that shows the object or symbol refered to (picture of a table, or of an indicative arrow, etc.). As in the previous case, the facilitation or interference effects are measured by the difference (smaller than or greater than) between the stimular configuration in which the two stimuli are words and/or pictures and the neutral condition in which the prime or distractor is of the type indicated (Glaser & Düngelhoff, 1984; Glaser & Glaser, 1989; La Heij, Van der Heijden, & Schreuder, 1985).

Finally, the neutral condition can be the isolated presentation of the target stimulus for contrast with the presentation of two paired stimuli (both words and/or pictures), the facilitation or interference in this case being entirely attributable to the presence of the irrelevant stimulus (Durso & Johnson, 1979). This neutral condition has not been used very much, maybe because it has been considered that the neutral condition — a single stimulus — is not equal to the experimental condition — two stimuli. This supposed argument is not very convincing, because in the previous case neither was it equal or totally equal. For example, in the neutral condition used by Glaser and Düngelhoff (1984), in which an empty frame appears, the participant can codify it as the picture of a frame and elicit a verbal response, which could be "frame", with which the neutral condition disappears as such.

In order to resolve the methodological vacilation between this type of neutral condition and the previous one, we have used a variant of the isolated presentation of the target: The prime or distractor is a blank card that generically activates the processing system of the respondent on presentation, but this activation is totally nonspecific, because it has neither semantic content nor definite form. The double stimulation is thus maintained and neutrality totally guaranteed with respect to the processing of words and pictures. In an unpublished study in which we compared the different neutral conditions, we confirmed the consistency and usefulness of the earlier-mentioned neutral condition, although, in the final analysis the choice of the most suitable neutral condition is a question of convenience, if the shortcomings of construction of the said conditions are remedied (see González-Marqués & Mayor, in press; Klein, 1964; La Heij, 1988).

Recently two neutral conditions have frequently been used, the no relation and some mode of the ones mentioned above (La Heij, 1988; McEvoy, 1988; Schriefers, Meyer, & Levelt, 1990; Sereno, 1991). Attempts have been made to explain facilitation and interference effects in terms of different models and different mechanisms. One of the most frequently invoked explanations for priming effects is the spreading-activation theory of semantic processing (Collins & Loftus, 1975) interpreted by Posner and

Snyder (1975), Neely (1977), and Stanovich and West (1979): The presentation of a stimulus (prime) produces an automatic spreading-activation that facilitates the processing of a subsequent stimulus (target) semantically related with it, this effect declining with the increase of the Stimulus onset asynchrony (SOA); if the participant puts into use his limited capacity of attention, facilitation effects can also be produced when the two stimuli are related, but inhibition effects are produced if they are not related. Thus whenever facilitation effects appear without interference it is due to an automatic processing, and whenever interference effects appear there are also facilitation effects (the former as a consequence of attending to the unrelated prime, the latter the result of attending to the target to which is added the effect of the automatic activation). Another explanation is based on models like the logogen model of Morton (1969), reelaborated as the verification model by Becker (1980): The facilitation and interference effects arise, in the interpretation of Schubert and Eimas (1977), from the increase in information on the semantic features of a target that is produced by a related context and from the decrease that results from an unrelated context. Becker (1980) characterized the semantic facilitation on the basis of a generation of a few semantic features, precisely those that are appropriate to a singular connotation of the cue, whereas the interference is connected to the appearance of semantic features appropriate to all the possible interpretations of the cue; the former implies a strategy of specific prediction and the later a strategy of generic expectation.

Another important aspect in understanding the nature of facilitation and interference effects is related to the locus in which they are produced within the processing system. With regard to the effects produced in priming conditions, the facilitation effects in related primes are situated in a prelexic phase (based on naming implying less postlexic processing than the lexic decision, for which reason the similar effects in both tasks must be attributed to prelexic processing), whereas the inhibition effects in unrelated primes must be considered postlexic in the lexic decision task (but not in the naming task as they do not occur or are very doubtful; Lorch, Balota, & Stamm, 1986). With regard to the effects produced in the Stroop condition, there are basically three hypotheses about the locus in which they occur: In the perceptual codification phase (the perception of the distractor reduces the respondent's capacity to perceive the target; Hock & Egeth, 1970); in the response production phase (because the automatic processing of the distractor leads to the production of a response that enters into competition with the response that the participant must give in relation to the target stimulus and in accordance with the requirements of the task, with the result that the effort to suppress a response has inhibitory effects (Dyer, 1973); and in the semantic decision phase (Seymour, 1977).

Variables that Affect Word and Picture Processing

Experimental Condition.   We give this name to what in the literature is usually called task, paradigm, or effect referred to priming and Stroop. We do this because both priming and Stroop are defined in the final instance by a peculiar combination of certain experimental conditions that have in common the presentation of two paired stimuli, one that is considered irrelevant (which is called prime in priming and distractor in Stroop) and another that is relevant for the task and, thus, is the one that the respondent considers as target for producing the response.

The radical distinction between the two conditions is, in our opinion, the successive presentation of the two stimuli in priming and their simultaneous presentation in Stroop. Other differences can be considered conventional, because in the successive modifications that have been introduced they have disappeared in applying the same conditions to priming as to Stroop.

Initially, and in its classic form, priming was an experimental condition with which it was attempted to obtain facilitation effects as a consequence of semantic relations existing between prime and target (semantic priming). Soon this semantic priming condition was applied to the orthographic and phonologic relations and was called phonologic priming. On varying certain conditions, other types emerge, among them repetition priming-when prime and target were identical-and backward priming-when the prime follows the target (in contrast to the classic form which was forward). For semantic priming, see Meyer and Schvaneveldt, (1976); Neely (1977); Sperber, McCauley, Ragain, and Well, (1979); Irwin and Lupker, (1983); Lupker, (1984); den Heyer, Briand, and Smith, (1985); Ratcliff and McKoon, (1988); for graphemic or phonological priming, see Hillinger, (1980); Evett and Humphreys, (1981); Forster and Davis, (1984); Sereno, (1991); for repetition priming, see Koriat, (1981); den Heyer, Goring, and Dannenbring, (1983); Logan, (1990); Rueckl (1990); Brown, Neblett, Jones, and Mitchell, (1991); for backward priming, see Koriat, (1981); Kiger and Glass, (1983); Dark, (1988); Seidenberg and McClelland, (1989); Peterson and Simpson, (1989). On the other hand, Fischler (1977), Lupker (1984), or Whittlesea and Jacoby (1990) deal with the distinction between semantic priming and associative priming, which had been pointed out by Meyer and Schvaneveldt (1971). It must be pointed out that studies of priming use, as well as the tasks of naming and categorizing, the task of lexic decision, which we are not going to deal with here; on the other hand, in contrast to semantic priming, one can also talk about perceptual priming (Farah, 1989).

Two characteristics have usually been attributed to the priming condition: The target stimulus was not used as prime and the responses were numerous and not repeated in the different items (Glaser & Glaser, 1989; La

Heij et al.,1985). The effects looked for were basically those of facilitation; thus priming and facilitation have come to be identified with one another, although some authors such as Tipper and Driver (1988) find a negative priming.

The Stroop effect was discovered by Stroop (1935) when he noted that to name a color is made difficult if the name of another color is written with that color, whereas to read a color word written with another color is hardly affected. A variant (called Stroop-like) consisted in using a picture and a word that were incongruent, the same pattern of results being obtained: The incongruent word inhibited the naming of the picture, whereas the incongruent picture hardly affected the reading of the word (Rosinki, 1977; Rosinki, Golinkoff, & Kukish, 1975). Soon pure stimuli were used together with the mixed ones (WW, PP, together with WP and PW) (see Glaser & Glaser, 1989; Mayor, Sainz, & González-Marqués, 1988). But new investigations discovered new effects: In categorization tasks, the reverse of the Stroop effect was produced (the picture as distractor increased the processing time of the word, whereas the effect of the word on the categorization of the picture was very weak or nonexistent); the belonging of the word and picture to the same category increased the processing time, and so forth. A characteristic of the Stroop-like condition was that the same words and pictures were used as distractors and targets, thus the responses were usually few and repeated (Glaser & Glaser, 1989; La Heij et al., 1985). The classic effects were those of inhibition or interference of the responses, so that Stroop and interference have come to be identified with one another (sometimes "Stroop-like interference" is used to indicate that the initial Stroop effect was a particular case of a general effect of interference, as proposed by Glaser & Glaser, 1989). For the variables and effects of the Stroop condition, as well as for the various explanatory hypotheses, see also Dyer (1973), Lupker (1979), Glaser and Glaser (1982), McLeod and Dunbar (1988), La Heij (1988), and Schriefers et al. (1990).

However, on varying the characteristics of the priming condition and the Stroop condition, the two have noticeably approximated to one another, especially when different stimulus onset asynchronies have been introduced and it has been found that they both produce facilitation and interference effects; thus they have come to be compared in an attempt to establish similarities and differences between them (La Heij et al., 1985; Mayor et al., 1988), and to decide if the same mechanisms do or do not underlie each of them.

We have investigated this question from different perspectives, using the two conditions in combined form, analyzing the behavior of words and pictures as primes or distractors and as targets in both conditions, comparing in each the effects of the taxonomic and parthonomic relations González-Marqués & Mayor, 1990; Mayor et al., 1988; Sainz, Mayor, &

González-Marqués 1991) and this study is on the same line. The results obtained up to now seem to confirm that the two conditions are basically similar, that they put the same mechanism into play, but that, because of their different temporal courses (with reference to the presentation of the two stimuli), they interact differently in the active memory as a function of the SOAs and the different combinations between the stimuli.

Naming and Categorization Tasks.   In the study of word and picture processing, in the priming and Stroop conditions, naming and categorization tasks have been very greatly used, as has already been mentioned. This has led to such studies being frequently included in wider areas and topics of investigation, such as word (and picture) processing and the process of categorization that helps to give meaning to the data obtained; in reverse fashion, in the study of these processes the effects obtained in the said conditions are frequently used.

With the term *naming* we cover both the "reading of the word" and the "naming of the picture," although many authors keep these two terms to underline the fact that the two tasks are different. However, the difference between the two is related to the different mode of the stimulus and consequently to the different processes implied. For this reason we consider that we are dealing, in a strict sense, with the same task, because the task is defined by the instructions that the experimenters give to the participant with regard to the response that is required of them and this response consists in both cases of pronouncing the word that corresponds to the stimulus (be it a word or a picture) and with which it is named. On word reading the investigations are innumerable; suffice it to mention the works on the topics of reading (see, for example, those contained in Balota, Flores, D'Arcais, & Rayner 1990) or of lexic representation (see the works contained in Marslen-Wilson, 1989) or of word recognition (see the revision of Norris, 1986). On the naming of drawings there are not so many studies, although one can refer to Warren and Morton (1982), Lupker (1988), La Heij (1988), McEvoy (1988), Reinitz, Wright, & Loftus (1989), and Levelt et al. (1991). The comparison between word and picture naming constitutes the topic that this work deals with, and the references are very abundant; see, for example, Potter and Faulconer (1975), Snodgrass (1980), Glaser and Glaser (1982), Huttenlocher and Kubicek (1983), Kroll and Potter (1984), La Heij et al. (1985), Theios and Amrhein (1989), and Biggs and Marmurek (1990).

Another different task is that of categorization, because the participant has to respond to certain stimuli (word or picture), not with its name, but with another word that symbolizes a category in which are included as examples the concepts corresponding to the word or picture that appears as the stimulus (Guenther & Klatzky, 1977; Wilkins, 1971).

In the results obtained in these tasks it is systematically demonstrated that the RT of categorization is far greater than that of naming and that numerous asymmetries are produced between them (Durso & Johnson, 1979; Glaser & Düngelhoff, 1984; Glaser & Glaser, 1989; Mayor et al., 1988; Smith & Magee, 1980). Isolated or combined use depends on the purpose of the investigators, because one starts with the supposition—implicit or explicit—that categorization always implies semantic processing (this generally considered to be a strategic type of process) and that naming can demand or not demand that semantic processing (being generally an automatic process; Carr, McCauley, Sperber, & Parmelee 1982; McCauley, Parmelee, Sperber & Carr, 1980; McEvoy, 1988; McLeod & Dunbar, 1988). Reality is not as simple as would appear in these basic assumptions, and this justifies the study of the nature of these tasks through the effects that other variables might have on them.

Modality of the Stimuli.   Both stimuli used in the mentioned conditions and tasks are usually presented in the word modality (written) and the picture modality. The target stimulus is the one that is relevant for the requirements of the task. The prime or distractor stimulus (that is irrelevant for the task), and the stimular configuration in which it participates together with the target are those that basically define the experimental conditions (priming and Stroop).

As we have seen, the central axis of investigation in this field (one could say, in this paradigm) is the processing of words and pictures. It is, thus, words and pictures that tend to appear systematically in studies of priming and Stroop, although initially in priming only words were used, and in Stroop words and colors (in the Stroop-like condition, words and pictures are necessarily used).

These two modes of target and of prime or distractor, being at the center of this type of investigation, allow it to be located within the large topic of present day cognitive psychology, which is none other than the analysis of the system of representation—of its form and of the processes and mechanisms involved; Potter and Faulconer (1975) or Guenther and Klatzky (1977) proposed a common code, based on the similarity of the responses to either modality of the stimulus; Durso and Johnson (1979), Te Linde (1982), and Paivio (1986) underlined the importance of the two levels of representation; Snodgrass (1984), Glucksberg (1984), Theios and Amrhein (1989), and Mayor et al. (1988) tended to prefer models that include three codes—one of them of an abstract and amodal character.

Semantic Relations.   The semantic relation between each of the paired stimuli has been systematically used to try to infer whether or not in certain tasks and conditions word and picture processing involves semantic processing.

The type of priming most frequently studied is in fact semantic, which has incorporated associative relations and semantic relations, sometimes contrasting them, although this is only reasonable if the type of associative relations is well controlled, because the majority of them are also semantic relations, as we have discovered in our laboratory. At the same time, the most commonly used semantic relations are taxonomic, although we have tried to compare them with parthonomic relations (Sainz, Mayor, & González-Marqués, 1991), and on occasion they have been contrasted with antonomic relations (Becker, 1980; Hodgson, 1991).

Of the taxonomic relations, the belonging of the two stimuli to the same category has been habitually chosen, this being called relation of category (Guenther & Klatzky, 1977; Lupker, 1988). The relation of identity is also considered to be a type of semantic relation, sometimes called relation of conceptual congruence and which includes, as a specific example, the so-called repetition priming; here the prime is identical to the target in its structure and in its semantic content. In addition to this, it is also possible in the relation of identity for the target and prime to differ in their modality and structure, so long as the same concept corresponds to both of them in the semantic memory. Sometimes synonyms have been used and even different pictures of the same object (Biggs & Marmurek, 1990; Hodgson, 1991).

In general, pairs of semantically related stimuli have been compared with pairs of unrelated stimuli. Recently, more than one type of semantic relation has been used (McEvoy, 1988) to try to prove the existence of a semantic gradient that is frequently the result of differences ranging from less to greater or from greater to less between the relation of identity, of category, and no relation (Glaser & Düngelhoff, 1984, Glaser & Glaser, 1989; La Heij, 1988; Mayor et al., 1988; Tipper & Driver, 1988). The basic hypothesis establishes differences between semantically related pairs (shorter RT, facilitation) and unrelated pairs (longer RT, interference). In regard to the semantic gradient, the hypothesis of its systematic appearance (in all conditions and tasks) can be made, but also the hypothesis of asymmetry, which denies its existence in the naming task, but affirms it for the categorization task (Glaser & Glaser, 1989).

Stimulus Onset Asynchrony (SOA) The demonstrated fact that word and picture processing consumes a time that varies as a function of the intervening variables has lead researchers to establish different intervals between the appearance of the stimulus and that of the target in the priming condition, whereas in the Stroop condition total synchrony of presentation of stimuli has been maintained. However, different SOAs have come to be used in the Stroop condition in the same way as was done in the priming condition. in reciprocal fashion, synchrony of presentation of stimuli has been used in priming (Dallas & Merikle, 1976), and with this the two conditions have become equal with regard to this variable.

In general, this difference in the processing time as a function of these synchronies and asynchronies of presentation of stimuli has proved to be a variable of powerful effects and of extraordinary usefulness for making inferences about the nature of word and picture processing (Glaser & Düngelhoff, 1984; Glaser & Glaser, 1982; Glaser & Glaser, 1989; González-Marqués & Mayor, 1990; Hodgson, 1991; Mayor et al., 1988; Schriefers et al., 1990; Smith & Magee, 1980).

Model of Word and Picture Processing

In the final instance, all the variables that we have analyzed up to now have been associated with various processing models, in some cases so that the model might serve as an explanatory framework for the functioning of the variable and in other cases in order to infer, on the basis of the effects of the variables, the structure and functioning of the processing system, and from there to be able to construct the model.

In research on this topic, in which the different variables are combined — conditions, tasks, modality of the stimuli (as primes or distractors and as targets), semantic relations and SOAs — models and general theories frequently appear with that double function; they are used to provide explanatory mechanisms for the data obtained, or the data are taken as a basis for their empirical verification (sometimes calling on a vague consistency between the data and the model).

Representation models of an amodal and abstract character have been called upon, together with dual code models, with a recent tendency towards mixed models (Snodgrass, 1984; Theios & Amrhein, 1989). Memory models such as activation diffusion have also been used (Collins & Loftus, 1975) or that of retrieval (Ratcliff & McKoon, 1988) or parallel distributed processing models (Cohen, Dunbar, & McClelland, 1990; Seidenberg & McClelland, 1989). Abundant use has been made of word recognition and lexic access models (Allport, 1979; Becker, 1980; Den Heyer et al., 1985; Levelt et al., 1991; Marslen-Wilson, 1989; Warren & Morton, 1982). But above all, and this is what most interests us, specific models have been constructed to explain word and picture processing using naming and categorization tasks in priming and Stroop conditions. Only these, and among these only the most recent, are referred to in what follows.

In Virzi and Egeth (1985) a translational model is proposed to explain the

Stroop interference. Two independent systems exist: one that processes spatial relations and the other that processes linguistic information. Each of these is subdivided into three subsystems, that act in different stages carrying out different processes: analysis of information, central decision, and response production. There exists a translation mechanism between the two systems.

Glaser and Glaser (1989) constructed a model based on the existence of two independent but interrelated subsystems: the semantic memory, to which pictures accede directly (through an executive semantic system), and the lexicon, to which words accede directly (through the graphemic or phonemic executive systems). To each conceptual node in the semantic memory there corresponds a lexical node in the lexicon, and vice versa. The model proposes a series of paths that the processing follows according to whether the stimuli are words or pictures and according to whether the task is naming or categorization. To these paths are applied a series of principles, some of which are very general and others extremely specific.

Theios and Amrhein (1989) established two subsystems, one for early visual processing and another for the production of the response (which can be verbal, analogic, or binary), between which are situated three processing subsystems that are substantially differentiated by the codes that they use: The superficial linguistic system codifies phonetically the information received from the early visual processing system, the superficial pictorial system codifies the information in images, and the abstract conceptual system codifies semantically the information that it receives from the two superficial systems.

Biggs and Marmurek (1990) proposed a processing overlap model to explain the effects of facilitation in naming and categorizing: The pictures, analyzed visually, pass over to the semantic memory, from which the categorization response is produced; if the response is naming, the processing includes a subprocess that has its roots in the lexicon; the words, analyzed visually, pass directly to a phonemic processer, which produces the naming response; they can also pass directly to the lexicon, from which can be produced the naming response, or, through processing in the semantic memory, the categorization response.

The model that we propose, shown in Fig. 7.1, is similar in many, respects to those mentioned, but as a whole it is different than all of them. The establishing of three processing stages in which different systems operate would seem to be beyond dispute. In the first stage, an analysis of the information is carried out by an early visual processing system (on this all the models are in agreement). In the third and final stage the response is executed by a response production system that in our case, is verbal (on this also all the models are in agreement). In the second and intermediate stage are situated the central processing systems (and here there are differences

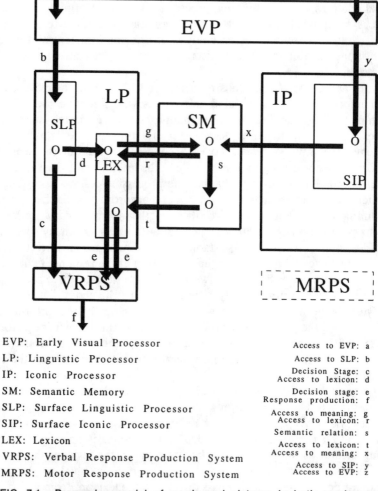

FIG. 7.1. Processing model of words and pictures in both naming and categorization tasks.

EVP: Early Visual Processor

LP: Linguistic Processor

IP: Iconic Processor

SM: Semantic Memory

SLP: Surface Linguistic Processor

SIP: Surface Iconic Processor

LEX: Lexicon

VRPS: Verbal Response Production System

MRPS: Motor Response Production System

Access to EVP: a
Access to SLP: b
Decision Stage: c
Access to lexicon: d
Decision stage: e
Response production: f
Access to meaning: g
Access to lexicon: r
Semantic relation: s
Access to lexicon: t
Access to meaning: x
Access to SIP: y
Access to EVP: z

between the various models). The linguistic processing system incorporates a graphemic–phonologic subsystem and a lexic subsystem; the iconic processing system only includes a subsystem of superficial analysis of images, because there is no iconic equivalent of the lexicon; the semantic processing system (semantic memory) codifies in an abstract and conceptual form the information received in the previous systems.

As specified in Table 7.1, this model establishes a different pattern of processing for words and pictures and also for the tasks of naming and categorization.

TABLE 7.1
Subprocesses Involved in the Tasks of Naming and Categorizing Words and
Pictures (see Fig. 7.1)

NAM W	a	b	d(-)	-	-	-	e(c)	f
NAM P	z	y	-	x	-	r	e	f
CAT P	z	y	-	x	s	t	e	f
CAT W	a	b	d	g	s	t	e	f

This model permits the analysis of facilitation and interference effects and the investigation of the locus where these effects are produced. It is neutral, however, with respect to the mechanisms that operate to produce them (spreading activation, retrieval, overlap, etc.). It also permits the analysis of the different variables that affect word and picture processing and their interactions.

Taking this model into account together with what we have said about the variables that modulate the facilitation and interference effects in the processing of words and pictures, predictions can be made that allow it to be empirically verified.

In conclusion of what has been said up to now about word and picture processing and in order to test it empirically, we are going to formulate two series of predictions, in the first place on facilitation and interference effects, and in the second place on the variables that affect processing and produce these effects.

(a) With regard to the facilitation and interference effects that are observed in word and picture processing, we maintain that basically they depend on the definition of the neutral condition and are modulated by the different experimental variables. To be precise, we can make the following predictions:

(a1) If we define facilitation and interference in terms of the longer or shorter RT produced by one of the values of each variable with respect to the other value of values of the same variable, we can predict that all the variables produce facilitation and interference effects, whose size and direction will be specified later (predictions b).

(a2) If we consider as the neutral condition the presentation of a prime or distractor consisting of a blank card (and thus without semantic content or any discernible stimular form or structure) followed by the presentation of another stimulus with a certain form and structure (a series of letters or a picture) and with semantic content, then the presentation of two paired stimuli (succesively and/or simultaneously paired) with these characteristics (each with form and semantic content) will require systematically a longer processing time than the neutral condition, these interference effects being a function of the different experimental variables (specified in b).

(a3) If we consider as the neutral condition the presentation of two stimuli with discernible form or structure and with informational content, but semantically unrelated to each other, then the presentation of two stimuli of the same characteristics but semantically related to each other will systematically require less processing time, these facilitation effects being a function of the different experimental variables (specified in b).

(b) The adoption of our proposed model for word and picture processing implies a differential processing of both stimulus modes in naming and categorization tasks, together with processing flexibility (measured through the variability of the RT) as a function of the different relevant variables and their mutual interaction. To be precise, we can specify the following predictions, which are susceptible to experimental verifications:

(b1) The categorization task consumes more time than the naming task; the word as a whole is processed more slowly than the picture; the naming of the word will be, according to the model, quicker than of the picture, and the categorization of the word will be slower than that of the picture (NAM W < NAM P < CAT P < CAT W).

(b2) If the experimental conditions of priming and Stroop are made completely equal, the pattern of responses that they produce will be similar, and differences between the two conditions will only be found as a function of the variables that define them; that is to say, of the modality and combination of the pairs of stimuli and of the asynchrony of presentation of the irrelevant stimulus with respect to the target.

(b3) The modality of the irrelevant stimulus—which is processed involuntarily in spite of being irrelevant—affects the processing time of the target; as prime or distractor the word slows the processing more than the picture; the combination of the modes of the prime or distractor and the target is slower in its pure form (WW,PP) than in its mixed form (WP,PW); the neutral condition—prime or distractor substituted by a blank card—will be slower than when the irrelevant stimulus is a word or a picture.

(b4) The different semantic relations between the two paired stimuli will modulate the processing in the form of a semantic gradient, with shorter RTs when the relation is of conceptual identity, longer RTs when no semantic relation exists, and intermediate RTs for the relation of category (the belonging of the two stimuli to the same category). The relation of category will tend to approximate in its effects to no relation in naming tasks (for in both cases the names of the primes or distractors are different to the names of the targets) and to the relation of identity in categorization tasks (because the two stimuli, in both cases, belong to the same category).

(b5) The effects of the different temporal courses of presentation of the stimuli will be systematically produced and will affect all the experimental variables, with the RTs corresponding to the shorter SOAs being similar to each other, but shorter than in the case of the simultaneous presentation of stimuli (SOA-O).

(b6) The conditions will only produce significant interactions with the specific variables that define them (mode of the target and SOAs). In the same way there will be significant interactions between the tasks and the variables that most specifically define them (mode of the target and semantic relations). The conditions and the tasks are independent variables; the remaining variables will produce less significant interactions, it being foreseeable that even OxDxRxS will be significant, because in the given experimental conditions and tasks these variables are not independent.

EXPERIMENT

In line with some previous studies (González-Marqués & Mayor, 1990; La Heij et al., 1985; Mayor et al., 1988; Sainz et al., 1991), an experiment on word and picture processing was carried out to compare the experimental conditions in which two paired stimuli are presented to interfere with or facilitate processing, which we call priming and Stroop, although the latter is really Stroop-like. In the experiment we try to orthogonally combine the variables that we have considered in the first part: the experimental condition (priming and Stroop), the task required of the respondent (naming and categorizing), the modality of the relevant stimulus presented and which is the objective that the respondent must take into account in his response (word and picture), the modality of the irrelevant stimulus that functions as prime or distractor (word and picture, to which was added a neutral condition consisting of the presentation of a blank card as prime or distractor), the semantic relation between the pairs of stimuli — relevant and irrelevant — (relation of identity, in which prime or distractor and target have the same meaning, although they can be presented in the pure modality — WW, PP — or mixed — WP, PW; relation of category, in which both stimuli belong to the same category; no relation, neither semantic nor associative) and the stimulus onset asynchrony (preexposure of the prime or distractor 100 ms before the target, total overlapping and post-exposure of the prime or distractor 100 ms after the target). A prior decision — equalization to the maximum of the priming and Stroop conditions — has led us to restrict the number of SOAs and the size of the intervals (100 ms), a characteristic that should be taken very much into account in the analysis of the results. The purpose of the experiment is to prove that all these variables influence word and picture processing and that they interact with one another; more precisely, it is to test the specific predictions that we made previously.

Method

Participants. Forty Psychology students at Complutense University (Madrid) aged 21 to 25 took part in this experiment. They were all native Spanish speakers and their collaboration was voluntary, though it was taken into account in their academic assessment.

Materials and Instrumentation. For the carrying out of this experiment 40 bysillabic four-letter words were chosen, 20 of high frequency of use and 20 of low frequency (indices above 18 and below 15, respectively, in accordance with Juilland and Chang-Rodríguez, 1964). Each of these words belongs to one of the following six categories: animal, furniture, vehicles, buildings, kitchen utensils, and parts of the body. Two cards were made up for each word; on one the word was written and on the other was the corresponding picture; 24 of them were used as targets and were grouped in three blocks: in the first, eight of them (and their corresponding pictures were used also in identical form (repeated) as primes or distractors (semantic relation of identity, ID): in the second, to each of the eight words or drawings used as a target, there corresponded eight words or drawings used as primes or distractors and belonging to the same semantic category as each of them (semantic relation of category, CAT); in the third, between the eight words and drawings used as targets and the corresponding words and pictures used as primes and distractors, there was no semantic (no semantic relation, NOR).

The targets were made up in red and the primes or distractors in blue to avoid confusion as a consequence of the different intervals between stimuli and their different orders of presentation. To these materials was added a blank card as the most adequate neutral condition (González-Marqués & Mayor, in press).

All the stimuli were presented to the participants by means of a three channel tachistoscope Electronic Developments Hampton Middx with Auto Card Changer registered by a Campden 565 time counter controlled by means of a Campden 340 key voice.

Design. The first variable was the condition (priming and Stroop, PRIM and STRO) that establishes a distinction between the sequential presentation of prime and target and the joint presentation of both stimuli (except in the SOA O), having equated other differences between both conditions (see Glaser & Düngelhoff, 1984; La Heij et al., 1985; Mayor et al., 1988). The second variable is the task (naming and categorization, NAM and CAT). The third is the stimulus onset asynchrony (SOA) (-100, 0, 100). The fourth is the target modality (word and picture, W and P). The fifth is the prime or distractor modality (word, picture, and neutral condition or blank card, W, P, and N). The last is the earlier-mentioned semantic relation between the prime or distractor and the target (relation of identity, relation of category and no relation, ID, CAT, NOR).

Procedure. The presentation of stimuli was organized in 12 blocks resulting from combining the variables that affect the experimental procedure (two conditions, two tasks, and three SOAs); within each block the stimuli were presented haphazardly (orthogonally combining the two targets, the three primes or distractors, and the three semantic relations).

In the priming condition, the irrelevant stimulus (prime or distractor) was presented for 90 ms and the relevant stimulus (target) also for 90 ms. The stimulus onset asynchrony was -100 ms, 0 ms, and 100 ms; in SOA (-100) the prime precedes the target; in SOA (0) both stimuli coincide exactly; in SOA (100) the target precedes the prime. In the Stroop condition there is always some time in which distractor and target coincide; in SOA (-100) the distractor is presented first and 100 ms later the target appears without the distractor disappearing, during 90 ms; in SOA (0) distractor and target are presented together for 90 ms; in SOA (100) first the target appears and 100 ms later the distractor is presented, both stimuli being then maintained for 90 ms. See Fig. 7.2.

One of the tasks consisted in naming the picture or reading the word that appeared as target (in red); the other task required that the participant pronounce aloud the category to which the words or pictures presented as targets (in red) belonged. Neither in the naming task nor in that of categorizing was there to be an open response to the stimulus presented as prime or distractor (in blue, or in the neutral condition, a blank card).

Only correct replies were considered; when a respondent made a mistake in any particular stimulus configuration, this was presented again at the end of the block.

Results and Discussion

In describing the results we shall first mention the influence of each of the variables on the RTs obtained, then we shall present the facilitations and interferences resulting from the subtraction from these data of the neutral condition (N) — in which the prime or distractor was replaced by a blank card — and the neutral condition (NOR) — defined as the nonexistence of semantic relation between the two pairs of stimuli. The data corresponding to the four basic groupings (from combining conditions x tasks: PRIM-NAM, PRIMCAT, STRONAM, and STROCAT) are presented, followed by the data for each of the conditions (PRIM and STRO) and tasks (NAM and CAT) and for the totality of all the data (GLOBAL). The mean values of the variables corresponding to all these groupings are shown in Table 7.2.

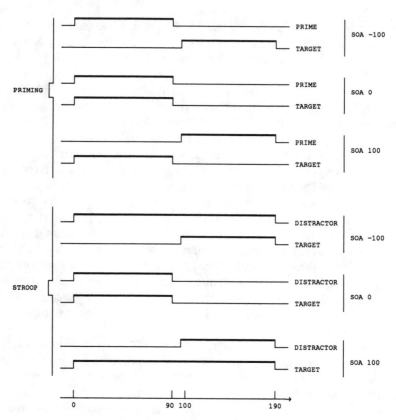

FIG. 7.2. Stimulus Onset Asynchrony (SOA) in priming and Stroop conditions.

For the analysis of the data the BMDP2V and BMDP7D statistical programs were used in their 1988 version with the aim of obtaining the corresponding ANOVAs, the histograms, and the significance of the differences between means.

The variable *condition* refers to the disposition and form of presentation of the stimuli. The differences observed between the global RT corresponding to the PRIM condition (810.57 ms) and the STRO condition (820.14) were not significant, $F(1, 8423) = 2.55$, $p > .1103$; the same occurred when the data were analized in isolation when the task required of the respondent was naming, $F(1, 4212) = 1.55$, $p > .2138$, or categorizing, $F(1, 4212) = 1.17$, $p > .2801$.

The *task* variable, as usual, systematically produces significant differences; categorization is about 332 ms slower than naming, both in the PRIM condition (976.00 ms vs. 645.14 ms), and in the STRO condition (987.01 ms vs. 653.26 ms) and in the combination of each (981.50 ms vs.

TABLE 7.2

Mean RTs of the Six Main Variables (global, from priming and Stroop Conditions, from Naming and Categorizing Tasks, and from the Combination of These Variables)

			GROUPINGS								
			CONDITIONS		TASKS		PRIMING		STROOP		
		GLOBAL	PRIMING	STROOP	NAMING	CATEGOR	NAMING	CATEGOR	NAMING	CATEGOR	
CONDITION	PR	810.57	—	—	645.14	976.00	—	—	—	—	
	ST	820.14	—	—	653.26	987.01	—	—	—	—	
TASK	NAM	649.20	645.14	653.26	—	—	—	—	—	—	
	CAT	981.50	976.00	987.01	—	—	—	—	—	—	
TARGET	W	828.42	820.79	836.04	604.41	1052.42	597.50	1044.08	611.33	1060.75	
	P	802.55	800.88	804.23	693.99	911.12	692.79	908.97	695.19	913.27	
DISTRACTOR	W	880.44	869.87	891.01	717.13	1043.75	723.99	1015.76	710.26	1071.75	
	P	805.19	809.28	801.10	637.85	972.54	631.76	986.80	643.93	958.27	
	N	760.33	753.36	768.30	592.63	929.04	579.67	927.06	605.59	931.02	
	ID	763.22	763.36	763.38	601.49	924.96	594.95	931.77	608.03	918.14	
SEMANT.REL	CAT	804.96	793.54	816.38	663.76	946.16	660.61	926.47	666.92	965.85	
	NOR	878.26	875.59	880.93	682.34	1074.19	679.86	1071.33	684.82	1077.04	
SOAS	100	791.94	791.67	792.21	625.10	958.77	627.69	955.65	622.52	961.90	
	0	910.79	918.16	903.42	743.30	1078.27	755.97	1080.36	730.63	1076.22	
	-100	743.72	722.67	764.77	579.20	908.25	551.77	893.57	606.63	922.92	

Note. (—indicates that grouping does not exist in this variable.)

173

649.20 ms)' to which correspond $F(1, 4212) = 2200.42, p < .001; F(1, 4212) = 1287.89, p < .001;$ and $F(1, 8423) = 3242.23, p < .001.$ If we consider the neutral condition to be that which we established in the experimental procedure (blank card as prime or distractor), the processing of the target (W or P) in the PRIM condition is more greatly interfered with in the naming task (+98.26 ms) than in categorization (+74.24 ms), whereas in the STRO condition the reverse occurs: Naming (+86.77 ms) interferes more than categorization (+71.51 ms). Now, if we consider no semantic relation as a neutral condition, the processing of the semantically related targets is facilitated in a similar fashion in the two conditions, but more facilitated in the categorization task (−170.71 ms in the PRIM condition and −167.32 ms in the STRO condition) than in naming (−73.22 ms in the PRIM condition and −53.24 ms in the STRO condition). See Fig. 7.3a.

The *target modality* is significant in the four groupings that arise from the combination of conditions and tasks. In the naming task, the processing of pictures is slower than that of words, both in the PRIM condition (95.29 ms difference), and in the STRO condition (83.86 ms); on the other hand, the reverse occurs in the categorization task, the processing of pictures is faster than that of words, both in the PRIM condition (135.12 ms) and in the STRO condition (147.48 ms)—all these differences being significant. Taken together (for the task, the conditions, and the global data), the target modality also presents significant differences. For the interferences and

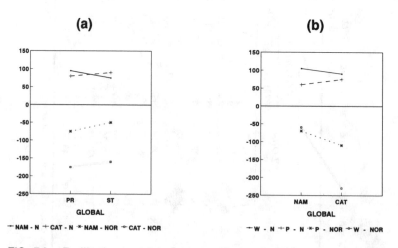

FIG. 7.3. Facilitation and interference effects of naming and categorization tasks (a) in Stroop and priming conditions, and (b) with words and pictures as targets (interference effects are present in the N neutral condition, and facilitation effects are present in the NOR neutral condition).

facilitations produced in the processing of W and P in the tasks of naming and categorization, see Fig. 7.3b.

Taking the obtained RTs as a baseline, the processing of pictures is generally facilitated with respect to the processing of words, though there is an important asymmetry in the naming task (P > W) with respect to the categorization task (W > P). See Fig. 7.4a.

The *irrelevant stimulus modality* (prime, in the priming condition; distractor, in the Stroop condition) is also a systematically significant variable, the processing of the target being slower when the prime or distractor is W than when it is P (with both of them making the processing slower than when the prime or distractor is the neutral condition N). In the four blocks (conditions x tasks), these differences are maintained, all of them being significant.

Taken as a whole, in the naming task the prime or distractor W produces a slower processing than P and both produce a slower processing than the neutral condition N, $F(2, 4212) = 124.26, p < .001$), the difference (W − P) being 78.28 ms ($t = 8.81, p < .001$), (W − N) being 124.50 ms ($t = 13.84, p < .001$), and (P − N) being 45.22 ms ($t = 5.03, p < .001$); similarly, in the categorization task the prime or distractor W is slower than P and both are slower than the neutral condition N, $F(2, 4212) = 47.58, p < .001$, the difference (W − P) being 71.24 ms ($t = 5.54, p < .001$), (W − N) being 114.74 ms ($t = 8.93, p < .001$) and (P − N) being 43.50 ms ($t = 3.39, p < .01$). See Fig. 7.4b.

If we take into consideration the neutral condition N, the result that is systematically observed is that both W and P as prime or distractor produce interference with respect to N and that the interference of W (119.77 ms) is greater than that of P (45.79 ms).

If we take as the neutral condition the responses to pairs of unrelated stimuli (prime–target), the processing of the targets is generally facilitated both by the prime or distractor W and by P, the facilitation of W (− 141.82 ms) being greater than that of P (− 90.35 ms). See Fig. 7.5a.

Another main variable is the type of *semantic relation* between the prime (or distractor) and the target. The differences between no relation (NOR), relation of category (CAT), and relation of identity (ID) are significant throughout the majority of the main groupings, a clear semantic gradient being observed that, in general, adopts the pattern NOR > CAT > ID.

Taken as a whole, the same pattern of differences is maintained: In the naming task the difference between NOR and CAT is 18.58 ms ($t = 2.04$, not significant), between NOR and ID 80.85 ms ($t = 8.88, p < .001$, and between CAT and ID 62.27 ms ($t = 6.84, p < .001$), with $F(2, 4212) = 56.11, p < .001$; in the categorization task the difference between NOR and CAT is 128.02 ms ($t = 10.05, p < .001$), between NOR and ID 149.23 ms ($t = 11.72, p < .001$) and between CAT and ID 21.21 ms ($t = 1.67$, not

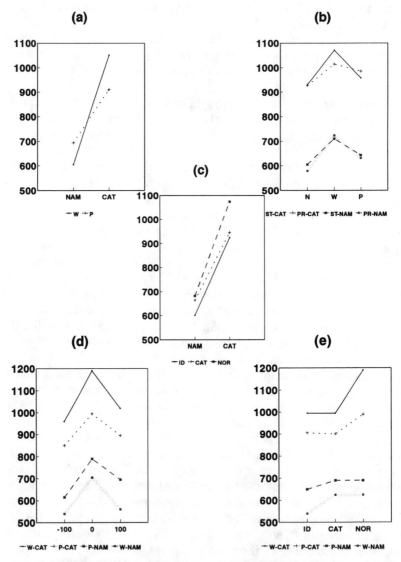

FIG. 7.4. RTs of the interaction between (a) tasks (NAM, CAT) × modality of the target (W, P); (b) modality of the prime or distractor (N, W, P) × tasks (NAM, CAT) × condition (PR, ST); (c) tasks (NAM, CAT) × semantic relationships (ID, CAT, NOR); (d) SOAs (−100, 0, 100) × tasks (NAM, CAT) × modality of the target (W, P); and (e) semantic relationships (ID, CAT, NOR) × tasks (NAM, CAT) × modality of the target (W, P).

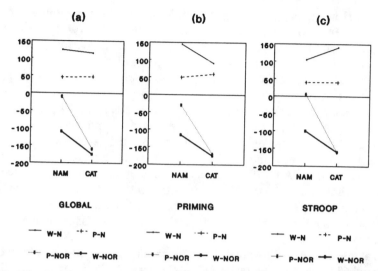

FIG. 7.5. Facilitation and interference effects of naming and categorizing tasks with words and pictures as primes or distractors from (a) global data, (b) priming condition, (c) Stroop condition (interference effects are present in the N neutral condition, and facilitation effects are present in the NOR neutral condition).

significant), with $F(2, 4212) = 92.64$, $p < .001$. Note that in the naming task the relation of category is not significantly different from no relation, whereas in the categorization task the relation of category does not differ from the relation of identity. See Fig. 7.4c.

If we take into consideration the neutral condition N and compare it with the rest of the data, a systematic pattern of interference is observed in all types of semantic relation together with a semantic gradient of interference that coincides with that already detected in the RTs (NOR > CAT > ID). Taken as a whole, the interferences conform to the semantic gradient indicated, except in the naming task, which turns out to be CAT (116.41 ms) > NOR (114.61 ms) > ID (23.60 ms), there being once more a certain equivalence between CAT and NOR; however, in the categorization task the classic gradient appears NOR (114.06 ms) > CAT (68.90 ms) > ID (28.52 ms).

If we consider no relation as the neutral condition, we have already seen that, in general, a systematic pattern of facilitation is produced, both when the semantic relation is of identity and when it is of category, the relation of identity (that is, the repetition of the semantic information of the prime stimulus as target or semantic coincidence between distractor and target) always being more facilitating than that of category (that is, the belonging of both stimuli—prime or distractor and target—to the same semantic category). Taken as a whole, the facilitation effects are much greater in ID

(– 112.01 ms) than in CAT (– 14.44 ms) when the task is naming, whereas the differences between ID (– 186.31 ms) and CAT (– 151.72 ms) are smaller when the task is categorization. Figure 7.6 shows, for both priming and Stroop conditions, the interference effects with the neutral condition N, and the facilitation effects with the neutral condition NOR for all types of semantic relationships.

The final main variable is *stimulus onset asynchrony (SOA)*, which in this experiment takes into account only three intervals and those very close to one another; in spite of this it is a variable that systematically attains statistical significance and that in general produces a pattern of more rapid responses with SOA (– 100) (where the prime or distractor is presented 100 ms before the target) and slower ones with SOA (0) (where both stimuli are presented together, completely overlapping), with SOA (100) producing slower responses than SOA (– 100) and considerably faster than SOA (0). See Fig. 7.4d.

Taking the data as a whole, the same pattern of responses is observed in general. In the naming task, $F(2, 4212) = 224.25$, $p < .001$, all the differences are significant: SOA (0) – SOA (100) = 118.20 ms; in the categorization task, $F(2, 4212) = 108.39$, $p < .001$, all the differences are also significant: SOA (0) – SOA (100) = 119.51 ms ($t = 9.42$, $p < .001$), SOA (0) – SOA (– 100) = 170.04 ms ($t = 13.40$, $p < .001$) and SOA (100) – SOA (– 100) = 50.53 ($t = 3.98$, $p < .001$). In the PRIM condition, $F(2,$

(a)   **(b)**

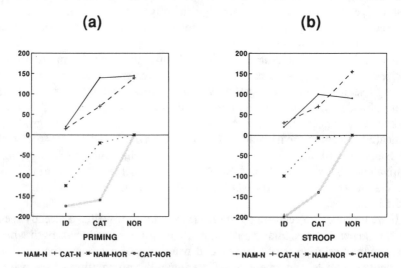

FIG. 7.6. Facilitation and interference effects of naming and categorizing tasks when the semantic relationships between the stimuli are either identity, categorial, or none (a) in priming condition, (b) in Stroop condition (interference effects are present in the N neutral condition, and facilitation effects are present in the NOR neutral condition).

4212) = 262.58, $p < .001$, the differences are also significant: SOA (0) − SOA (100) = 126.49 ms (t = 14.54, p < .001), SOA (0) − SOA (−100) = 195.49 ms ($t = 22.33, p < .001$) and SOA (100) − SOA (−100) = 69.00 ($t = 7.79, p < .001$) in the STRO condition, $F(2, 4212) = 83.10, p < .001$ only two differences are significant: SOA (0) − SOA (100) = 111.21 ms ($t = 10.50, p < .001$), SOA (0) − SOA (−100) = 138.65 ms ($t = 11.03, p < .001$), whereas SOA (100) − SOA (−100) = 27.44 ms does not reach statistical significance. Finally, in the global data, $F(2, 8423) = 289.11, p < .001$, all the differences are also significant: SOA (0) − SOA (100) = 118.85 ms ($t = 17.30, p < .001$), SOA (0) − SOA (−100) = 167.07 ms ($t = 22.64, p < .001$) and SOA (100) − SOA (−100) = 48.22 ms ($t = 5.34, p < .001$).

Note that all the differences are highly significant, except for the difference between preexposure (SOA −100) and postexposure (SOA 100) of the distractor in the case of the STRO condition (data as a whole, STRONAM and STROCAT).

If we take the neutral condition (N) into consideration, in relation to this all the data in general show interference, sometimes very marked. SOA (−100) causes the least interference and in certain configurations it even produces facilitation. SOA (0) produces the highest interferences and SOA (100) produces medium interference. Taken as a whole, the interferences conform to the patterns already mentioned: In the naming task SOA (0) (127.93 ms) > SOA (100) (72.59 ms) > SOA (−100) (54.12 ms) and in the categorization task SOA (0) (135.24 ms) > SOA (100) (68.31 ms) > SOA (−100) (37.95 ms). In the two conditions, however, there is a reversal of the amount of interference produced by pre-and postexposure: In the PRIM condition there is conformation to the more general pattern, SOA (0) (144.77 ms) > SOA (100) (80.63 ms) > SOA (−100) (33.34 ms), whereas in the STRO condition, SOA (0) (118.40 ms) > SOA (100) (60.27 ms) > SOA (−100) (58.73 ms). Note the asymmetry between the interference produced in STRONAM and STROCAT by SOAs (−100) and (100). Taken as a whole, SOA (0) (131.58 ms) > SOA (100) (70.45 ms) > SOA (−100) (46.03 ms).

If we take no semantic relation as the neutral condition, the two types of semantic relation produce a general facilitation in all the SOAs, SOA (0) being the one that produces the greatest effects, and SOA (100) and SOA (−100) behaving in a similar fashion, though with some significant asymmetries. Taking the data as a whole, in the naming task, SOA (0) (−109.04 ms) < SOA (100) (−41.79 ms) < SOA (−100) (−38.84 ms) and in the categorization task, SOA (0) (−223.30 ms) < SOA (100) (−143.15 ms) < SOA (−100) (−140.60 ms) in the conditions there is a reversal of the facilitation produced by pre- and postexposure: In priming, SOA (0) (−168.76 ms) < SOA (100) (−115.06 ms) < SOA (−100) (−82.08 ms), whereas in Stroop SOA (0) (-163.58 ms)$<$SOA (-100) (-97.36 ms)$<$SOA (100) (-69.88 ms). In the global data SOA (100) (-97.36 ms) and SOA (-100) (-89.72 ms) are equalized, these effects being almost doubled in SOA (0) (-166.17 ms).

The significant double *interactions* are very numerous, which indicates the complexity of the processing of words and pictures in the conditions, tasks and variables that we have manipulated (C = condition; T = task; O = target; D = distractor or prime; R = semantic relation; S = SOA). Of the possible interactions in which the experimental condition (priming and Stroop) or the task (naming and categorizing) intervenes as a variable, it can be said that the following reach significance in an inverted fashion: In the first place the $C \times T$ interaction is not significant; in the second place, of all the interactions in which the condition intervenes, only $C \times S$ (in the global data, $F(2, 4212) = 8.45$, $p < .001$; and in the naming task, $F(2, 4212) = 13.62$, $p < .001$; because in the categorization task, $F(2, 4212) = 1.05$, $p = .3416$, is not the significant), and $C \times D$ (in the naming task, $F(2, 4212) = 3.17$, $p < .05$; and in the categorization task, $F(2, 4212) = 6.51$, $p < .01$; because in the data as a whole, $F(2, 8423) = 2.34$, $p = .0963$, is not significant) are significant, the already mentioned $C \times T$, together with $C \times O$ and $C \times R$, not being significant; in the third place, of all the interactions in which the task intervenes, the only ones that are not significant are the equivalents of the above, $T \times S$ (not significant in the global data, nor in the conditions PRIM and STRO) and $T \times D$ (although it is significant in the PRIM condition, $F(2, 4212) = 8.04$, $p < .001$), $T \times O$ and $T \times R$ being significant; in the fourth place, all the interactions in which the condition and the task do not intervene are significant: $O \times D$, $O \times R$, $O \times S$, $D \times R$, $D \times S$, and $R \times S$, as can be seen in Table 7.3.

Some triple and quadruple interactions turn out to be significant in many of the various goupings that were considered. Among these $T \times O \times R$ and $T \times D \times R$ stand out in the global data and in the conditions PRIM and STRO, and $O \times D \times R$, $O \times D \times S$ and $D \times R \times S$ stand out in almost all groupings. Among the quadruple interactions the one that stands out is the one that combines the four variables, $O \times D \times R \times S$, which appear in all groupings and which in the majority of them is significant. See Table 7.3.

The most striking aspect of the interactions between the type of condition (PRIM and STRO) and the rest of the variables is the reversal that is produced in the effects by the SOAs and the modality of the irrelevant stimulus (prime or distractor), a fact that proves the importance of the SOA variable and the modality of the prime or distractor in defining the experimental condition as priming or as Stroop.

Among the interactions between the task and the rest of the variables, $T \times O$ and $T \times R$ deserve to be mentioned, which is coherent with the importance and close connection of the modality of the target and the semantic relation between prime or distractor and target in the carrying out of the task. Furthermore, the triple interaction $T \times O \times R$ is significant in the global data, as well as separately in the PRIM and STRO conditions. In Fig. 7.4e can be seen the effects produced by the interaction $T \times O \times R$: The semantic gradient is modulated by the equality that occurs between CAT and NOR in the naming task and between ID and CAT in the categorization task (the same in the processing of W as in that of P). Also, there exists a now classical asymmetry between the facilitation produced by the processing of W with respect to P (85.5 ms) in the naming task and the interference (141.30 ms) that it produces in the categorization task. Finally, the differences are greater when W is processed (with respect to P), and when the task is CAT (with respect to NAM).

The six double interactions between the four variables that make up the four basic blocks (the result of combining two conditions × two tasks, PRIMNAM, STRONAM, PRIMCAT, and STROCAT), that is to say $O \times D$, $O \times R$, $O \times S$, $D \times R$, $D \times S$, and $R \times S$, are all significant in the global data, in the PRIM condition (except $O \times R$), in the STRO condition, in the naming task, and in the categorization task (except $O \times D$). Whithin the four blocks, $D \times R$, and $D \times S$ are also all significant, whereas $O \times D$ is significant in PRIMNAM and STRONAM, $O \times R$ in STRONAM, PRIM-CAT, and STROCAT, $O \times S$ only in STROCAT, and $R \times S$ in PRIMNAM and STROCAT. This strong interaction is reinforced if we consider that the triple interactions $O \times D \times R$, $O \times D \times S$, and $D \times R \times S$ are significant in the global data, in the PRIM condition, in the STRO condition (except $D \times R \times S$), in the naming task, in the categorization task (except, once again, $D \times R \times S$), and on five more occasions in the four blocks, always in PRIMNAM and $O \times D \times S$ also in STRONAM and PRIMCAT. At the same time, the interaction between $O \times D \times R \times S$, shown in Fig. 7.7, is significant in the global data (also in PRIM and STRO, in NAM, in PRIMNAM, and STRONAM.)

The *predictions* that have been tested in this experiment have been confirmed in a clear and systematic way, although in some aspects it is necessary to make certain clarifications.

With regard to the facilitation and interference effects, meaning shorter or longer RTs between the values of the different variables (*prediction a1*), one must refer to the detailed description of the results that we have just made, although in essence it can be said that all the variables considered have produced significant facilitation and interference effects.

Prediction(a2) relative to the interference effects is overwhelmingly confirmed in the global data (and also in each of the conditions and tasks and in the different groupings). The neutral condition (that is the presentation of a single stimulus with a discernible form and semantic content) systematically requires less time than the processing of two stimuli (with

TABLE 7.3

F values corresponding to the interactions between two variables and some of the most significative ones between three and four variables. (In bold are the probabilities.)

	GLOBAL	GROUPINGS							
		CONDITIONS		TASKS		PRIMING		STROOP	
		PRIMING	STROOP	NAMING	CATEGORY	NAMING	CATEGORY	NAMING	CATEGORY
CT	0.04 **.8361**	—	—	—	—	—	—	—	—
CO	1.03 **.3106**	—	—	0.77 **.3816**	0.41 **.5218**	—	—	—	—
CD	2.34 **.0963**	—	—	3.17 **.0421**	6.51 **.0015**	—	—	—	—
CR	1.42 **.2412**	—	—	0.15 **.8626**	2.56 **.0771**	—	—	—	—
CS	8.45 **.0002**	—	—	13.62 **.0000**	1.05 **.3416**	—	—	—	—
TO	390.84 **.0000**	265.78 **.0000**	154.69 **.0000**	—	—	—	—	—	—
TD	0.27 **.7626**	8.04 **.0003**	2.34 **.0962**	—	—	—	—	—	—
TR	29.81 **.0000**	26.49 **.0000**	10.00 **.0000**	—	—	—	—	—	—
TS	0.09 **.9099**	0.56 **.5693**	0.92 **.3991**	—	—	—	—	—	—
OD	8.17 **.0003**	4.16 **.0156**	4.44 **.0119**	11.39 **.0000**	1.40 **.2460**	11.11 **.0000**	0.38 **.6813**	3.36 **.0349**	1.90 **.1498**
OR	5.12 **.0060**	6.26 **.0019**	4.04 **.0176**	7.19 **.0008**	12.07 **.0000**	1.33 **.3238**	11.89 **.0000**	6.34 **.0018**	4.44 **.0119**
OS	7.67 **.0005**	2.18 **.1130**	5.83 **.0030**	4.52 **.0109**	4.70 **.0092**	2.08 **.1249**	1.03 **.3563**	2.73 **.0653**	4.11 **.0165**

(Rows TO, TD, TR, TS, OD, OR, OS are grouped under the vertical label INTERACTIONS.)

DR	24.93 / .0000	14.40 / .0000	12.47 / .0000	33.47 / .0000	6.61 / .0000	26.61 / .0000	3.04 / .0163	12.85 / .0000	4.48 / .0013
DS	19.41 / .0000	14.46 / .0000	8.45 / .0000	12.02 / .0000	9.01 / .0000	19.19 / .0000	3.63 / .0059	2.48 / .0422	6.64 / .0000
RS	6.32 / .0000	2.85 / .0225	4.10 / .0025	2.69 / .0297	3.77 / .0046	2.83 / .0233	1.15 / .3316	1.48 / .2050	2.94 / .0195
CSD	1.88 / .1102	—	—	3.37 / .0093	1.92 / .1036	—	—	—	—
TOR	16.03 / .0000	17.78 / .0000	6.13 / .0022	—	—	—	—	—	—
TDR	5.05 / .0005	4.23 / .0020	2.17 / .0695	—	—	—	—	—	—
SOD	8.87 / .0000	11.15 / .0000	3.77 / .0045	9.06 / .0000	2.85 / .0227	11.45 / .0000	4.09 / .0026	5.10 / .0004	1.26 / .2848
ODR	8.80 / .0000	7.17 / .0000	2.89 / .0208	7.12 / .0000	3.51 / .0072	8.03 / .0000	2.36 / .0510	1.75 / .1362	1.37 / .2415
SDR	4.54 / .0000	4.04 / .0001	1.81 / .0704	4.31 / .0000	1.90 / .0554	6.99 / .0000	0.94 / .4796	0.88 / .5288	1.33 / .2257
CSOD	4.34 / .0016	—	—	5.10 / .0004	1.88 / .1113	—	—	—	—
TSOD	0.70 / .5934	—	—	—	—	—	—	—	—
SODR	4.91 / .0000	—	—	6.20 / .0000	1.25 / .2647	6.56 / .0000	1.40 / .1914	2.25 / .0214	0.81 / .5942

Note. (— indicates that grouping does not exist in this variable).

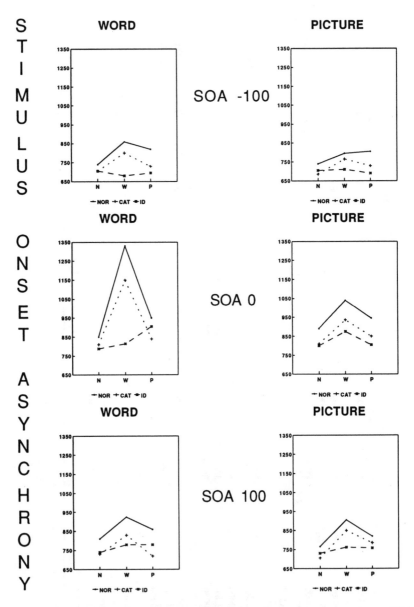

FIG. 7.7. Mean RTs of the interaction between modality of the target (W, P) × modality of the prime or distractor (N, W, P) × semantic relationships (ID, CAT, NOR) × SOAs (−100, 0, 100).

form and semantic content). Thus, far from the conventional idea that the priming condition produces facilitation and the Stroop condition interference, our data support the idea that both conditions produce interference in relation to the neutral condition, such as we have defined it. There are some exceptions, though they are not significant, such as the facilitation produced by the relation of identity in the categorization of W with SOA (−100) and the categorization of P prime P, or that produced by the relation of category in the categorization of W with prime P. To evaluate these systematic interference effects it is necessary to insist that our neutral condition is practically equivalent to the isolated presentation of the target stimulus (whereas frequently, for example in Glaser and Düngelhoff, 1984, it is practically equivalent to an unrelated prime or distractor, at least when the modality is P). It should also be noted that the SOAs are short (−100, 0, 100 ms), which would explain the nonappearence of some of the facilitation effects that appear in previous investigations with longer SOAs, especially in the priming condition.

If we consider no semantic relation as the neutral condition (*prediction a3*), systematic facilitation effects appear, as we have seen in the earlier description of results. Semantic relation between paired stimuli requires less processing time than no semantic relation and this occurs in the globality of the data, in the two conditions and the two tasks and in the different groupings, as well as in the different principle variables, target, prime or distractor, and SOAs. Only in certain very specific combinations of these variables does interference appear instead of facilitation, for example, in the STRO condition NAM W with distractor P, in the PRIM condition NAM W with prime P and with SOA (O).

The tendency for the effects of the relation of category to be similar to those of no relation in the naming task is fully confirmed. On the other hand, in the categorization task there appears a clear semantic gradient (ID < CAT < NOR), although the effects of the relation of category are more similar (closer) to those of the relation of identity than to those of no relation; earlier we offered an explanation that seems convincing.

Also the predictions about the variables that affect word and picture processing according to our proposed model are globally confirmed. This prediction obviously does not imply that other variables not considered in this experiment do not affect the processing of W and P, as has been revealed in different experiments, such as the frequency of vicinity, configural similarity, the presentation or not of identical stimuli, the belonging or not of the irrelevant stimuli to the set of responses, and so forth.

Naming and categorization of words and pictures exactly fit *prediction (b1)*. If we take in isolation the data of the neutral condition, we have NAM W (553) < NAM P (650) < CAT P (864) < CAT W (993) and, if we take the global data, in the same way NAM W (604)<NAM P (694)<CAT P (909)<CAT W (1052). As we have already seen, the processing of the picture is quicker in general than that of the word, because it does not have to pass through the filter of a mental lexicon, and the categorization task consumes more time than the naming task, but, if we take into account the different tasks of naming and categorization, the aforementioned asymetry is produced and reaches statistical significance (interaction $T \times O$). As is only to be expected, the relevant stimulus for the production of the response and the requirements of the task affect — in isolation and in interaction — the processing and contribute to the configuration of a consistent pattern of responses that allows the confirmation of the basic structure of the proposed model.

The second *prediction* (*b2*) is also fulfilled in all its parts: there is no significant difference in the processing of W and P in the priming condition and in the Stroop condition; furthermore, the pattern of responses is very similar in both conditions throughout variables such as the task, the target, and semantic relations (interactions $C \times T$, and $C \times O$, and $C \times R$, not significant; see, nevertheless, facilitation and interference effects of interaction $C \times T$ in Fig. 7.3a). However, the condition variable is affected by the different nature of the primes or distractors and by the different SOAs, as is revealed in the fact that interactions $C \times D$ and $C \times S$ are significant. The target stimulus, contrary to prediction, does not produce differences between the Stroop and priming conditions, although its interaction with the prime does differentially affect the said conditions (interaction $C \times O \times D$ is significant). The nature of the processing seems to be the same in both conditions, also the mechanism involved; the only differences are related to the experimental variables that specifically define the conditions. In this we basically coincide with La Heij et al., 1985, and with our results in other experiments (González-Marqués & Mayor, 1990; Mayor et al., 1988). We would point out again that the SOAs in this experiment have been restricted in number (3) and range (100, 0, − 100 ms), which might be responsible for the similarity in the patterns of response in both conditions.

The third *prediction* (*b3*) is also confirmed in general terms, but a sufficiently clear pattern of responses does not appear in relation to the various aspects considered here. In the global data, the presence of a word as prime or distractor results in a longer RT than that of a picture (the same occurs in both conditions and in both tasks and in the different groupings). The identical modality (WW, PP) does not turn out to be systematically slower than the mixed modality (WP, PW), although it does appear in the data relative to interferences (with respect to the neutral condition N), although a distinction must be made between the combination WW, which is the slower, and the combination PP, which is the faster. On the other hand, interactions $C \times D$ and $T \times D$ do not reach statistical significance. The greater effect of the prime or distractor W with respect to the prime or distractor P has frequently been found in previous investigations.

The fourth *prediction* (*b4*) with relation to the existence of a semantic gradient is systematically fulfilled in all the groupings analyzed (global data, in conditions PRIM and STRO, in tasks NAM and CAT, and in PRIM-NAM, STRONAM, PRIMCAT, and STROCAT). The interferences that result from comparing the data obtained with prime or distractor W and P with those obtained in the neutral condition (N) are also arranged on the same semantic gradient. According to our data, the inexistence of semantic relation requires a longer processing time than when there exists a semantic relation between the pairs of stimuli and, between these, processing the relation of category is slower than processing the relation of identity (NOR > CAT > ID). However, one must point out an important asymmetry in terms of the task:

1. In naming, the pattern of responses for the relation of category approximates to that of no relation (the differences are not significant) and this is reflected in the RTs and in the interferences (in comparison with the neutral condition N), and in a limited facilitation (to be precise, as a result of comparing the relation of category with the neutral condition NOR), with the interference of no relation in the Stroop condition being in exceptional cases smaller than in the relation of category.

2. On the other hand, in the categorization task the pattern of responses to the relation of category approximates to that of the relation of identity (the differences are not significant), which is reflected in the RTs, in a limited fashion in the interferences (with respect to N) and in a marked fashion in the facilitation (with respect to NOR).

This asymmetry should be interpreted in terms of the interaction $T \times R$:

1. When the task consists of naming a W or a P, the presence of a conceptually identical prime or distractor produces very little interference and a marked facilitation, whereas the relation of category and no relation both produce marked interference and almost no facilitation, since the naming task does not involve semantic processing.

2. However, in the categorization task semantic processing of the target is obligatory and is thus favored by the processing (also semantic) of the prime or distractor that is related with it (independently of whether the relation be of identity or of category, because both stimuli, in either case, are included in the same category: "table-table" are both examples of the same category "furniture," in the same way that "dog-cat" are also both examples of the same category "animal"), whereas in the case of there being no relation between prime and target, by definition each of the stimuli

belongs to a different category, which produces more interferences and no facilitation.

The semantic gradient, in general, is a robust effect, as has been revealed in various experiments with different conditions in the same way an asymmetry has frequently been found in the behavior of the relation of category with respect to the relation of identity and with respect to no relation in naming and categorization tasks.

The fifth *prediction* (*b5*) is also confirmed in the global data and in all the groupings. SOA (O) always increases the RT with respect to the other SOAs and produces greater effects of interference (with respect to N) and of facilitation (with respect to NOR). The explanation is to be found in the total synchrony of presentation of both stimuli, in contrast to what occurs in SOA (−100)and in SOA (100), in which the processing of one of the stimuli always commences 100 ms before (in the first place, the prime or distractor and in the second, the target), to which has to be added the time of presentation of the other stimulus (successively or simultaneosly with the previous one), which increases the global time that the stimular configuration is present to the participant and which consequently reduces the RT that is measured from the moment in which the target appears. To this reduction of the RTs in SOAs (−100) and (100) there corresponds also a reduction of the facilitation and interference effects due in fact to the aforementioned asynchrony of presentation of the stimuli. In spite of the fact that this asynchrony is very small − 100 ms of pre- or postexposure − it is a very sensitive variable that produces systematically significant differences and that interacts significantly with the other variables (except for the task).

The influence of the temporal course of the double processing of the relevant and irrelevant stimuli has been pointed out by Smith and Magee (1980), Glaser and Düngelhoff (1984), Glaser and Glaser (1989), and Sereno (1991), among many others. The different experimental conditions and their multiple interactions make it difficult to compare and generalize the results obtained; it seems, however, that with SOA(O) the greatest interference effects are produced and for larger SOAs there are greater facilitation effects especially in preexposure of the irrelevant stimulus, although a certain symmetry exists between pre- and postexposure. Our data conform to this pattern, although we find both facilitation and interference effects (greater or smaller) in each SOA given our definition of such effects in terms of different neutral conditions. With this consideration in mind the results of other authors and our own results are compatible.

The sixth and final *prediction* (*b6*) is confirmed in general terms, as has already been partially indicated. The conditions only give rise to significant interactions with the primes or distractors and with the SOAs. The tasks basically interact with the modality of the targets and with the semantic relations producing the characteristic asymmetries to which we have already referred. The interaction $O \times D \times R \times S$, also significant, confirms the hypothesis that in the processing of words and pictures (in naming and categorization, in priming and Stroop conditions), all the variables produce effects on the RT and consequently on the facilitation and interference effects. All these variables have not been dealt with in such a systematic manner in a single experiment, but they have been taken partialy into account, the possible interactions between these variables being significant in general terms.

The *model* that we propose (shown in Fig. 7.1) is confirmed in general terms by the data of our experiment. If we take into account the global RTs that correspond to the neutral condition (presentation of the word or picture in isolation), on the basis of the formula in Table 7.1, an estimate could be made of the time consumed by some of the subprocesses considered: $d = 129$ ms (because $d = \text{CAT W} - \text{CAT P} = 993$ ms $- 864$ ms $= 129$ ms); $s = 214$ ms (because $s = \text{CAT P} - \text{NAM P} = 864$ ms $- 650$ ms 214 ms); $(g + t)$ or $(x + t)$ or $(x + r) = 246$ ms (supposing that the reading route is $a + b + d + e + f$, then $(g + t) = (\text{CAT W} - 214) - \text{NAM W} = (993 - 214) - 553 = 246$ ms); and finally $(a + b + e + f)$ or $(z + y + e + f) = 404$ ms. If we take the RTs corresponding to the neutral condition and to the experimental conditions (that is to say all the data), these parameters would have values of 141 ms, 215 ms, 231 ms and 463 ms respectively. These data would alternatively support the hypothesis that the locus of the effects produced by the variables would be situated in the peripheral phases and not in the central phases, or the hypothesis that a strictly serial and additive processing does not take place. What these data do confirm without doubt is the basic prediction of the model, that is, that NAM W < NAM P < CAT P < CAT W with the global data and with the data of the neutral condition, as we have seen; with the data related to SOA (-100) $(533 < 624 < 847 < 963)$, to SOA (O) $(710 < 753 < 987 < 1168)$, and to SOA (100) $(563 < 681 < 892 < 1025)$; with the data related to the relation of identity $(544 < 658 < 859 < 989)$, to the relation of category $(636 < 692 < 896 < 991)$ and to no relation $(631 < 733 < 972 < 1176)$; in the priming condition $(637 < 718 < 930 < 1122)$ and in the Stroop condition $(642 < 712 < 993 < 1091)$; with prime or distractor being a word $(694 < 740 < 956 < 1125)$ or a picture $(585 < 690 < 908 < 1037)$.

This robust effect $(T \times O)$, which is not only significant at the global level $(F = 390.84, p = .0000)$, but also in the priming condition $(F = 265.78, p = .0000)$ and in the Stroop condition $(F = 154.69, p = .0000)$, and which is maintained throughout all the variables (only the interaction $T \times O \times R$ is significant), does not permit us, however, to decide as to whether the processing is serial (sequentially additive effects) or if it is produced in parallel with some effects overlapping others, although everything seems to indicate that the latter occurs.

On the other hand, the model does permit the investigation of the effects introduced by double stimulation, because for each of the situations (naming with WW, WP, PW and PP and categorization with WW, WP, PW and PP) the difference between the processing of the neutral condition (only one significant stimulus) and of the other experimental conditions (two significant stimuli) can be calculated, as can be seen in Fig. 7.8.

These data allow us to conclude that the processing time of two stimuli is increased above the processing of a single stimulus, more when the target is a word (97 ms) than when it is a picture, and thus, more when the double stimulation is WW (146 ms) and less when it is PP (42 ms), with WP being closer to the former (91 ms) and PW (48 ms) being closer to the latter.

In each of these eight situations, the variables responsible for these greater or lesser interference effects that arise in the naming and categorization of words and pictures (as primes or distractors and as targets) are the semantic relations and the SOAs (because the priming and Stroop conditions do not interact significantly with the task nor with the target). Thus, one could specify how many ms of interference (or facilitation) are due, in each of these eight situations, to the different semantic relations, the different SOAs, and their interaction, as can be seen in Fig. 7.9.

In NAM WW and CAT WW the greater interference is due to the relations of category and to no relations, especially when the two stimuli (which are words) are overlapped in SOA (0): To a lesser degree, the interference is also increased in NAM WP and CAT WP by the relations of category and no relations in SOAs (0) and (100). The reduced interference in CAT PW and CAT PP is due to the fact that the average interference produced by no relation is compensated by the facilitation produced by the relation of category and that of identity respectively; in NAM PW and NAM PP all the variables contribute in a similar fashion and to a small extent. Thus, the greater part of the interference effects are due to the increases in RT produced by no relations and SOA (0), with the relation of identity producing hardly any effect and SOA (-100) very little; overlapping and semantic incongruence are, according to our data, the main factors responsible for the interference effect (with respect to the neutral condition), which double processing introduces in these eight basic situations in which the way in which the processing systems functions according to our model is made manifest (in an operational form).

With reference to our model, in the four cases in which the two stimuli are of identical modality (NAM WW, NAM PP, CAT WW, and CAT PP), the path followed by the processing is also the same in each of these four cases (Fig. 7.8); if the relation between the two stimuli is of identity (repetition), obviously it will not produce interference and it could even

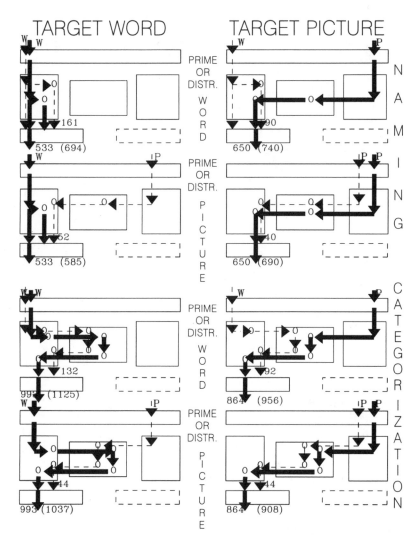

FIG. 7.8. Following the processing model from Fig. 7.1, processing pathways of words and pictures when used as primes and targets in naming and categorization tasks. The solid lines represents the target (the last number indicates the processing time in msec from the neutral condition); the dotted line represents the processing of either the prime or the distractor (the last number indicates the processing time in milliseconds of either prime or distractor that outlasts the time from the neutral condition); the last number in parenthesis indicates the processing time of the two stimuli in Stroop and priming conditions.

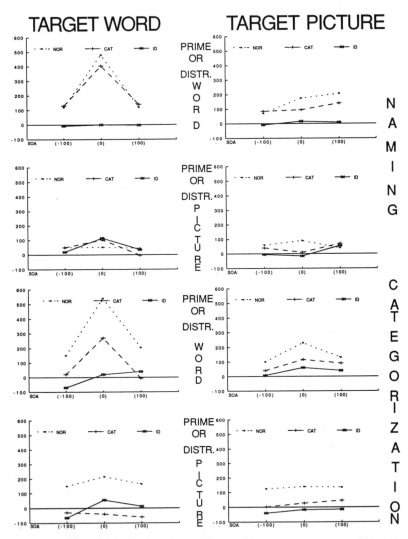

FIG. 7.9. Facilitation (and interference) effects that result from the interactions between the semantic relationships (ID, CAT, NOR) × SOAs (−100, 0, 100) in each of the eight situations depicted in Fig. 7.8. (NAM W target with W prime or distractor, NAM W with P; NAM P with W; NAM P with P; CAT W with W; CAT W with P; CAT P with W; and CAT P with P). The mean of all facilitation and interference effects corresponds to the processing time, in milliseconds, of the irrelevant stimulus in each of the eight situations (Fig. 7.8).

produce some facilitation (though limited because of the small intervals between them — 0 or 100 ms —). On the other hand, if the relation is of category or if there is no relation, interference will be produced, always greater in WW than in PP. This is exactly what occurs: relation of identity (NAM WW = − 2; NAM PP = + 9; CAT W = + 1; CAT PP = − 25); relation of category (+235, +44, +92, +24, respectively); no relation (+249, +67, +304, +132, respectively), the RTs being always compared with the neutral condition N; these data also conform to the predictions of Glaser and Glaser (1989) with some difference in the size of the effects.

In the four cases in which the stimuli are of different modality (which are those generally used in the Stroop-like condition), the paths followed by the processing are also different, with the possibility of overlapping in some phases. The model leaves open the interpretation of the results in terms of the semantic relations and the SOAs without the appearance of so clear a pattern as has sometimes been suggested. In the first place, in all the situations, the different modes of distractor or prime and of target produce interference (in CAT PW with relation of category facilitation appears); in the second place, when the relation is of conceptual identity, a double asymmetry is produced (P interferes moderately in the naming of W 56 ms but W does not interfere in the naming of P; whereas P does not interfere in the categorization of W, but W does interfere moderately in the categorization of P 43 ms); in the third place, semantic incongruence always produces interference (NAM PW = 49 ms; NAM WP = 151 ms; CAT PW = 177 ms; CAT WP = 153 ms), which does not conform to the predictions nor to the results of Glaser and Glaser (1989); in the fourth place, the relation of category should be similar to no relation in the naming task and in fact this is what occurs (NAM PW = 51 ms; NAM WP = 113 ms), but it should also produce similar effects to the relation of identity in the categorization task, and this does not occur (CAT PW = − 49; CAT WP = 78).

If we use no relation as the neutral condition, some of our data could be compared with those obtained by Biggs and Marmurek (1990) in their attempt to verify their overlap model of naming. Their predictions refer to the effects produced by the processing of a W or a P when the prime is a W or a P and the relation between them is of identity (the authors call this repetition) or of category (which they simply call relation). In the case of repeated stimuli, WW, WP, and PP will be facilitated (because they overlap visually, phonemically, semantically, and perhaps lexically), whereas in PW there will be no facilitation (because there is no overlapping because naming W is predominantly phonetic and naming P has to be semantic and lexical). In the case of related stimuli, naming word will not be facilitated either by W or by P because a word is read before acceding to the semantic system (where semantic relations are processed), but naming picture will be facilitated, both by W and by P, because a semantic overlap and perhaps a lexical overlap are produced. Our data conform exactly to these predictions that coincide with ours: If the relation is of identity, the facilitation in WW $= -250$ ms, in WP $= -148$ ms, and in PP $= -58$ ms, whereas in PW an interference of 8 ms is produced; if the relation is of category, in WP $= -38$ ms and in PP $= -23$ ms facilitation is found, whereas in WW $= -13$ ms and in PW $= 17$ ms facilitation is not found or interference is found.

Conclusion

The most important results of this experiment can be reduced to three:

1. The facilitation and interference effects are defined in terms of the neutral condition and of the variables that affect the processing; if a blank card is presented as the neutral condition (presentation of the target without a structurally and semantically discernible prime or distractor), of the presentation of two stimuli (with discernible structure and semantic information) more time is required for the processing of the target; if the neutral condition is the absence of semantic relation, any type of relation (in our case, of identity and of category) requires less time for the processing of the target: In the first case one can speak of interference effects and in the second case, of facilitation, with the different variables producing similar interference and facilitation effects.

2. All the variables considered—conditions, tasks, modality of target and prime, semantic relations, and SOAs—affect in a differential way the processing of words and pictures, there being multiple significant interactions between the said variables, all of which highlights the complexity and flexibility of the processing, naturally within certain limits and within a quite consistent pattern of RTs.

3. The basic characteristics of the model that we propose are amply confirmed: (a) the existence of three stages of processing; (b) the existence of three interconnected central systems: a linguistic processing system with two subsystems, graphemic-phonologic processing and lexic processing; a pictorial processing system with a single system for processing structural and formal features; and an amodal system of semantic processing; (c) the existence of different pathways for the processing of the primes or distractors and the targets in terms of the modality of both stimuli (W and P) and of the task (naming and categorization); and (d) modulation of these basic processing patterns in terms of the different semantic relations and presentation intervals between the two stimuli. This model does not permit us to decide about the mechanisms that operate on the facilitation and interference effects nor about the serial or parallel, automatic, and strategic

nature of the processing, although it can be inferred that different mechanisms of activation and inhibition (response competition) intervene and that the processing is partly serial and partly parallel, partly automatic, and partly strategic.

REFERENCES

Allport, A. D. (1979). Conscious and unconscious cognition: A computacional metaphor for the mechanism of attention and integration. In N. Lars-Goran (Ed.), *Perspectives in memory research* (pp.505-533). Hillsdale, NJ: Lawrence Erlbaum Associates.

Balota, D. A., Flores D'Arcais, G. B., & Rayner, K. (1990). *Comprehension processes in reading*. Hillsdale, NJ: Lawrence Erlbaum Associates.

Becker, C. A. (1980). Semantic context effects in visual word recognition: An analysis of semantics strategies. *Memory and Cognition, 8*, 493-512.

Biggs, T. C., & Marmurek, H. H. C. (1990). Picture and word naming: Is facilitation due to processing overlap? *American Journal of Psychology, 103*, 81-100.

Brown, A. S., Neblett, D. R., Jones, T. C., & Mitchell, D. B. (1991). Transfer of processing in repetition priming: Some inappropriate findings. *Journal of Experimental Psychology: Learning, Memory and Cognition, 17*, 514-525.

Carr, T. H., McCauley, Ch., Sperber, R. D., & Parmelee, C. M. (1982). Words, pictures, and priming: On semantic activation, conscious identification, and the automaticity of information processing. *Journal of Experimental Psychology: Human Perception and Performance, 8*, 757-777.

Cohen, J. D., Dunbar, K., & McClelland, J. L. (1990). On the control of automatic processes: A parallel distributed processing account of the Stroop effect. *Psychological Review, 97*, 332-361.

Collins, A. M., & Loftus, E. F. (1975). A spreading-activation theory of semantic processing. *Psychological Review, 82*, 407-428.

Dallas, M., & Merikle, P. M. (1976). Response processes and semantic-context effects. *Bulletin of the Psychonomic Society, 8*, 441-444.

Dark, V. J. (1988). Semantic priming, prime reportability, and retroactive priming are interdependent. *Memory and Cognition, 16*, 299-308.

den Heyer, K., Briand, K., & Smith, L. (1985). Automatic and strategic effects in semantic priming: An examination of Becker's verification model. *Memory and Cognition, 13*, 228-232.

den Heyer, K., Goring, A., K., Dannenbring, G. L. (1983). Semantic priming and word repetition: The two effects are additive. *Journal of Memory and Language, 24*, 699-716.

Durso, F. T., & Johnson, M. K. (1979). Facilitation in naming and categorizing repeated pictures and words. *Journal of Experimental Psychology: Human Learning and Memory, 5*, 449-459.

Dyer, F. N. (1973). The Stroop phenomenon and its use in the study of perceptual, cognitive, and response processes. *Memory and Cognition, 1*, 106-120.

Evett, L. J. Humphreys, G. W. (1981). The use of abstract graphemic information in lexical access. *Quarterly Journal of Experimental Psychology, 33A*, 325-350.

Farah, M. J. (1989). Semantic and perceptual priming: How similar are the understanding mechanisms. *Journal of Experimental Psychology: Human Perception and Performance, 8*, 188-194.

Fischler, I. (1977). Semantic facilitation without association in a lexical decision task. *Memory and Cognition, 5*, 335-339.

Forster, K. I., & Davis, C. (1984). Repetition priming and frequency attenuation in lexical access. *Journal of Experimental Psychology: Learning, Memory and Cognition, 10,* 680–698.

Glaser, M. O., & Glaser, W. R. (1982). Time course analysis of the Stroop phenomenon. *Journal of Experimental Psychology: Human Perception and Performance, 8,* 875–894.

Glaser, W. R., & Düngelhoff, F. J. (1984). The time course of picture-word interference. *Journal of Experimental Psychology: Human Perception and Performance, 10,* 640–654.

Glaser, W. R., & Glaser, M. O. (1989). Context effects in Stroop-like word and picture processing. *Journal of Experimental Psychology: General, 118,* 13–42.

Glucksberg, S. (1984). Commentary: The functional equivalence of common and multiple codes. *Journal of Verbal Learning and Verbal Behavior, 23,* 100–104.

González-Marqués, J., & Mayor, J. (1990, August). *Temporal course effects on the processing of words and pictures as primes and targets.* Paper presented at the Third European Workshop on Imagery and Cognition, University of Aberdeen, Scotland.

González-Marqués, J., & Mayor, J. (in press). Diferentes condiciones neutrales utilizadas en condiciones experimentales de priming y Stroop. [Different neutral conditions used in priming and Stroop experimental paradigms]. *Revista de Psicología del Lenguaje, 1.*

Guenther, R. K., & Klatzky, R. L. (1977). Semantic classification of pictures and words. *Journal of Experimental Psychology: Human Learning and Memory, 3,* 498–514.

Hillinger, M. L. (1980). Priming effects with phonemically similar words: The encoding-bias hypothesis reconsidered. *Memory and Cognition, 8,* 115–123.

Hock, H. S., & Egeth, H. E. (1970). Verbal interference with encoding in a perceptual classification task. *Journal of Experimental Psychology, 83,* 299–303.

Hodgson, J. M. (1991). Informational constraints on pre-lexical priming. *Language and Cognitive Process, 6,* 169–205.

Huttenlocher, J., & Kubicek, L. F. (1983). The source of relatedness effects on naming latency. *Journal of Experimental Psychology: Learning, Memory and Cognition, 9,* 486–496.

Irwin, D. I., & Lupker, S. J. (1983). Semantic priming of pictures and words: A levels of processing approach. *Journal of Verbal Learning and Verbal Behavior, 22,* 45–60.

Juilland, A., & Chang Rodríguez, E. (1964). *Frequency dictionary of Spanish words.* London: Mouton.

Kiger, J. I., & Glass, A. L. (1983). The facilitation of lexical decision by a prime ocurring after the target. *Memory and Cognition, 11,* 356–365.

Klein, G. S. (1964). Semantic power measured through the interference of words with color-naming. *American Journal of Psychology, 77,* 576–588.

Koriat, A. (1981). Semantic facilitation in a lexical decision as a function of prime-target association. *Memory and Cognition, 9,* 587–598.

Kroll, J. F., & Potter, M. C. (1984). Recognizing words, pictures, and concepts: A composition of lexical, object, and reality decisions. *Journal of Verbal Learning and Verbal Behavior, 23,* 39–66.

La Heij, W. (1988). Components of Stroop-like interference in picture naming. *Memory and Cognition, 16,* 400–410.

La Heij, W., Van der Heijden, A. N. C., & Schreuder, R. (1985). Semantic priming and Stroop-like interference in word-naming task. *Journal of Experimental Psychology: Human Perception and Performance, 11,* 62–80.

Levelt, W. J. M., Schriefers, H., Vorberg, D., Meyer, A. S., Pechmann, T., & Havinga, J. (1991). The time course of lexical access in speech production: A study of picture naming. *Psychological Review, 98,* 122–142.

Logan, G. D. (1990). Repetition priming and automaticity: Common underlying mechanisms? *Cognitive Psychology, 22,* 1–35.

Lorch, R. F., Balota, D. A., & Stamm, E. G. (1986). Locus of inhibition effects in the priming of lexical decisions: pre- or post lexical access? *Memory and Cognition, 14*, 95–103.

Lupker, S. J. (1979). The semantic nature of response competition in the picture-interference task. *Memory and Cognition, 7*, 485–495.

Lupker, S. J. (1984). Semantic priming without association: A second look. *Journal of Verbal Learning and Verbal Behavior, 23*, 709–733.

Lupker, S. J. (1988). Picture naming: An investigation of the nature of categorical priming. *Journal of Experimental Psychology: Learning, Memory and Cognition, 14*, 444–455.

McLeod, C. M., & Dunbar, K. (1988). Training and Stroop-like interference: Evidence for a continuum of automaticity. *Journal of Experimental Psychology: Learning, Memory and Cognition, 14*, 126–135.

Marslen-Wilson, W. (1989). *Lexical representation and process*. Cambridge, MA: The MIT Press.

Mayor, J., Sainz, J., & González-Marqués, J. (1988). Stroop and priming effects in naming and categorizing task using words and pictures. In M. Denis, J. Engelkamp, & J. Richardson (Eds.), *Neuropsychological and cognitive approach to mental imagery* (pp. 69–78). Amsterdam: Martinus Nijhoff.

McCauley, C., Parmelee, C. M., Sperber, R. D., & Carr, T. H. (1980). Early extraction of meaning from pictures and its relation to conscious identification. *Journal of Experimental Psychology: Human Perception and Performance, 6*, 265–276.

McEvoy, C. L. (1988). Automatic and strategic processes in picture naming. *Journal of Experimental Psychology: Learning, Memory and Cognition, 14*, 618–634.

Meyer, D. E., & Schvaneveldt, R. W. (1971). Facilitation in recognition pairs of words: Evidence of a dependence between retrieval operations. *Journal of Experimental Psychology, 90*, 227–234.

Meyer, D. E. & Schvaneveldt, R. W. (1976). Meaning, memory structure, and mental process. *Science, 192*, 27–33.

Morton, J. (1969). Interaction of information in word recognition. *Psychological Review, 76*, 165–178.

Neely, J. H. (1977). Semantic priming and retrieved from lexical memory: Roles of inhibitionless spreading activation and limited-capacity attention. *Journal of Experimental Psychology: General, 106*, 226–254.

Norris, D. (1986). Word recognition: Context effects without priming. *Cognition, 22*, 93–136.

Paivio, A. (1986). *Mental representation. A dual coding approach*. New York: Oxford.

Peterson, R. R., & Simpson, G. B. (1989). Effects on backward priming on word recognition in single-word and sentence contexts. *Journal of Experimental Psychology: Learning, Memory and Cognition, 15*, 1020–1032.

Posner, M. I., & Snyder, C. R. R. (1975). Facilitation and inhibition in the processing of signals. In P. M. A. Rabbitt & S. Dornič (Eds.), *Attention and performance V* (pp. 669–682). New York: Academic Press.

Potter, M. C., & Faulconer, B. A. (1975). Time to understand pictures and words. *Nature, 253*, 437–438.

Ratcliff, R., & McKoon, G. (1988). A retrieval theory of priming in memory. *Psychological Review, 95*, 385–408.

Reinitz, M. T., Wright, E., & Loftus, G. R. (1989). Effects of semantic priming on visual encoding of pictures. *Journal of Experimental Psychology: General, 118*, 280–297.

Rosinki, R. R. (1977). Picture-word interference is semantically based. *Child Development, 48*, 643–647.

Rosinki, R. R., Golinkoff, R. M., & Kukish, K. S. (1975). Automatic semantic processing in a picture-word interference task. *Child Development, 46*, 247–253.

Rueckl, J. G. (1990). Similarity effects in word and pseudowords repetition priming. *Journal of Experimental Psychology: Learning, Memory and Cognition, 16*, 374–391.

Sainz, J., Mayor, J., & González-Marqués, J. (1991, July). *Picture-word interference effects in part-whole and taxonomic decision task: Partial evidence for a functional dissociation between lexicon and semantic memory.* Paper presented at the International Conference on Memory, University of Lancaster, England.

Schriefers, H., Meyer, A, S., & Levelt, W. J. M. (1990). Exploring the time course of lexical access in language production: Picture-word interference studies. *Journal of Memory and Language, 29,* 86–102.

Schubert, R. E., & Eimas, P. D. (1977). Effects of context on the classification of words and no-words. *Journal of Experimental Psychology: Human Perception and Performance, 3,* 27–36.

Seidenberg, M. S., & McClelland, J. L. (1989). A distributed, developmental model of word recognition and naming. *Psychological Review, 96,* 523–568.

Sereno, J. A. (1991). Graphemic, associative, and syntactic priming effects at a brief stimulus onset asynchrony in lexical decision and naming. *Journal of Experimental Psychology: Learning, Memory and Cognition, 17,* 459–477.

Seymour, P. H. K. (1977). Conceptual encoding and locus of the Stroop effects. *Quarterly Journal of Experimental Psychology, 29,* 245–265.

Smith, M. C., & Magee, L. E. (1980). Tracing the time course of picture-word processing. *Journal of Experimental Psychology, General, 109,* 373–392.

Snodgrass, J. G. (1980). Toward a model for picture and word processing. In P. A. Kolers, M. E. Wrolstad, & H. Bouma (Eds.), *Processing of visible language, 2* (pp. 565–584). New York: Plenum.

Snodgrass, J. G. (1984). Concepts and the surface representation. *Journal of Verbal Learning and Verbal Behavior, 23,* 3–22.

Sperber, R. D., McCauley, C., Ragain, R. D., & Weil, C. M. (1979). Semantic priming effects on pictures and word recognition. *Memory and Cognition, 7,* 339–345.

Stanovich, K. E., & West, R. F. (1979). Mechanisms of sentence context effects in reading: Automatic activation and conscious attention. *Memory and Cognition, 7,* 77–85.

Stroop, J. R. (1935). Studies of interference in serial verbal reactions. *Journal of Experimental Psychology, 18,* 643–662.

Te Linde, J. (1982). Picture-words differences in decision latency: A test of common-coding assumptions. *Journal of Experimental Psychology: Learning, Memory and Cognition, 8,* 584–598.

Theios, J., & Amrhein, P. C. (1989). Theoretical analysis of the cognitive processing of lexical and pictorial stimuli: Reading, naming and visual and conceptual comparison. *Psychological Review, 96,* 5–24.

Tipper, S. P., & Driver, J. (1988). Negative priming between pictures and words in a selective attention task: Evidence for semantic processing of ignored stimuli. *Memory and Cognition, 16,* 64–70.

Virzi, R. A., & Egeth, H. E. (1985). Toward a translational model of Stroop interference. *Memory and Cognition, 13,* 304–319.

Warren, C., & Morton, J. (1982). The effects of priming on pictures recognition. *British Journal of Psychology, 73,* 117–129.

Whittlesea, B. W. A., & Jacoby, L. L. (1990). Interaction of prime repetition with visual degradation: Is priming a retrieval phenomenon? *Journal of Memory and Language, 29,* 546–565.

Wilkins, A. J. (1971). Conjoint frequency, category size, and categorization time. *Journal of Verbal Learning and Verbal Behavior, 10,* 382–385.

Probing the Nature of the Mental Representation of Visual Objects: Evidence From Cognitive Dissociations

8

Lynn A. Cooper
Columbia University

A pervasive yet seemingly unremarkable feature of our perceptual experience of the world is its phenomenal organization and continuity. Despite the vagaries of the proximal information available to our perceptual systems, those systems construct internal models of objects and events that are unified spatially and integrated over time. Individual objects and layouts of objects in the environment have spatial structure and coherence; events unfold temporally in a largely predictable and meaningful fashion. This continuity of experience seems curiously inconsistent with recent insights about the architecture of the perceptual/cognitive systems that support our awareness of and behavior in the world. In particular, a prevailing view in cognitive science that enjoys a good deal of popularity is that the representations and processes underlying both global functions like perception and language—as well as more specialized activities such as imagery, spatial attention, and object recognition—are organized in a modular fashion, or as sets of component subsystems (e.g., Farah, 1985; Kosslyn, 1987; Kosslyn, Flynn, Amsterdam, & Wang, 1990).

Arguments favoring the idea of modular organization can be mounted on logical and computational grounds (see, e.g., Fodor, 1983; Marr, 1982). As well, there is a growing body of empirical evidence based on functional dissociations among various sorts of processing systems that strongly implicates some form of modularity. The evidence comes primarily from two sources, historically distinct but increasingly complementary in their converging pictures of the structure of human cognition. The first is the clinical neuropsychological tradition of case reports and experimental studies of single patients or groups of patients exhibiting selective cognitive

199

deficits following damage to the brain (see, e.g., Farah, 1990; McCarthy & Warrington, 1990). The second is laboratory studies of intact adults in which dissociations among representational or processing systems for performing well-defined cognitive tasks are experimentally induced. Of particular relevance to the present paper are investigations of both kinds that point to dissociations (suggesting underlying modularity) in perceptual/cognitive systems for representing information about visual objects.

A functional dissociation that has recently received considerable attention in behavioral, cognitive, and clinical neuropsychology concerns the distinction between systems for determining *what* an object is, in the sense of its identity and visual characteristics, versus *where* an object is located in space. The search for behavioral dissociations in humans between the "what" and "where" systems has been fueled by the seminal work of Mishkin and Ungerleider (1982; Ungerleider & Mishkin, 1982) that demonstrates the existence of anatomically separable pathways hypothesized to carry information concerning these distinct properties of visual objects. The "what" pathway corresponds to the ventral system, receiving input from small retinal ganglion cells (the parvocellular pathway; see, e.g., Hubel & Livingstone, 1987) and running from the occipital lobe to inferior temporal cortex; the "where" pathway corresponds to the dorsal system, running from occipital to parietal areas and receiving input from large ganglion cells, or the magnocellular pathway. Furthermore, these anatomical distinctions are reflected in functional distinctions between the systems, as measured by response properties of single neurons and by selective behavioral deficits in monkeys with lesions in either parietal or inferior temporal (IT) areas. In particular, cells in IT areas appear to be sensitive to complex shapes but not selective to properties like retinal location or size of visual patterns (see, e.g., Desimone, Albright, Gross, & Bruce, 1984; Gross, Desimone, Albright, & Schwartz, 1984; for a review, Plaut & Farah, 1990), and animals with lesions in this area show corresponding difficulties in pattern-based discrimination performance. Lesions in the parietal area, by contrast, produce deficits in learning discriminations based on object location (e.g., Ungerleider & Mishkin, 1982), and single units in this area appear more sensitive to motion and location information than to pattern shape (Andersen, Essick, & Siegal, 1985).

Various investigators have recently extended this "what/where" distinction to analyses of human performance on selected cognitive tasks. For example, Kosslyn and his colleagues (Kosslyn, 1987; Kosslyn et al., 1990) distinguished between the coding of "categorical" relations among the parts of an object, or the qualitative representation of relative location information, and "coordinate" relations, or the metric representation of high-precision information of the sort needed to navigate in space. The idea behind this account is that both sorts of relations are mediated by distinct subsystems of a "where"-type system, corresponding to the dorsal pathway, whereas pattern analysis and object identification are accomplished by an analog of the ventral system. Within the domain of attention, Farah, Wallace, and Vecera (in press) used the "what" (ventral)/"where" (dorsal) distinction as a framework for interpreting clinical and behavioral evidence on brain-damaged patients exhibiting unilateral neglect. Biederman and his colleagues (e.g., Biederman & Cooper, 1992) appealed to this same distinction as an account of their finding of dissociable patterns of recognition and priming in object naming experiments.

The work described in the present chapter follows in this tradition of providing evidence for a striking pattern of behavioral dissociations, and then advancing some tentative speculations concerning underlying neural systems that might support the observed functional pattern. It departs from the work cited earlier in two major respects: First, the emphasis is on what can be learned about the organization of cognition by observing the range of task and stimulus conditions under which behavioral dissociations occur. That is, behavioral findings play the central role in the account that follows, and relationships to known or hypothesized neural systems are of secondary importance. Second, the dissociation(s) to be described do not correspond naturally to the influential "what/where" or ventral/dorsal distinction. Rather, they consist of dissociable aspects of the representation of objects that operate within the "what" system.

Of particular interest is the distinction between two rather different functions that mental representations of objects seem to serve in guiding ongoing behavior. The first includes the automatic and unconscious computations involved in locating objects and in anticipating their continuing structure, particularly as the objects and/or the observer move or transform in space. The second class of functions served by representations of objects are those that require conscious knowledge of the identity of an object, both in the sense of the object's meaning and in the visual characteristics that differentiate recognizable objects from one another. The sources of information on which these functions of object representations are based seem, on analysis, to be quite different. Information about the global structure of individual objects, as well as the layout of objects in the environment, is required to generate expectations about hidden surfaces of occluded objects and about changes in object structure under transformation. By contrast, information about semantic, functional, and particular visual attributes of objects forms the basis for determining the identity of objects.

In the program of research reviewed here (which is part of an ongoing project being conducted in collaboration with Daniel L. Schacter of Harvard University and various of our students and associates), we establish that these two aspects of representations of objects can be functionally dissociated in laboratory experiments with intact, adult participants (see Cooper, Schacter, Ballesteros, & Moore, 1992; Schacter, Cooper, & Delaney, 1990a, 1990b; Schacter, Cooper, Delaney, Peterson, & Tharan, 1991). Questions that we address include: How, experimentally, can we investigate and isolate distinguishable functions of representations of visual objects? What information is preserved in and accessible from such representations? How are aspects of these mental representations retrieved when we remember things about external objects and events? In formulating answers to questions like these, we are seeking to unite theoretical perspectives on the representation and recognition of visual objects with fundamental issues in the study of human memory. The description of our ongoing program of research is divided into three sections. The first provides a brief review of some of our evidence for a dissociation between structural and episodic representations of visual objects. The second describes work using this dissociation as a tool for exploring the nature of the information preserved in the underlying mental representations. The final section considers some theoretical implications of the body of findings for the organization of memory systems generally, for issues in object recognition, and for speculations concerning possible neural bases of the dissociable representations.

DISSOCIATION BETWEEN STRUCTURAL AND EPISODIC REPRESENTATIONS OF OBJECTS: EVIDENCE FROM ENCODING MANIPULATIONS

An experimental approach and conceptual framework that has been central to our investigations comes from Schacter's (1987) distinction between implicit and explicit forms of remembering in the domain of verbal memory processes (see, also, Tulving & Schacter, 1990). Explicit memory refers to intentional or conscious recollection of recent experiences, that is, the familiar sort of episodic memory that is generally measured by standard tests of recognition and recall. Implicit memory, in contrast, refers to the unintentional retrieval of previously acquired information on tasks that do not require conscious recollection of a specific past experience or study situation. The existence of this latter sort of memory has generally been inferred from performance facilitation or priming effects on verbal tasks that nonetheless have strong perceptual components, including lexical decision, word fragment completion, and word identification (e.g., Graf & Schacter, 1985; Schacter, 1987). In the domain of nonverbal memory processes, Biederman and his associates (e.g., Biederman & Cooper, 1991, 1992) documented priming effects in an object naming task, and Musen &

Treisman (1990) reported a dissociation between implicit and explicit memory for relatively simple two-dimensional patterns.

On the basis of this and other work on dissociable memory processes — coupled with the observations earlier concerning different functions served by mental representations of objects — Schacter and I, along with Suzanne Delaney (cf. Schacter, Cooper, & Delaney, 1990a), formulated some initial hypotheses concerning the representation of objects in memory and its relationship to implicit and explicit tests of remembering. First, we reasoned that information about the relationships among components of an object, or its global three-dimensional structure, might be represented in a system funtionally separable from the system for representing information about an object's meaning, function, and distinctive visual characteristics. Second, we reasoned that the former structural aspects of object representations might be accessible primarily to nonconscious or implicit tests of memory, whereas the latter semantic or episodic aspects might be available to retrieval processes underlying conscious, explicit memory performance.

We devised a modification of an object decision task (cf. Kroll & Potter, 1984) to assess implicit memory for specifically three-dimensional objects. Participants studied sets of drawings of unfamiliar, three-dimensional structures of the sort illustrated in Fig. 8.1. Half of the drawings on the study list depicted *possible objects*, that is, objects whose surfaces and edges were connected in such a way that they could potentially exist in the world. The other half of the drawings displayed *impossible objects*, that is objects containing subtle surface and edge violations that would make it impossible for them to exist as actual three-dimensional structures. Conscious, explicit memory for the objects was tested by a standard "yes/no" recognition task. Implicit memory was assessed by our object decision task, in which respondents were required to determine whether briefly presented studied or nonstudied objects represented possible or impossible structures. Note that facilitation of performance or priming on this object decision task for studied (possible or impossible) drawings, compared with nonstudied drawings, constitutes evidence of implicit memory for the objects. This is because the task made no reference to nor required any conscious recollection of a specific previous exposure to the objects (cf. Schacter, 1987). Figure 8.2 provides a schematic illustration of the study phase and both the implicit and explicit test phases of our basic experimental paradigm.

Manipulation of the conditions under which the objects were studied or encoded is a crucial part of the logic of our initial series of experiments. Briefly, we reasoned that to perform the object decision task, information would have to be extracted about the three-dimensional structure of the object. That is, an object can only be judged possible following an analysis of the structural relations among its various components. We reasoned, further, that facilitation or priming of object decision performance should

POSSIBLE OBJECTS

IMPOSSIBLE OBJECTS

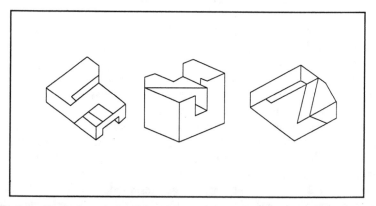

FIG. 8.1.   Examples of possible (top) and impossible (bottom) objects used in object decision and recognition tasks.

only be obtained following study tasks that lead to the encoding of information about global, three-dimensional object structure. In contrast, encoding tasks that fail to promote the extraction of structural information should not produce facilitation of subsequent object decision performance. Such encoding tasks might, however, contribute to levels of explicit recognition memory, as long as those tasks permitted participants to acquire distinctive information about each of the studied objects. (Note that

STRUCTURE OF EXPERIMENTAL TRIALS

STUDY PHASE:

36 objects (18 possible, 18 impossible) presented individually
for 5 seconds each, with instructions concerning encoding.

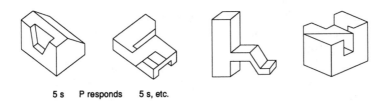

5 s   P responds   5 s, etc.

TEST PHASE:

OBJECT DECISION   OR   RECOGNITION

50-ms presentation of
72 individual objects

5-s presentation of
72 individual objects

Participant responds "possible"
or "impossible" to each

Participant responds "yes" (seen
previously) or "no"(a new item)

"possible"   "impossible"   "no" (new)   "yes" (old)

FIG. 8.2. Schematic illustration of the structure of experimental trials.

this prediction follows from the well-documented relationship between item
distinctiveness and level of recognition memory performance in the literature on episodic memory for verbal materials, e.g., Craik & Tulving, 1975;
Tulving, 1983). Thus, we expected that recognition processes should be able
to use a variety of different forms of encoded information about visual
objects; however, implicit memory should only be observed following
encoding of information specifically about the three-dimensional structure
of an object.

In an initial series of experiments (Schacter et al., 1990a, 1990b), we demonstrated a functional dissociation between the representation of structural and semantic information about objects. In one condition—designed to encourage encoding of information about global object structure and relations among components—respondents indicated during study whether each presented object appeared to be facing primarily to the left or to the right. In a second, elaborative encoding condition, a different group of participants examined each object and indicated something familiar that the (meaningless) depicted structure reminded them of most strongly. Note that this second study task required relating the unfamiliar objects to preexisting knowledge structures and creating semantically rich and distinctive encodings for each item.

The results of this experiment, for both implicit (object decision) and explicit (recognition) memory tasks are displayed in Fig. 8.3. Data in the upper panel show performance on the object decision task, expressed as *priming scores* or accuracy on previously studied objects minus accuracy on objects not shown during study. Results are plotted separately for the two encoding conditions and for possible and impossible objects. In the lower panel, recognition performance is shown as the difference between hits (correct "yes" or "old" responses) and false alarms (incorrect "yes" or "old" responses), as a function of the same encoding and object variables. The anticipated double dissociation, or interaction between structural versus semantic conditions of encoding and implicit versus explicit test tasks is apparent: Elaborative or semantic encoding yielded significantly higher levels of recognition memory than did left/right or structural encoding. However, evidence for priming of possible/impossible object decision judgments was only obtained under conditions of structural encoding.

This pattern of results demonstrates that implicit and explicit memory for unfamiliar, three-dimensional objects can be dissociated experimentally. It supports, further, the idea that our object decision task accesses information about the global structural relations among components of an object, whereas episodic information—including the meaningful identity of an object—is represented by a system accessible to explicit tests of memory. The selectivity of priming to conditions requiring the representation of specifically structural information about objects is underscored by the results of a second experiment comparing left/right encoding with encoding of local visual information. In this latter condition, participants were required during study to indicate whether each object appeared to contain more horizontal or vertical lines. Although this horizontal/vertical study situation was designed to draw attention to visual aspects of the unfamiliar structures, the encoded information concerned features of the two-dimensional pattern of line segments rather than the overall structure of the drawings interpreted as three-dimensional objects. As expected, the results shown in Fig. 8.4 confirm

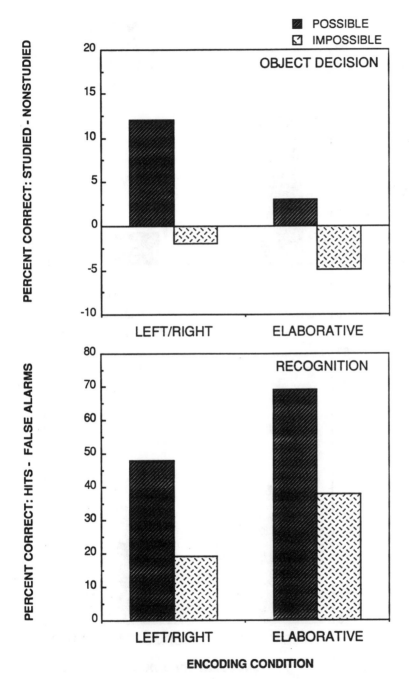

FIG. 8.3. Results for the object decision (top) and recognition (bottom) tasks, as a function of structural vs. elaborative encoding conditions and possible vs. impossible object types. Data adapted from Schacter, Cooper, and Delaney, 1990a, Experiment 2.

SUMMARY OF PRIMING AND RECOGNITION RESULTS

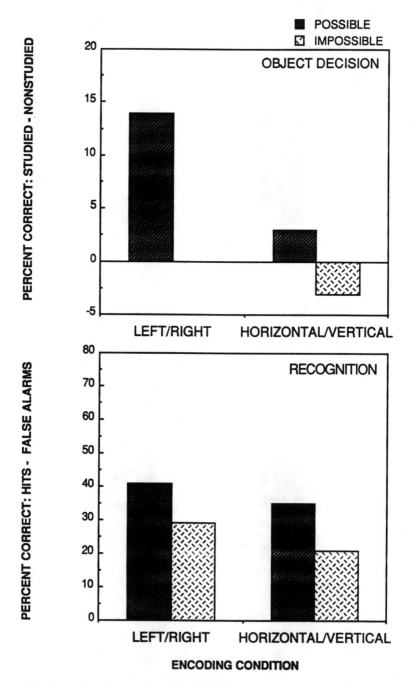

FIG. 8.4. Results for the object decision (top) and recognition (bottom) tasks, as a function of structural vs. local encoding conditions and possible vs. impossible object types. Data adapted from Schacter, Cooper, and Delaney, 1990a, Experiment 1.

that priming on the object decision task is confined to the left/right encoding condition, which enabled the acquisition of a three-dimensional structural description of each studied object. Facilitation of object decision performance is essentially absent under conditions requiring encoding of the local orientation of the line segments from which the objects were composed.

One salient feature of the results displayed in Figs. 8.3 and 8.4 is that priming, when obtained, occurs only for possible and not for impossible objects. This result is highly consistent across a variety of experimental manipulations; initially, the finding was puzzling and seemed problematic for our account of dissociable systems for the representation of structural and episodic information about visual objects. Accordingly, we undertook a series of experiments exploring factors that might contribute to the failure to obtain priming of impossible objects (Schacter, Cooper, Delaney, et al., 1991). These studies evaluated a number of explanations for the absence of priming, and they employed conditions designed to maximize the opportunity for observing facilitation of object decision performance with impossible structures. To summarize this series of experiments briefly, we have been unable to obtain priming of impossible objects despite changes in task instructions emphasizing the "impossible" response, and regardless of the number, duration, or quality of exposure to objects during study.

The data from one experiment in this series — in which one 5s exposure of the study items, under conditions of structural or left/right encoding, was compared with four such separate exposures — are shown in Fig.8.5. Surprisingly, roughly equivalent levels of priming for possible objects are obtained after one or four full exposures of the study items; however, no priming of "impossible" responses is evident even in the four-exposure condition. Results for recognition again reveal a striking dissociation between conditions affecting implicit and explicit memory for objects. Recognition performance is significantly enhanced when the left/right encoding task is performed four times, compared with a single study exposure, for both possible and impossible objects. This finding contrasts sharply with the lack of effect of the study-task manipulation on implicit memory for both object types.

From this and other experiments (see Schacter, Cooper, Delaney et al., 1991), we have come to believe that the failure to obtain priming of "impossible" judgments reflects computational constraints on the ability of the system carrying information about global object structure to form representations of objects that are not realizable in three-dimensional space. That is, structural impossibility cannot be represented at a global level; instead, respondents apparently rely on detection of local surface and edge violations in judging that line drawings of unfamiliar objects are, in fact, physically impossible. This account is consistent with our general theoretical perspective. Furthermore, it emphasizes the importance of representing

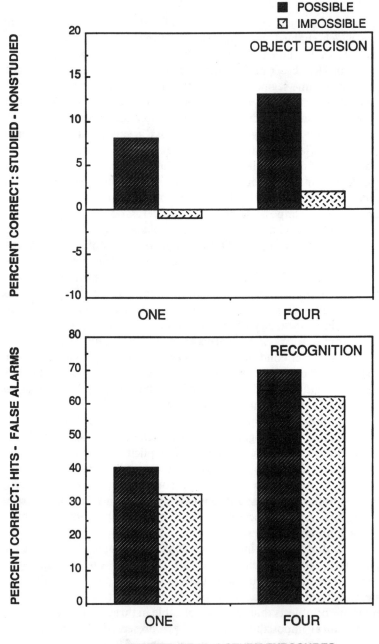

FIG. 8.5. Results for the object decision (top) and recognition (bottom) tasks, as a function of number of study exposures and possible vs. impossible object types. Data adapted from Schacter, Cooper, Delaney, Peterson, and Tharan, 1991, Experiment 1.

global three-dimensional structure to the system that supports priming on the object decision task. The central role of three-dimensional organization in the computation of structural descriptions of object is a theme that will be reiterated in the final section of this chapter.

To summarize thus far, a number of lines of evidence point to the existence of a functional dissociation between a system for representing the global structural relations among components of an object, and a system that represents episodic information concerning object meaning and the visual properties that make individual objects distinctive. First, only under conditions enabling the coding of information about object structure (i.e., left/right study) is priming or implicit memory for visual objects exhibited. Second, this facilitation of object decision performance is only evident for possible objects, whose global structures can be described by the underlying representational system. Third, conditions of object encoding that selectively improve explicit recognition memory are those that require semantic interpretation of unfamiliar structures (elaborative study), extraction of local visual features (horizontal/vertical study), and repetition of study exposures. Note that these are just the sorts of conditions that should be expected to enhance the distinctiveness of an object's representation in episodic memory. In addition, in as yet unpublished experiments (Schacter & Cooper, 1991), we have found that encoding objects with respect to their potential functions (e.g., whether each object could be used as a tool or for support) leads to reduced priming but enhanced recognition, compared with results obtained under left/right or structural conditions of study.

NATURE OF THE INFORMATION CODED IN STRUCTURAL AND EPISODIC REPRESENTATIONS OF OBJECTS: EVIDENCE FROM STUDY-TO-TEST STIMULUS TRANSFORMATIONS

Another thrust of our program of research complements the work described above. In this second line of investigation, we are probing the nature of the information preserved in structural and episodic representations of visual objects by introducing changes in attributes of objects from the time of study to the time of testing (object decision or recognition). That is, rather than documenting dissociations between structural and episodic aspects of memory for objects — deriving from manipulations of conditions of encoding — we are using the dissociations as a tool for examining the nature of the information coded in the underlying representational systems. The structure of the experimental approach and the logic generating it can be summarized as follows: Study-to-test changes in visual attributes *preserved* in representations of objects should produce measurable impairments in performance on tasks requiring retrieval of those representations. However, if a particular attribute or form of visual information is irrelevant to or not preserved in the underlying mental representation, then performance on an appropriate test task should remain invariant over transformation of the property in question.

The analysis in the preceding section of the dissociable systems for representing information about visual objects characterizes the structural description system that mediates performance on the object decision task as preserving information about the global three-dimensional structure and the relationships among the component parts of an object. The episodic system, by contrast, has been characterized as using any source of information that makes the memorial representation of an object distinctive. These sources of information include semantic and functional properties of objects, as well as visual attributes that serve to distinguish individual objects from one another.

This characterization leads to hypotheses about the effects of types of study-to-test object transformations on performance on implicit and explicit memory tasks. In particular, we should expect that transformations that are irrelevant to representing the global structure of an object would leave priming on the object decision task intact, despite discriminable differences between study and test items. Candidate transformations that change an object's appearance, but leave the description of its three-dimensional structure unchanged, include transformations of size, position, color, and texture. Changes in an object's dimensional structure, its orientation, and the direction from which it is illuminated might alter the structural description by enhancing or revealing particular relations among component parts while obscuring others. Episodic representations of objects should be affected by all of the transformations noted above, because all of these visual attributes contribute to the distinctiveness of any particular object in memory.

Many of our explorations of the effects of study-to-test changes on performance on the implicit object decision task and the explicit test of recognition memory are still in the "in progress" stage. Already, though, some compelling results have emerged that are sharpening our theoretical notions concerning the kinds of information preserved in the underlying representational systems. In an initial series of experiments (Cooper et al., 1992), we have examined the effects of changes in object size and parity, from the time of study to the time of testing, on performance on our implicit and explicit memory tasks.

The experiment manipulating object size consisted of a study phase during which possible and impossible objects were encoded under structural or left/right conditions (cf. Fig. 8.2). One group of participants studied "small" objects (about 8 degrees of visual angle), and another group studied objects enlarged by a factor of 2.5 (about 19 degrees of visual angle). Thus, the difference in the sizes of the encoded objects was substantial—well above levels that might produce difficulties in discriminability of the size change. Each of the size-defined study groups was further divided into two test groups, one group viewing same-size objects and the other group viewing changed-size (smaller or larger) objects. These groups were divided again, such that separate groups of participants participated in the object decision and the recognition test tasks.

Figure 8.6 displays the results of this experiment for both implicit (left panel) and explicit (right panel) memory performance. Data are averaged over absolute size of the objects, as this factor produced no significant effects. In addition, for simplicity of presentation, the data are averaged over possible and impossible object types. As in the experiments described above, no priming and reduced levels of recognition were exhibited for impossible objects; thus, the data shown in Fig. 8.6 represent levels of both sorts of test performance that are substantially lower than those generally obtained when possible objects are considered in isolation.

The two central outcomes of this experiment are readily apparent in Fig. 8.6. First, robust priming is obtained on the object decision task, and the

STUDY-TO-TEST TRANSFORMATION: SIZE

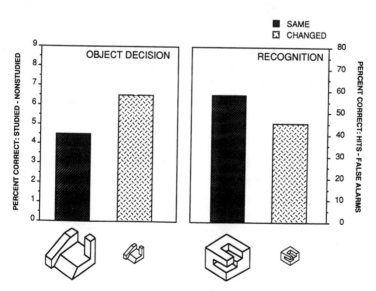

FIG. 8.6. Results for the object decision (left) and recognition (right) tasks, as a function of same vs. changed size of test objects. Data adapted from Cooper, Schacter, Ballesteros, and Moore, 1992, Experiment 1.

level of facilitation is not reduced (indeed, it is even greater) when object size is changed from study to test. Second, performance on the explicit recognition task is significantly impaired when studied and tested objects differ in size. Once again, a dissociation between implicit and explicit memory processes has emerged. In the case of the present experiment, the dissociation is a manifestation of the differential responsiveness of the two underlying systems to stimulus transformations of size; in the previous experiments, the dissociation resulted from differences in object encoding produced by manipulation of the study tasks. The data in Fig. 8.6 provide additional support for the idea of separate representational systems for structural and episodic information about objects. They indicate, as well, that size is an attribute to which the structural description system is indifferent. The episodic system, by contrast, clearly codes size as a property of an object's distinctive representation in memory.

A second experiment in this series (see Cooper et al., 1992) examined changes in the parity or overall left/right orientation of objects from study to recognition or object decision testing. A within-participant version of the experimental design described above was used such that participants studied objects displayed in an arbitrarily selected left/right orientation and were tested with both identical objects and their reflected or mirror-image versions. Figure 8.7 illustrates the results of this experiment, for both object decision and recognition performance, averaged over the same factors described in connection with Fig. 8.6.

The pattern of data from this experiment, in which objects were transformed by reflection from study to test, is strikingly similar to that obtained with the transformation of size (cf. Fig. 8.6). Magnitude of priming on the object decision task is not reduced by the mirror-image transformation, but explicit recognition of transformed test objects is clearly impaired. These outcomes suggest that standard/reflected orientation, like object size, is not preserved in the mental representations that support priming. However, parity does appear to be an important aspect of the representations of objects underlying explicit recognition. In a subsequent unpublished experiment, we have also assessed the effects of changing object color from study to test. Like size and reflection, color changes produce no decrement in amount of facilitation on the object decision task. Somewhat surprisingly, transformations of color have little effect on recognition performance either. Apparently, the attribute of color is sufficiently separable from the attribute of object shape to allow shape recognition processes to operate with essentially no interference from irrelevant color variation (cf. Garner, 1974).

The failure of reflection to affect level of priming on the object decision task may seem surprising at first blush. Reflection is one form of orientation change, and object orientation seems a priori to be an attribute likely

STUDY -TO -TEST TRANSFORMATION: REFLECTION

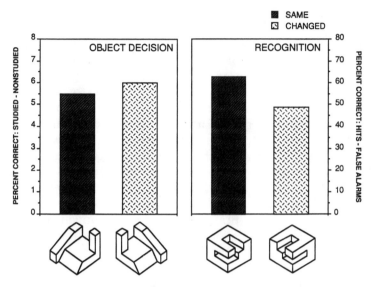

FIG. 8.7.   Results for the object decision (left) and recognition (right) tasks, as a function of standard vs. reflected versions of test objects. Data adapted from Cooper, Schacter, Ballesteros, and Moore, 1992, Experiment 2.

to influence structural description representations. On closer examination, however, it is evident that the reflection transformation leaves the relationship of an object's central axis to its component parts and its more global frame of reference unchanged. Hence, the lack of effect of mirror-image transformation on object decision priming may be understandable. The importance of an object's major axis and its relation to a global (perhaps gravitationally based) frame of reference is becoming clear in some recent as yet unpublished experimental findings (Cooper, Schacter, & Moore, 1991). In these studies, we transformed test objects by rotation in the picture plane, and compared levels of object decision and recognition performance to those obtained under conditions without the study-to-test transformation. The outcomes were clear, and they stand in marked contrast to those displayed in Fig. 8.7 for the transformation of reflection. Priming was virtually eliminated with test objects transformed by rotation in the plane; recognition, as well, was markedly reduced. There are certain complexities in the findings, which will be reported elsewhere in detail, but they suggest quite strongly that structural descriptions of three-dimensional objects are axis-based. That is, not only are relationships among components of objects themselves coded in such structural representations, but also the relationship of these components to an object's major axis and to a frame of reference is preserved. Adequate evaluation of this idea will require experimental work using transformations other than reflection and rotation in the plane, some of which honor and others that violate this axis-to-reference-frame relation.

In summary, the line of research examining the effects of study-to-test changes in object attributes on priming and recognition holds considerable promise for providing a detailed characterization of the information coded in structural description and episodic representations of visual objects. Already, we have established that priming of performance on our implicit memory task persists over transformations of size, color, and reflection. This pattern of results supports our central theoretical notions, in that none of these transformations affect the global three-dimensional structure or relationships among parts of objects. As in the experiments manipulating conditions of encoding, in studies involving attribute changes from study to test, explicit recognition exhibits some marked dissociations from object decision performance. Specifically, all stimulus transformations (except for color change) cause deterioration in explicit memory performance. Again, this pattern of results makes sense from our general theoretical perspective. With respect to the outcomes summarized in Figs. 8.6 and 8.7, size and reflection are properties that render individual objects distinctive and, thus, should be coded by the episodic system that supports explicit recognition.

THEORETICAL IMPLICATIONS

In this final section, I consider briefly the implications of certain of our experimental findings for theoretical issues in the areas of object representation and memory system structure. The most significant point is that the behavioral dissociations demonstrated in this program of research place strong constraints on the functional organization of the underlying representational systems. The pattern of results obtained under different conditions of object encoding suggest the operation of a presemantic system for computing the global structure and relations among components of objects that is distinguishable from an episodic system that represents individual objects by virtue of meaning, function, and particular (nonstructural) visual characteristics (cf. Schacter, 1990). Note that the systems being tapped in our experimental situations are operating at a precategorical level of analysis, in that the stimuli are unfamiliar and the tasks do not require that objects be named, identified, or otherwise categorized conceptually.

This functional dissociation between structural and episodic representations of objects, coupled with the differential sensitivity of these representations to transformations of object attributes, argues for a multiple-systems view of memory, as contrasted with alternative single-system accounts based on the principle of transfer-appropriate processing (e.g., Roediger, Weldon, & Challis, 1989). The distinction between these approaches and the evidence that our experiments provide for a multiple-systems perspective have been discussed in detail elsewhere (see Cooper et al., 1992; Schacter et al., 1990a).

In addition to relying on experiments that show cognitive dissociations in normal adult respondents as support for this view of memory organization, we, like others (e.g., Gabrieli, Milberg, Keane, & Corkin, 1990; Shimamura & Squire, 1984; for a review, see Shimamura, 1986), have turned to amnesic patients and elderly adults to obtain more compelling evidence for the idea that multiple, separable systems underlie performance on implicit and explicit tests of memory. In one study, Schacter, Cooper, Tharan, and Rubens, (1991) compared performance of a group of six amnesic patients with that of matched and student control participants on our object decision and recognition tasks. The results were clear and dramatic: Not surprisingly, explicit recognition memory of the amnesic group was severely impaired, when compared with that of both sorts of control participants. Nonetheless, all three participant groups showed considerable levels of object decision priming of strikingly similar magnitudes (for each group, about 10%). More recently, we also obtained essentially the same findings (though no so dramatic) when performance of elderly respondents was compared with that of younger adult controls (Schacter, Cooper, & Valdiserri, 1992). As with the amnesic group, older participants exhibited notable decreases in object recognition performance; however, amount of object decision priming did not differ with age. The results of both of these experiments suggest that the ability to form and retrieve structural representations of objects remains intact despite aging and certain forms of brain damage, although explicit recognition processes suffer impairment.

Our results also point to the beginnings of a theoretical account of the nature of structural description representations that support priming on the object decision task. The experiments described above employing the study-to-test transformation procedure indicate that these representations are invariant over changes in visual attributes like size, parity, and color; however, the axis-based nature of the representations is suggested by the sensitivity of priming to rotations in the picture plane. Furthermore, aspects of our findings support the idea that what is being modeled by the structural representation system is the global three-dimensional structure of an object — as opposed to one or a set of two-dimensional representations. Evidence for this conclusion comes from the fact that priming is only obtained under encoding conditions or with stimuli that permit three-dimensional structure to be computed. That is, local visual encoding and elaborative encoding — which do not require the extraction of a three-dimensional representation of studied objects—fail to produce subsequent facilitation of object decision performance. In addition, and quite importantly, priming is not exhibited with stimuli—the impossible objects—for which three-dimensional representations are unavailable.

The idea that the representations mediating performance on the implicit memory task are of three-dimensional object structure is also supported by preliminary results from a series of experiments initiated very recently. In these studies, we are using more realistic renderings of solid, depth-cued objects, and an implicit task that requires participants to determine whether (studied or nonstudied) briefly presented objects are symmetric or asymmetric. Under such conditions—where the three-dimensional structure of the depth-cued objects is readily available and highly salient—it appears difficult to create situations in which priming fails to be obtained. This tentative finding is also consistent with a related line of research (Cooper, 1988, 1989, 1990, 1991) demonstrating that participants form mental representations of the three-dimensional structure of objects even when tasks can be performed on the basis of selected sets of two-dimensional projections. More precise characterization of the nature of the representations of objects computed by the structural description system remains a central objective in the ongoing program of research.

Finally, the apparent modularity of the underlying functional systems leads naturally to the speculation that distinct neural pathways support structural and episodic representations of objects. Although we are a long way from being able to advance hypotheses about neural locus with any degree of confidence, the results of the experimental work described above give intriguing clues about what neuroanatomical regions might contribute to the functional systems. In particular, we (Cooper et al., 1992; Schacter, Cooper, Tharan, et al.,1991) have proposed that regions of inferior temporal (IT) cortex could constitute a neural locus of the structural description system that produces priming on the object decision task. Evidence from behavioral studies on nonhuman primates with lesions in IT and of the response properties of single units in this area is consistent with this suggestion (for a review, see Plaut & Farah, 1990). In general, cells in IT appear sensitive to complex shapes, but they respond invariantly over changes in object attributes that are correlated with minor variation in conditions of viewing. The similarity of this description of IT coding to properties of the structural representation system revealed in our behavioral studies with humans is striking; however, considerably more work—both analytic and experimental—must be done to determine whether the similarity is more than simply superficial.

In conclusion, I wish to emphasize the importance of evidence from cognitive dissociations in developing a picture of the functional systems supporting the mental representation of visual objects. The initial dissociation between structural and semantic aspects of objects led us to probe more deeply the nature of the information preserved in the underlying representational systems. The resulting characterizations generate hypotheses about neural systems that can be evaluated with coverging methods, including the testing of brain-injured patients and possibly future work employing techniques of brain imaging and electrophysiological recording. Whether or not particular preliminary ideas about the neural systems that underlie the representation of visual objects prove correct, behavioral experiments like those described here can uncover rich and compelling patterns of functional dissociation that must ultimately be explained at both computational and neural levels.

ACKNOWLEDGMENT

The research reported in this chapter was supported by Grant 90-0187 from the Air Force Office of Scientific Research to Daniel L. Schacter and Lynn A. Cooper.

REFERENCES

Andersen, R. A., Essick, G. K., & Siegel, R. M. (1985). Encoding of spatial location by posterior parietal neurons. *Science, 191,* 572–575.

Biederman, I., & Cooper, E. E. (1991). Priming contour-deleted images: Evidence for intermediate representations in visual object recognition. *Cognitive Psychology, 23,* 393–419.

Biederman, I., & Cooper, E. E. (1992). Size invariance in visual object priming. *Journal of Experimental Psychology: Human Perception and Performance, 18,* 121–133.

Cooper, L. A. (1988). The role of spatial representations in complex problem solving. In S. Steele & S. Shiffer (Eds.), *Cognition and representation* (pp. 53–86). Boulder, CO: Westview Press.

Cooper, L. A. (1989). Mental models of the structure of three-dimensional objects. In B. Shepp & S. Ballesteros (Eds.), *Object perception: Structure and process* (pp. 91–119). Hillsdale, NJ: Lawrence Erlbaum Associates.

Cooper, L. A. (1990). Mental representation of three-dimensional objects in visual problem solving and recognition. *Journal of Experimental Psychology: Learning, Memory, and Cognition, 16,* 1097–1106.

Cooper, L. A. (1991). Dissociable aspects of the mental representation of objects. In R. H. Logie & M. Denis (Eds.), *Images in human cognition* (pp. 3–34). New York: Elsevier.

Cooper, L. A., Schacter, D. L., Ballesteros, S., & Moore, C. (1992). Priming and recognition of transformed three-dimensional objects: Effects of size and reflection. *Journal of Experimental Psychology: Learning, Memory, and Cognition, 18,* 43–57.

Cooper, L. A., Schacter, D. L., & Moore, C. (1991, November). *Orientation affects both structural and episodic representations of three-dimensional objects.* Paper presented at the 32nd annual meeting of the Psychonomic Society, San Francisco, CA.

Craik, F. I. M., & Tulving, E. (1975). Depth of processing and the retention of words in episodic memory. *Journal of Experimental Psychology: General, 104,* 268–294.

Desimone, R., Albright, T. D., Gross, C. G., & Bruce, C. (1984). Stimulus selective properties of inferior temporal neurons in the macaque. *Journal of Neuroscience, 4,* 2051-2062.

Farah, M. J. (1985). The neurological basis of mental imagery: A componential analysis. In S. Pinker (ED.), *Visual cognition* (pp. 245-271). Cambridge, MA: MIT Press.

Farah, M. J. (1990). *Visual agnosia: Disorders of object recognition and what they tell us about normal vision.* Cambridge, MA: MIT Press.

Farah, M. J., Wallace, M. A., & Vecera, S. P. (in press). "What" and "where" in visual attention: Evidence from the neglect syndrome. In I. A. Robertson & J. C. Marshall (Eds.), *Unilateral neglect: Clinical and experimental studies.*

Fodor, J. A. (1983). *Modularity of mind.* Cambridge, MA: MIT Press.

Gabrieli, J. D. E., Milberg, W., Keane, M. M., & Corkin, S. (1990). Intact priming of patterns despite impaired memory. *Neuropsychologia, 28,* 417-428.

Garner, W. R. (1974). *The processing of information and structure.* Hillsdale, NJ: Lawrence Erlbaum Associates.

Graf, P., & Schacter, D. L. (1985). Implicit and explicit memory for new associations in normal and amnesic patients. *Journal of Experimental Psychology: Learning, Memory, and Cognition, 11,* 501-518.

Gross, C. G., Desimone, R., Albright, T. D., & Schwartz, E. L. (1984). Inferior temporal cortex as a visual integration area. In F. Reinoso-Suarez & C. Ajmone-Marsan (Eds.), *Cortical integration* (pp. 291-315) New York: Raven Press.

Hubel, D. H., & Livingstone, M. S. (1987). Segregation of form, color, and stereopsis in primate area 18. *Journal of Neuroscience, 7,* 3378-3415.

Kosslyn, S. M. (1987). Seeing and imagining in the cerebral hemispheres: A computational approach. *Psychological Review, 94,* 148-175.

Kosslyn, S. M., Flynn, R. A., Amsterdam, J. B., & Wang, G. (1990). Components of high-level vision: A cognitive neuroscience analysis and accounts of neurological syndromes. *Cognition, 34,* 203-277.

Kroll, J. F., & Potter, M. C. (1984). Recognizing words, pictures, and concepts: A comparison of lexical, object, and reality decisions. *Journal of Verbal Learning and Verbal Behavior, 23,* 39-66.

Marr, D. (1982). *Vision.* San Francisco, CA: Freeman.

McCarthy, R. A., & Warrington, E. K. (1990). *Cognitive neuropsychology: A clinical introduction.* San Diego, CA: Academic Press.

Mishkin, M., & Ungerleider, L. G. (1982). Contribution of striate inputs to the visuospatial functions of parieto-preoccipital cortex in monkeys. *Behavioural Brain Research, 6,* 57-77.

Musen, G., & Treisman, A. (1990). Implicit and explicit memory for visual patterns. *Journal of Experimental Psychology: Learning, Memory, and Cognition, 15,* 127-137.

Plaut, C. D., & Farah. M. J. (1990). Visual object representation: Interpreting neuropsychological data within a computational framework. *Journal of Cognitive Neuroscience, 2,* 320-343.

Roediger, H. L. III, Weldon, M. S., & Challis, B. H. (1989). Explaining dissociations between implicit and explicit measures of retention: A processing account. In H. L. Roediger, III, & F. I. M. Craik (Eds.), *Varieties of memory and consciousness: Essays in honor of Endel Tulving* (pp. 3-41). Hillsdale, NJ: Lawrence Erlbaum Associates.

Schacter, D. L. (1987). Implicit memory: History and current status. *Journal of Experimental Psychology: Learning, Memory, and Cognition, 13,* 501-518.

Schacter, D. L. (1990). Perceptual representation systems and implicit memory: Toward a resolution of the multiple memory systems debate. In A. Diamond (Ed.), *Development and neural bases of higher cognition. Annals of the New York Academy of Sciences, 608,* 543-571.

Schacter, D. L., & Cooper, L. A. (1991, November). *Implicit memory for novel visual objects: Function and structure.* Paper presented at the 32nd annual meeting of the Psychonomic

Society, San Francisco, CA.

Schacter, D. L., Cooper, L. A., & Delaney, S. M. (1990a). Implicit memory for unfamiliar objects depends on access to structural descriptions. *Journal of Experimental Psychology: General, 119*, 5-24.

Schacter, D. L., Cooper, L. A., & Delaney, S. M. (1990b). Implicit memory for visual objects and the structural description system. *Bulletin of the Psychonomic Society, 28*, 367-372.

Schacter, D. L., Cooper, L. A., Delaney, S. M., Peterson, M. A., & Tharan, M. (1991). Implicit memory for possible and impossible objects: Constraints on the construction of structural descriptions. *Journal of Experimental Psychology: Learning, Memory, & Cognition, 17*, 3-19.

Schacter, D. L., Cooper, L. A., Tharan, M., & Rubens, A. B. (1991). Preserved priming of novel objects in patients with memory disorders. *Journal of Cognitive Neuroscience, 3*, 118-131.

Schacter, D. L., Cooper, L. A., & Valdiserri, M. (1992). Implicit and explicit memory for novel visual objects in older and younger adults. *Psychology & Aging, 7*, 299-308.

Shimamura, A. P. (1986). Priming effects in amnesia: Evidence for a dissociable memory function. *Quarterly Journal of Experimental Psychology, 38A*, 619-644.

Shimamura, A. P., & Squire, L. R. (1984). Paired-associate learning and priming effects in amnesia: A neuropsychological study. *Journal of Experimental Psychology: General, 113*, 556-570.

Tulving, E. (1983). *Elements of episodic memory.* New York: Oxford University Press.

Tulving, E., & Schacter, D. L. (1990). Priming and human memory systems. *Science, 247*, 301-396.

Ungerleider, L. G., & Mishkin, M. (1982). Two cortical visual systems. In D. J. Ingle, M. A. Goodale, & R. J. W. Mansfield (Eds.), *Analysis of visual behavior* (pp. 549-586). Cambridge, MA: MIT Press.

9 Objects of the Mind: Mental Representations in Visual Perception and Cognition

Lynn A. Cooper
Julian Hochberg
Columbia University

The goal of this chapter is to provide an explicit statement of the theoretical orientation that underlies each of our contributions to the present volume (Cooper, chapter 8; Hochberg, chapter 11). This point of view fuels, as well, our individual and joint programs of research on object perception and representation; it underscores the centrality of mental representations of objects to theory and research in visual cognition. The discussion is divided into two parts. In the first section, we argue for the necessity of a conceptual level corresponding to a "mentally represented object," and we offer two examples of phenomena based on perceptual couplings (Hochberg, 1974) that compel us to conclude that mental representations comprise a necessary analytic tool for studying visual cognition. In the second section, we consider the idea that mental representations of visual objects and events reflect the internalization of properties of their external physical counterparts. We cite several examples of phenomena and experimental results that show this solution to be overly simple; we suggest, instead, that the central challenge is to study and understand just those cases in which the analogy between mental representations and physical objects breaks down.

Objects, not attributes (or sensations), are the distinctive subject matter of visual cognition. Indeed, it is hard to see what we gain by studying the perception of abstracted attributes like color and motion, unless those studies ultimately contribute to an understanding of our perception of objects and events. Unfortunately, the physical stimuli for the perception of objects are not as well defined as those for attributes can be. This is so because objects are not physical entities as such; they are units of analysis or description that derive as much from the task to be performed as from measurable aspects of physical structure.

In its dictionary meaning, an object is a "material thing; a person or thing to which action or feeling is directed; thing sought or aimed at." (A thing, in turn, is "any possible object of thought.") This is not bad for a start: A rock, a cloud, a swarm of bees — each has very different physical properties, but they are alike in a set of important opportunities for action that they afford the observer. Most significant here are the possibilities that objects offer for the *perceptual* acts that provide the information on which visual cognition is based, as well as the input to other, subsequent cognitive acts (e.g., of imaginal manipulation, problem-solving, and public or private report). We distinguish such dispositions for perceptual and cognitive actions from the instrumental uses to which objects might be put (e.g., sitting, cutting, etc.), referred to as "affordances" by J. J. Gibson (1979).

WHY ARE MENTAL REPRESENTATIONS NEEDED IN OBJECT PERCEPTION?

The specific information that a physical object affords the observer's perceptual systems sets the stage for what we can expect to gain, conceptually, from the construct of a mentally represented object. In general, a physical object provides structure — mutually constrained, or redundant, multidimensional information. To take a very simple example, if we know that an object is a square, then the answers to many questions about it are fixed (e.g., the diagonals are equal; if we look from one corner to the next, we will find the same corner angle rotated 180 deg, etc.). The structure of an object, whether fixed or changing, and that of its optical environment, for example, its relationship to light sources and to the eye of the observer, jointly determine the optic array that confronts the observer. That is, the structures of objects and environments together constrain the distribution of luminance gradients and embedded texture gradients (e.g., a ball with the sun overhead is shaded below, whereas a concave hemispherical depression under the same illumination is shaded above). Finally, as objects and observers move and change their spatial relationships — whether in two or in three dimensions — the structures of motion, layout, and objects all contribute lawfully to the resulting optic array.

Most of the purposive behavior of which we are aware is directed toward the still and moving objects around us, or at the layout of surfaces within which we move. We must assume that evolutionary endowment and individual learning provide an accuracy of perceiving and remembering the objects of our behaviors, that is, at least at the level required for survival. Thus, our reports of objects' surface reflectances and shapes are often in better correspondence with the objects in the world than one might expect from local measures of their retinal images. In experimental research on the object constancies, for example, observers' reports of such attributes as object shape, size, and lightness remain relatively invariant over changes in the retinal image due (respectively) to changes in orientation or slant, distance, or illumination on the object's surfaces. *Indeed, the very conception of mental representations was introduced as an essential component of perceptual theory in order to explain how such object constancy can hold, despite changes in the sensory information impinging on the receptor surface.*

If such object constancy were perfect, and if we were interested only in locomotion or manipulation, we might dismiss both the visual sensory system and the ordered light it receives as being "merely mediating variables" (Brunswik, 1956). Or, we might assert that the two-dimensional pattern of light to the eye, properly considered, contains all of the information needed to specify directly the distal object's attributes. Thus, if an object's *configuration* itself were the stimulus basis of form perception – regardless of where on the retinal mosaic it fell – then *shape constancy* would be direct. No further explanation would be needed, because the configuration itself remains invariant when transformed by rotation and/or translation (Koffka, 1935). Again, an object and its surroundings present the eye with a luminance ratio that remains invariant despite changes in the overall illumination, so proximal luminance ratios can specify the ratio of distal object-to-surround reflectances (Wallach, 1948). Many such potentially informative invariances in proximal stimulus patterns are provided to an observer who is moving in a normal environment; if used, these invariant patterns offer a form of explanation for perception that has no need and, indeed, no room for mental representations of any kind.

The physical structure of a real object and that of its viewing context constrain the possible patterns of light in the retinal image. Those constraints provide for measures that are *physically coupled* (Hochberg, 1956). For example, if some object's surface provides the eye with a luminance, L, reflected from some source of illumination, I, according to some function $f(\beta)$, where β is the surface's angle to that source, then for a given illumination any measure of L will be physically coupled to any measure of β. Helmholtz's (1866/1962) commitment to the idea that each sensory element in the retinal mosaic functions independently led him to just this argument in his famous proposal concerning unconscious inference in perception. That is, from the premises of independent sensory channels as the elements of visual processing and of constraints deriving from physically coupled regularities in the world, an unconscious inference from nonnoticed (and nonnoticeable) sensations *must interpose a process of mental representation between the early sensory response and final percept* (the latter term meaning, today, what we can potentially report to ourselves or to others).

We know now that Helmholtz's assumption of independent sensory elements is no longer viable. Can we then explain what was thought to be a "taking of illumination into account"—with its bothersome baggage of mental representation—as the direct effect of higher order variables of stimulus information, such as luminance ratios? If so, conceptions of mental representation would be unnecessary to accounts of perception. The direct explanation fails, however, because we can change an object's perceived lightness by changing its perceived slant *without changing stimulus luminance ratios in any consistent fashion*. More importantly, we can accomplish this using diverse manipulations (e.g., Hochberg & Beck, 1954) that are equivalent *only in their effects on perceived slant* (see Hochberg, chapter 11, this volume). Furthermore, as we discuss later, identical physical stimulus patterns can give rise to the perception, in alternation, of very different objects. *The perceptual coupling, in short, resides in the viewer and not in the stimulus measures.* Such convergent interresponse couplings are not to be explained by couplings in the present stimulation. Their demonstrable existence makes it problematic to deny the role of mental representations in the perception of objects.

Let us consider another robust instance of the mental representation of an object, before returning to the issue of perceptual couplings. If two objects are judged identical, despite differences in orientation, then some form of shape constancy is evident. In a Helmholtzian explanation, such shape constancy is achieved by taking the object's displacements into account, and thus some form of inference and mental representation is required. Recall that the Gestalt theorists (e.g., Koffka, 1935) held an object's configuration—invariant under rotation and translation—to be the effective and direct stimulus for form perception. The retinal image itself thus became irrelevant, as it was for the same reason to J. J. Gibson (1979). Those who develop computational models to explain object-centered, as distinguished from viewer-centered, shape recognition (e.g., Marr, 1982) also assume some level of representation at which retinal transformations are irrelevant. There are many demonstrations, however, that the appearance of a particular shape fails to remain invariant under sufficient rotation (e.g., Mach, 1906/1959; Rock, 1973). Regardless of whether shape constancy is present or absent under specified conditions, it will become clear, later, that we must still appeal to mental representations to explain relevant experimental findings.

Shepard and his colleagues (Shepard & Cooper, 1982; Shepard & Metzler, 1971) showed that when participants are asked to judge whether two objects presented at different orientations are identical or mirror images, the time required to make the judgment about the objects' parities is a simple linear function of the objects' angular separation. The idea that a mental representation of the object(s) to be judged is imagined as being rotated in real time—or "mental rotation", as measured by judgment times—is a plausible hypothetical construct in this paradigm. As Attneave (1981) noted, these data are incompatible with the invariance hypothesis. Even more importantly, these findings lead to a new experimental paradigm (cf. Cooper, 1976) in which inferred mental rotation serves a causal role, just as inferred apparent slant did in the perceived lightness example above.

If participants are asked to rotate mentally some object whose shape they know, starting at time t_0, and at some time, t_1, in the course of that rotation they are shown a probe object and asked to judge its parity, then the additional time, Δt, needed to make the judgment is a joint function of each participant's mental rotation rate, ω', (as determined in previous experiments), and of the angular displacement, γ, of the probe shape relative to the reference object. If $\gamma = (\omega' \times t)$, the additional judgment time $\Delta t = 0$; otherwise, more time is needed.

This is just what we would expect if the respondents were actually comparing a physically rotating reference object to the probe object. In that case, any feature's initial displacement, α_1, from its starting point is physically coupled to a measure, t_1, of the time from the start of the rotation to the point at which the probe object is presented, by the function $\alpha_1 = (\omega_1 \times t_1)$; the subsequent rotation required to bring the probe object to the orientation of the reference object would be $\alpha_2 = (\gamma - \alpha_1)$. But, in this experiment there is no physical reference object and no physical rotation. There is only our assumption that a mental representation of the object is available to the respondent, and that it undergoes a purely *cognitively coupled* pair of response variables—rotation rate and attendant orientation at each elapsed time—to explain the experimental data. Presentation time t_1 and presentation angle γ do comprise the experimental manipulations, of course. But it is the hypothetical construct of mental rotation, at a rate consistent with each respondent's performance in a previous experiment, that is the effective if inferred variable. And, we must note that the displacements in mental space, α_1 and α_2, that are implicated in each period of the rotation, t_1, and t_2, respectively, appear to be additive, as they would be in physical space.

This last point provides a transition between our discussion of the need for mental representations in perception and our consideration of what properties those representations might have. In the case of mental rotation, we cannot explain the properties of the mentally represented object in terms of any physical stimulus variable or invariances; however, a simple internalized kinematics does seem, at least approximately, to apply (cf. Shepard, 1984). Thus, the mental event (of rotation) seems to reflect some aspects of the physical world. Before developing this idea (and its difficulties) further, three cautionary notes are needed: (a) we do not know whether mental representations are important in object perception when conditions are not such as to reveal their operation; (b) not all that is coupled in stimulation is perceptually coupled, and perception tolerates structural inconsistencies that violate consistencies and couplings expected in the physical world (Hochberg, 1968; Hochberg & Peterson, 1987); and (c) we have not specified what couplings are subsumed in a mental representation.

WHAT IS THE NATURE OF A MENTALLY REPRESENTED OBJECT?

This last point is most important, if mental representations are to be meaningful or conceptually useful. Before we attempt to explain or model a mental representation, we should have a clear idea about what is to be explained or modeled. The most common attempts along these lines follow Helmholtz in asserting that mental representations embody physical laws and/or ecological probabilities. This generalization must in some measure be true, else we could not survive. But evolutionary needs fare better as explanations than as predictions. To apply an evolutionary explanation requires detailed knowledge about the demands of the ecological niche; the aspects of the environment that a mental representation must reflect depend on the functions that the representation must serve—the set of behaviors that it must guide. Indeed, we do not as yet know what diverse functions mental representations of objects serve, and what degrees of correspondence with properties of physical objects those functions impose (Cooper, this volume; Cooper & Munger, in press).

We do know, however, that the properties of perceived objects may differ in important ways from properties expected of objects in the world. For example, mentally represented objects—but not their physical counterparts—may exhibit spatial inconsistencies, nonrigidity, and abrupt exchange of near and far in perceived reversals of perspective (Hochberg, this volume). It will be important to flesh out more fully this litany of noncorresponding properties in undertaking definitions and descriptions of mental representations of objects. Below, we begin this task by pointing to four cases in which experimental evidence reveals properties of perceived representations of objects that do not reflect properties of objects as they behave in the physical world. These include: (a) the dependence of mental representations of objects on a frame of reference, whether it be retinally or gravitationally based; (b) the failure, in certain cases, of imagined or extrapolated transformations on objects to conform to predictions from physical dynamics; (c) the tendency for a single stimulus pattern to give rise to different perceived objects, often in spontaneous alternation; and (d) the dependence of a mentally represented object's attributes on the conditions under which such a representation is acquired, and on the purposes for which it must be used.

Let us consider, again, the mental rotation experiment in general, and the coupling between mental rotation time and mentally represented object orientation in particular, to illustrate the first case cited above. We have already noted that if perceived shape were invariant over transformation, then the parity judgment should not depend on angle. This is because the viewer should have equal knowledge about the configuration at all orientations. Note that the *physical object* (to which a mental representation corresponds, in this task) is indeed invariant in its orientation, *in that the relationship between its parts and the various couplings implied by its structural description are, for rigid objects, independent of orientation to either gravity or to the observer's axis.* The mentally represented object, by contrast, is clearly not invariant over rotation, in that its characteristics are a function of what features the object-in-an-orientation would present to the viewer's gaze from a narrow range of viewing angles.

Despite relevant mental rotation research (e.g., Corballis, 1988; Corballis, Zbrodoff, & Roldan, 1976) and recent studies of object priming (e.g., Cooper, Schacter, Ballesteros, & Moore, 1992; Cooper, Schacter, & Moore, 1991)—both of which reveal strong effects of orientation—it is still not clear whether the object's orientation with respect to gravity, or with respect to the viewer's retina, is the important factor. Research on the recognition of complex shapes shows effects of retinal, rather than gravitational, orientation (Rock, 1973); as Kohler (1929) noted, upright letters and faces viewed with one's head inverted seem just as hard to recognize as the same objects viewed when they are inverted and one's head is upright. Observations like these suggest that the retinal image will probably turn out to be relevant to visual cognition, both empirically and theoretically. Indeed, the retinal image and the framework it provides for gathering information about object properties may prove central to an analysis of the nature of representations of objects.

The core idea here is that our construction of the visual world—the stitching together of the visual space that provides the "where," and the convergence of object properties that provides the "what"—is achieved by sequences of individual glances that are themselves guided by the viewer's decision to query some region within the current retinal image. Such perceptual inquiry proceeds by highly skilled and very frequent ($\sim$ 200,000 per day) elective, purposive, ballistic actions that are directed to bring different regions of the retinal image into foveal vision. Because only information in the low spatial frequencies is available to peripheral vision, most answers to questions about detail must be sought by intelligently directed eye movements, and those queries must usually be directed at an object that is not fully present in foveal stimulation. If one finds merit in Helmholtz's (1866/1962) observation that his "idea of a table is what he would see if he looked at it from any position," that formula must apply as well to the viewer's idea of some object that is only partly present in clear vision for any direction of gaze.

What, specifically, does this guided sampling by individual glances suggest about how an object is represented? We know that only a limited number of separate chunks of information within each glance can be encoded in a form that the viewer can report, or can *pass through* for further cognitive manipulation (Hochberg, this volume). In addition, there is but a narrow window of time within which such encoding can occur (Sperling, 1960). This strongly suggests that selected information is represented in some form (perhaps a visual working memory or "visual sketch pad," cf. Baddeley, 1992) to be added to, or to confirm the entry encoded from a previous glance. Under usual conditions of laboratory experiments, that is, normal, self-initiated glances at very simple objects requiring little information to categorize or recognize, this process should appear as seamless as casual reading of familiar or redundant text. With a sequence of rapid glances at rich and detailed environments, as well as in sequential presentations of partial views of relatively complex objects, it has been shown that a great deal of information fails to be encoded (e.g., Hochberg, 1968; Intraub, 1985; Rock, 1983). Moreover, the contents of each glimpse, along with the viewer's perceptual/cognitive task, must affect the sequences of subsequent glances that bring different parts of the retinal image to the fovea; they must affect as well the information encoded about an object from those retinal regions.

Our point is this: *The ecological niche that these information-gathering behaviors serve derives at least as much from the proximal retinal image as from the distal physical world.* In short, there are good theoretical reasons to believe that viewer-centered reference frames will be relevant to our understanding of the nature of mentally represented objects. Whether the effective framework is retinal, gravitational, or both, the fact remains that mentally represented and perceived objects depend on their frames of reference in ways that their physical counterparts do not. And, this is only one way in which objects in the world and our mental representations of them differ.

The attraction of various versions of the "mind-reflects-world" formula lies in their substitution of the orderly, mathematically tractable measures and relationships of physics for the uncharted mysteries of mental structure (Cooper & Munger, in press; Hochberg, 1988; Shepard, 1984). There are many examples in which this approach does seem to describe the attributes of perceived and imagined objects, for example, Shepard and his colleagues' elegant experiments on apparent motion of alternating views of two-dimensional shapes (Farrell & Shepard, 1981; Shepard & Farrell, 1985) and three-dimensional objects (Shepard & Judd, 1976). Other examples of the approach, however, are readily matched by cases in which internalized physics fails to predict experimental outcomes consistently. Thus, Freyd and her collaborators (Freyd, 1987; Freyd & Finke, 1984, 1985; Freyd & Johnson, 1987) have demonstrated that motion implied by ordered sequences of static views of simple, two-dimensional shapes continues slightly beyond the point at which the motion is terminated by the requirement of a "same–different" judgment. This finding of an "overshoot" for mentally represented motion suggests that principles of dynamics (i.e., "representational momentum") could be used to predict the apparent position of a pictured object. But Cooper and her colleagues (Cooper, 1989; Cooper, Gibson, Mowafy, & Tataryn, 1987) reported the opposite effect (i.e., an undershoot) in imagined continuations of real perceived motion. They also found that changes in the apparent mass of objects fail to affect parameters of extrapolated motion (Cooper & Munger, in press; Munger & Cooper, in preparation); such effects should clearly be predicted if internalized dynamics governed the mentally represented motion of objects. Indeed, there is a substantial literature on the failure of cognitive judgments about the motion of objects (their trajectories, collisions, etc.) to conform to principles of kinetics or kinematics (e.g., Gilden, 1991; Kaiser & Proffitt, 1987; McCloskey, Washburn, & Felch, 1983; Proffitt, Gilden, Kaiser, & Whelan, 1988; Runeson, 1975). It is clear, then, that physical models of the perceived or extrapolated motion of represented objects are not uniformly successful in accounting for relevant experimental results. The divergences and anomalies must be understood, not ignored, if we are ever to predict and understand mentally represented events.

A third and important case in which mental representations of objects fail to reflect fundamental characteristics of physical objects concerns spontaneous fluctuations in perception. Figure-ground alternation, perspective reversals, and re-organizations in event perception are all examples of the perception of two (or more) objects, in more or less spontaneous alternation, in response to a single stimulus pattern or event. Responses in these cases are constrained by the stimulus information, to be sure. However, the mental representation that the viewer is asked to "fit" to the stimulus pattern significantly affects the relative durations with which the alternative perceived objects are reported. Note that these reports of seeing one or the other object are not just responses that viewers can vary to please the experimenter; rather, they meet the criterion of *perceptual coupling*. For example, an observer shown a wire cube that is actually in clockwise rotation reports that it is rotating counterclockwise when asked to try to perceive the cube in reversed perspective.

Such phenomena suggest (but do not demand, cf. Hochberg, 1974;

chapter 11, this volume) that alternative mental representations of objects stand between the stimulus information and the final response. Such representations display a wide range of exceptions to the "mind-reflects-world" formula, as indexed by the perceptual reports they generate. Perfectly consistent physical objects are perceived and reported in ways that are inconsistent with their structure (Gillam, 1972; Hochberg & Peterson, 1987; Peterson & Hochberg, 1983), even when the objects are in motion and the error in depth thus results in both a coupled error in perceived motion and a continuous nonrigid deformation of structure (Hochberg & Peterson, 1987). Local depth cues in the proximal stimulus pattern are sometimes decisive in determining which alternative structure is perceived. In such cases, the "wrong" object is perceived because the viewer has attended to a local feature that is easy to misconstrue. For example, when attending to intersection 2 in Fig. 9.1A, the object is free to reverse in perceived depth (Hochberg & Peterson, 1987), accompanied by appropriate illusory concomitant motion (dotted arrow) when the object is in real motion (solid arrow).

There is a seeming paradox here: Robust errors occur when the retinal shape of the object fits tolerably well, at each separate moment, with the projection of a different and more regular object viewed in perspective at a

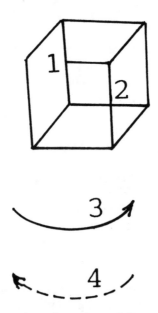

FIG. 9.1. Apparent rotation of a cube and its parts
A. A partly covered rigid wire cube rotating as shown by arrow 3. Although its orientation is fixed at intersection 1, it appears to reverse in depth, spontaneously, when intersection 2 is fixated, and, when it reverses, appears to rotate as shown by arrow 4.

different orientation—as in an oscillating "Ames window"—and again nonrigid deformations are seen, perceptually coupled to the illusory motion (Hochberg & Peterson, 1987). In both this and the previous example, the illusions seem to result from attending to specific proximal features that evidently encourage misconstrual—either by leading to the selection of one of two or more competing mental representations, or by biasing fluctuations of attention between quite different sources of information. Note that reversals of orientation can also occur *against* such proximal information (von Hornbostel, 1922). For example, a rigid rotating cube (Fig. 9.1B) in strong perspective presents at least two sides that, were they to function as "Ames trapezoids," would support the correct perception of the cube and its motion (Fig. 9.1C). Nevertheless, such cubes appear to reverse—against striking information from motion perspective, rigidity deformation, and local depth cues (Fig. 9.1D). Strangely enough, this robust phenomenon seems to increase in frequency and strength with increasing knowledge and practice (Cooper, personal communication; Cutting, personal communication). It is important to learn why this occurs, and whether the phenomenon is evidence of alternation between purely internally based mental representations of objects. We are currently trying to understand these issues in experimental work in progress (Hochberg & Cooper, in preparation).

The fact that viewers seem willing to perceive inconsistent objects stands in bold contrast to cases in which some figural organization, usually involving completion or subjective contours, is taken as evidence that the mind necessarily mirrors the structure of objects in the world. These latter

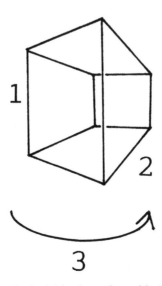

FIG. 9.1. (Continued) B. A rigid wire cube, with the face marked 2 the nearer, rotating as shown by arrow 3.

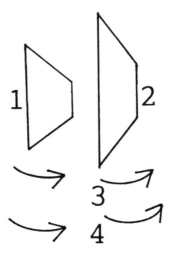

FIG. 9.1. (Continued) C. The two faces of cube B, 1 and 2, when viewed alone appear to rotate as shown by arrow 4, in agreement with their actual motions (arrow 3) and with what would be expected of them if they were actually "Ames trapezoids." They remain rigid in appearance as they move in depth.

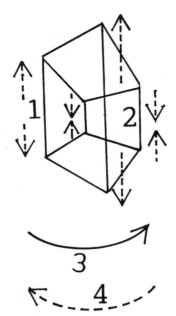

FIG. 9.1. (Continued) D. The whole cube, actually rigid and moving as in B and C (arrow 3) nevertheless soon reverses its depth against both its pictorial and motion perspective and then appears to rotate as shown by arrow 4, even though it then appears strongly nonrigid (appearing to expand and to compress as shown by the vertical arrows) as it proceeds in its illusory trajectory.

demonstrations usually rest implicitly or explicitly on the assumption that object perception is structurally consistent. They often leave unmeasured the effects of viewing instructions, which can be substantial (Hochberg & Peterson, 1987; Peterson & Hochberg, 1983), so the sensitivity of the demonstrated effects to implicit suggestions or demands cannot be assessed. It would be interesting and useful for any attempt at theoretical synthesis to reexamine the more interesting completion phenomena/experiments with these points in mind. All that we can say right now is that rigidity does not appear to be a strong default attribute of perceptual representations of objects; whether this is true as well for purely mental representations of objects (i.e., when no relevant stimulus information is present) is a question for future research.

We noted above that there are two possible reasons why a viewer might perceive different objects while looking at the same stimulus pattern. It could be that different information is extracted in the two cases, owing to changes in the direction of gaze or by less externally evident fluctuations in attention, leading to perception of different objects. We do not know yet whether such an attention-based explanation is competitive with the notion that perceptual alternations reveal alternative mental representations. We do know, however, that a viewer's task can significantly alter the nature of the mental representations that are available for further perceptual and cognitive use. This fact removes us further from the comfortable assumption that the attributes of a mentally represented object follow in any simple way from those of its physical referent. Relevant experimental evidence constitutes our final case casting doubt on a strict "mind-reflects-world" formulation.

In an ongoing program of research, Schacter, Cooper, and their collaborators (e.g., Cooper, 1991, chapter 8, this volume; Cooper & Schacter, 1992; Schacter, Cooper, & Delaney, 1990a, 1990b; Schacter, Cooper, Delaney, Peterson, & Tharan, 1991) showed that the conditions under which novel, three-dimensional objects are encoded have strong effects on what kinds of information about the objects can be accessed for subsequent tests of memory. Requiring participants to study objects in a way that emphasizes their global structure (i.e., determining whether each object appears to be facing to the left or the right) leads to robust priming on an implicit test of memory (i.e., deciding whether briefly presented individual objects represent physically possible or impossible structures). Encoding objects in ways that emphasize their local features (i.e., determining whether each object contains more horizontal or vertical line segments) fails to produce priming. Finally, encoding the objects by attributing semantic or functional properties to them not only fails to produce priming, but also leads to greatly enhanced performance on an explicit "yes/no" test of conscious recognition.

These findings provide striking evidence that accessible properties of mental representations derived from the same view of the same object can differ greatly, depending on the conditions under which they were initially acquired and subsequently tested. Such representations can differ greatly, as well, in the information they preserve and pass through to further cognitive processing, and they can serve functions quite apart from those of conscious or reportable recognition. We are currently trying to apply similar experimental techniques to studying the kinds of mental representations of objects manifested by the perceptual couplings described in earlier sections. We must understand these very different situations in which invoking the concept of mental representation is appropriate, before we can attempt to generalize about what the attributes of mentally represented objects might be. It seems clear that such attributes do not necessarily correspond to those of external physical objects; in addition, there is task dependency in even what descriptors are appropriate.

CONCLUDING REMARKS

In the first section of this chapter, we examined some situations in which the conception of mental representations of objects emerged almost of necessity in attempting to organize behavioral data. We defined the construct not by introspections about consciousness, but by the convergence and coupling of input and response variables. The value of this notion therefore depends not on its intuitive appeal, but rather on its systematic predictive power. If the construct is to be more than a vague metaphor, we need some system for specifying what the coupled attributes of a mentally represented object will be under particular conditions. This is a difficult task, implying an enormous program of research.

Having constructed "objects of the mind" because of the imperatives of behavioral evidence, we have had to begin *deconstructing* them, again from behavioral necessity. Mental analogues of physical structures offer the vital start needed to move from the level of sensory thresholds to that of object-oriented perception. Obviously, we should seek to uncover as many parallels as we can between attributes of objects in the world and attributes of their corresponding mental representations. But we must examine these analogues with care, determining which cases fail, as well as when and why they do. Only after we have surveyed where distal physics can and cannot be used to predict perceptual and cognitive constructs, and only after we have brought order to that survey, will we be able to tackle the task of neural explanation that will render the metaphor of "object" superfluous. Conversely, any experimental manipulation that reveals a dissociation of aspects of psychological objects from properties of the distal objects that they represent demands rapt attention. Such distinctions—and not the separation into sensory modalities, into computational processing units, or into categories of ecological adaptation—offer the introductory tools for understanding how objects of the mind represent objects in the world.

REFERENCES

Attneave, F. (1981). Three approaches to perceptual organization: Comments on views of Hochberg, and Shepard and Shaw and Turvey. In M. Kubovy & J. Pomerantz (Eds.), *Perceptual organization* (pp. 417–421). Hillsdale, NJ: Lawerence Erlbaum associates.

Baddeley, A. (1992). Consciousness and working memory. *Consciousness and Cognition, 11,* 3–6.

Brunswik, E. (1956). *Perception and the representative design of psychological experiments* (2nd ed.). Berkeley: University of California Press.

Cooper, L. A. (1976). Demonstration of a mental analog of an external rotation. *Perception & Psychophysics, 19,* 296–302.

Cooper, L. A. (1989). Mental models of the structure of three-dimensional objects. In B. Shepp & S. Ballesteros (Eds.), *Object perception: Structure and process* (pp. 91–119). Hillsdale, NJ: Lawrence Erlbaum Associates.

Cooper, L. A. (1991). Dissociable aspects of the mental representation of objects. In R. H. Logie & M. Denis (Eds.), *Images in human cognition* (pp. 3–34). North Holland: Elsevier Science Publishers.

Cooper, L. A., Gibson, B. S., Mowafy, L., & Tataryn, D. J. (1987, November). *Mental extrapolation of perceptually-driven spatial transformations.* Paper presented at the 28th annual meeting of the Psychonomic Society, Seattle, Washington.

Cooper, L. A., & Munger, M. P. (1993). Extrapolating and remembering positions along cognitive trajectories: Uses and limitations of analogies to physical motion. In N. Eilan & W. Brewer (Eds.), *Spatial representation.* London: Blackwell.

Cooper, L. A., & Schacter, D. L. (1992), Dissociations between structural and episodic representations of visual objects. *Current Directions in Psychological Science, 1,* 141–146.

Cooper, L. A., Schachter, D. L., Ballesteros, S., & Moore, C. (1992). Priming and recognition of transformed three-dimensional objects: Effects of size and reflection. *Journal of Experimental Psychology: Learning, Memory, and Cognition, 18,* 43–57.

Cooper, L. A., Schacter, D. L., & Moore, C. (1991, November). *Orientation affects both structural and episodic representations of three-dimensional objects.* Paper presented at the 32nd annual meeting of the Psychonomic Society, San Francisco, CA.

Corballis, M. C. (1988). Recognition of disoriented shapes. *Psychological Review, 95,* 115–123.

Corballis, M. C., Zbrodoff, N. J., & Roldan, C. E. (1976). What's up in a mental rotation? *Perception & Psychophysics, 19,* 525–530.

Farrell, J. E., Shepard, R. N. (1981). Shape, orientation, and apparent rotational motion. *Journal of Experimental Psychology: Human Perception and Performance, 7,* 477–486.

Freyd, J. J. (1987). Dynamic mental representations. *Psychological Review, 94,* 427–438.

Freyd, J. J., & Finke, R. A. (1984). Representational momentum. *Journal of Experimental Psychology: Learning, Memory, and Cognition, 10,* 126–132.

Freyd, J. J., & Finke, R. A. (1985). A velocity effect for representational momentum. *Bulletin of the Psychonomic Society, 23,* 443–446.

Freyd, J. J., & Johnson, J. Q. (1987). Probing the time course of representational momentum. *Journal of Experimental Psychology: Learning, Memory, and Cognition, 13,* 259–268.

Gibson, J. J. (1979). *The ecological approach to visual perception*. Boston: Houghton Mifflin

Gilden, D. L. (1991). On the origins of dynamical awareness. *Psychological Review, 98*, 554–568.

Gillam, B. (1972). Perceived common rotary motion of ambiguous stimuli as a criterion of perceptual grouping. *Perception & Psychophysics, 11*, 99–101.

Helmholtz, H. von. (1962). *Treatise on physiological optics*. New York: Dover. (Original work published 1866)

Hochberg, J. (1956). Perception: Toward the recovery of a definition. *Psychological Review, 63*, 400–405.

Hochberg, J. (1968). In the mind's eye. In R. N. Haber (Ed.), *Contemporary, theory and research in visual perception* (pp. 304–331). NY: Appleton-Century-Crofts.

Hochberg, J. (1974). Higher-order stimuli and interresponse coupling in the perception of the visual world. In R. B. Macleod & H. L. Pick (Eds.), *Perception: Essays in honor of James J. Gibson* (pp. 17–39). Ithaca, NY: Cornell University Press.

Hochberg, J. (1988). Visual perception. In R. Atkinson, R. Herrnstein, G. Lindzey, & D. Luce (Eds.), *Stevens' handbook of experimental psychology, Vol.1* (pp. 295–375). NY: Wiley

Hochberg, J., & Beck, J. (1954). Apparent spatial arrangement and perceived brightness. *Journal of Experimental Psychology, 47*, 263–266.

Hochberg, J., & Cooper, L. A. (In prep.) *As the cube turns*.

Hochberg, J., & Peterson, M. A. (1987). Piecemeal organization and cognitive components in object perception: Perceptually coupled responses to moving objects. *Journal of Experimental Psychology: General, 116*, 370–380.

Hornbostel, E. M. von (1922). Ueber optische inversion. *Psychologische Forschung, 1*, 130–156.

Intraub, H. (1985). Visual dissociation: An illusory conjunction of pictures and forms. *Journal of Experimental Psychology: Human Perception and Performance. 7*, 604–610.

Kaiser, M. K., & Proffitt, D. R. (1987). Observers' sensitivity to dynamic anomalies in collisions. *Perception and Psychophysics, 42*, 275–280.

Koffka, K. (1935). *Principles of Gestalt psychology*. NY: Harcourt, Brace & World.

Kohler, W. (1929). *Gestalt psychology*. NY: Liveright.

Mach, E, (1959). *The analysis of sensation and the relation of the physical to the psychical*.(S. Waterlow, Trans.) NY: Dover. (Original work published 1906)

Marr, D. (1982). *Vision*. San Francisco: Freeman.

McCloskey, M., Washburn, A., & Felch, L. (1983). Intuitive physics: The straight-down belief and its origin. *Journal of Experimental Psychology: Learning, Memory, and Cognition, 9*, 636–649.

Munger, M. P., & Cooper, L. A. (in prep.). *What is represented in representational momentum?*

Peterson, M. A., & Hochberg, J. (1983). Opposed-set measurement procedure: A quantitative analysis of the role of local cues and intention in form perception. *Journal of Experimental Psychology: Human Perception and Performance, 9*, 183–193.

Proffitt, D. R., Gilden, D. J., Kaiser, M. K., & Whelan, S. M. (1988). The effect of configural orientation on perceived trajectory in apparent motion. *Perception & Psychophysics, 43*, 465–474.

Rock, I. (1973). *Orientation and form*. New York: Academic Press.

Rock, I. (1983). *The logic of perception*. Cambridge, MA: MIT Press.

Runeson, S. (1975). Visual prediction of collision with natural and non-natural motion functions. *Perception & Psychophysics, 18*, 261–266.

Schacter, D. L., Cooper, L. A., & Delaney, S. M. (1990a). Implicit memory for unfamiliar objects depends on access to structural descriptions. *Journal of Experimental Psychology: General, 119*, 9–24.

Schacter, D. L., Cooper, L. A., & Delaney, S. M. (1990b). Implicit memory for visual objects and the structural description system. *Bulletin of the Psychonomic Society, 28*, 367–372.

Schacter, D. L., Cooper, L. A., Delaney, S. M., Peterson, M. A., & Tharan, M. (1991). Implicit memory for possible and impossible objects: Constraints on the construction of structural descriptions. *Journal of Experimental Psychology: Learning, Memory, & Cognition, 17*, 3–19.

Shepard, R. N. (1984). Ecological constraints on internal representation: Resonant kinematics of perceiving, imagining, thinking, and dreaming. *Psychological Review, 91*, 417–447.

Shepard, R. N., & Cooper, L. A. (1982). *Mental images and their transformations.* Cambridge, MA: MIT Press.

Shepard, R. N., & Farrell., J. E. (1985). Representations of the orientations of shapes. *Acta Psychologica, 59*, 104–121.

Shepard, R. N., & Judd, S. A. (1976). Perceptual illusion of rotation of three-dimensional objects. *Science, 191*, 952–954.

Shepard, R. N., & Metzler, J. (1971). Mental rotation of three-dimensional objects. *Science, 171*, 701–703.

Sperling, G. (1960). The information available in brief visual presentations. *Psychological Monographs. 74* (11, Whole no. 498).

Wallach, H. (1948) Brightness constancy and the nature of achromatic colors. *Journal of Experimental Psychology, 38*, 310–324.

IV PERCEPTUAL THEORY

10 The Foundations of Veridical and Illusory Perception

R. H. Day
La Trobe University, Victoria, Australia

It is proposed here to present a general theory in terms of which perception in its veridical and nonveridical (or illusory) aspects can be comprehended and explained. The theory is an expansion and refinement of views set out earlier (Day, 1989). A basic assumption is that veridical and illusory perception are coextensive and can be accounted for in the same terms, and much of what follows is concerned with demonstrating the validity of that assumption. The essential identity of veridical and illusory perception implies that an explanation can be developed via the data of either. The present explanation is based mainly on the data of illusory perception.

Perception is treated throughout as the representation to the individual of real, physical states of affairs of both the external environment and of the self. The former include objects, persons, scenery events, and extended terrain and spaces. States of the self include postures, movements, and activities such as reaching, standing, running, and speaking. Although it is obvious that our own physical states are represented to us — we readily and immediately perceive what we are doing — this aspect of perception is usually overlooked in the theoretical treatments, with notable exceptions (see Gibson, 1979; Howard, 1982).

Another basic assumption is that perception as representation is essentially a biological process in that it serves the functions of adaption and survival in the natural physical environments in which humans have evolved. The natural environments are taken to include plains, forests, hills, caves, and sky but not the constructed environments of houses, streets, and vehicles. This view is of particular significance in connection with illusory perception in constructed spaces.

Another point to make by way of introduction is that a good deal of perception involves several sensory modes. We frequently see, hear, and feel an object at the same time. Furthermore, a stimulus correlate for a particular property of a state of affairs perceived via one mode can derive from stimulation via another. For example, proprioceptive correlates are involved in visual distance perception and vestibular correlates in visual orientation perception. It follows that a general theory must account for both intermodal and unimodal perception in their veridical and illusory aspects.

The theory is outline is as follows. Numerous features of the proximal stimulus array, also known as cues, are commonly correlated with one property of a physical state of affairs. In the normal course of events these multiple stimulus correlates undergo a process of integration leading to a veridical or near-veridical representation of that property or attribute in perception. The stimulus correlates of a particular physical property can be experimentally manipulated in a variety of ways. They can be varied in number, arranged so that they are in conflict, artificially contrived in the absence of the physical property from which they normally derive, and selected so that they are equally representative of two or more situations. No matter how the proximal correlates (i.e., cues) are manipulated, they are combined in the same way as naturally occurring correlates. However, even though the outcome is a unitary representation, it is illusory with each type of manipulation giving rise to characteristic groups of illusions. These include underconstancy with reduction in the number of stimulus correlates, compromise representations with conflicting cues, the appearance of properties where none exist physically when artificial correlates are contrived, and unstable (fluctuating) representations when the correlates derive equally from two or more situations.

PHYSICAL PROPERTIES AND THEIR STIMULUS CORRELATES

Proximal Stimulus Correlates (Cues)

Physical states of both the environment and the individual give rise to patterns of energy at the sensory receptors. These patterns, which usually vary over time as well as space, are the proximal stimuli that initiate the chain of neural activity and culminate in a perceptual representation. Certain features of these proximal energy patterns correlate with particular properties (or attributes) of a physical state of affairs. For example, both the size of the retinal image and the degree of convergence of the eyes correlate with the size of an external object. Likewise, a pattern of stimulation in the joints, tendons, and muscles of an arm correlates with its position. A point to be emphasized is that the features of the proximal stimulus pattern are not simply replicas or necessarily even rough copies of the physical properties that give rise to them. Rather they correlate with them. For example, binocular disparity is in no sense a replica of observer–object distance; it is a correlate of it. This view was first adumbrated clearly by Gibson (1950, 1959) and is emphasized here.

Proximal correlates of physical properties are commonly referred to as cues. Here the two terms are treated as synonymous and used interchangeably. However, the term cue is frequently used in reference to an external physical situation rather than to a proximal feature of the stimulation. Overlay as a cue for distance is a case in point. It is sometimes used with reference to physical overlap of objects at different distances along an axis, as depicted in countless textbooks. Here overlay refers to a particular spatiotemporal pattern of light at the retina. The distinction being made is that between distal and proximal stimuli, introduced originally in Gestalt psychology (see Pastore, 1971) and clearly made by Gibson (1968) between sources of stimulation and patterns of receptor energy.

Two characteristics of stimulus correlates are to be noted; they are commonly complex or higher order and can involve features that do not derive directly from the property itself. The first characteristic is central to Gibsons' (1950, 1959) argument. He has emphasized the texturing, patterning, and movement of stimulus correlates and their temporal transformations consequent on observer movement. Attention has already been drawn to the second characteristic. It is that proximal correlates do not necessarily derive directly from an object or event. Vergence as a cue for distance (Hochberg, 1971), distance as a cue for size (Gilinsky, 1955; Holway & Boring, 1941), and shape as a cue for direction of motion in depth (Day & Power, 1963; Power, 1967) are cases in point.

Multiple Stimulus Correlates of Single Properties

Numerous features of a proximal stimulus array are commonly correlated with a single attribute of a physical situation. This was clearly recognized by Gibson when he pointed out that "two or more variables of stimulation can yield the same quality of experience as in the case of visual depth or the case of kinesthesis where the variables are ordinarily multiple and concomitant" (Gibson, 1959, p. 466).

Multiple stimulus correlates of single attributes are well documented in the cases of visual depth and distance (see Hochberg, 1971) and auditory direction (see Gulick, 1971; Irvine, 1986). They occur also in the cases of visual edge (Day, 1987), visual size (Day & Parks, 1989), and numerous other properties, but are neither well documented nor widely recognized.

Therefore, after briefly reviewing the cues for visual depth and distance and auditory direction, some less recognized instances of multiple correlates are described.

Visual Depth and Distance.   The stimulus correlates for the third dimension of space have been extensively studied and documented (see Boring, 1942; Gibson, 1950; Hochberg, 1971) and a convenient system of classification has been devised by Sekuler and Blake (1985). A version of this is shown in Fig. 10.1

A distinction is made between oculomotor and visual cues with the former divided into accommodation and vergence and the latter into binocular and monocular cues. Monocular cues are then broken down into static and motion cues.

Two points relevant to present considerations can be made. First, visual accommodation as a cue for distance remains controversial (Hochberg, 1971; Kunnapas, 1968; Sekuler & Blake, 1985) and if it operates at all, it does so for only some observers under narrowly specified conditions (Fisher & Cuiffreda, 1988). Second, the stimulus correlates of depth and distance vary widely in respect to the range over which they are effective. For example, vergence works up to about 20m (Gibson, 1950), binocular disparity up to about 450m (Davson, 1980), and overlay, linear perspective, and aerial perspective presumably as far as the visible horizon.

Auditory Direction.   The stimulus correlates for the egocentric direction of a sound source are shown in Fig. 10.2. The main division is between auditory and head cues, with the former consisting of binaural and monaural cues and the latter of head-position and head-movement cues. Binaural and monaural cues are well documented (see Gulick, 1971; Irvine, 1986; Wightman, Kistler, & Aruda, 1989). The former consist of interaural time-of-arrival differences and interaural intensity differences, and the latter of direction-dependent interactions of incoming sounds with the folds of the pinnas (see Wightman & Kistler, 1989a). Head-position (Day, 1968)

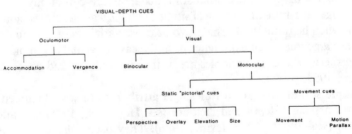

FIG. 10.1. Some of the multiple stimulus correlates (cues) for visual depth.

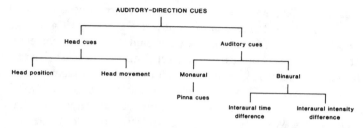

FIG. 10.2. Some of the multiple stimulus correlates (cues) for auditory direction.

and head-movement cues (Wallach, 1939, 1940), presumably involving both muscular and labyrinthine receptors, are critical for the resolution of ambiguities of apparent direction that arise with binaural cues (see Day, 1969).

Visual Edge. Physical edges generate numerous proximal stimulus correlates some of which have been described by Day (1987), who has distinguished between two-dimensional (2D) edges on a surface and the three-dimensional (3D) edges of objects and layered surfaces. The correlates of these two classes of edge are set out in Fig. 10.3. Those for 2D edges are divided into static and moving correlates. The first group consists of step-function discontinuities in surface luminance, color, and texture. The movement cues include discontinuities in the amplitude and direction of the movement of texture elements. The stimulus correlates of 3D edges, that is, corners and ridges, consist of various cues to depth (see Fig. 10.1) along with discontinuities correlated with 2D edges. For example, a ridge formed at the junction of two surfaces may give rise to retinal disparity, motion parallax, and linear perspective, along with step function differences in surface luminance and texture density. It can be noted that Kaplan (1969) showed that the differential rate of accretion and deletion of texture elements as surfaces at different depths move relative to each other also serve as cues to 3D edges.

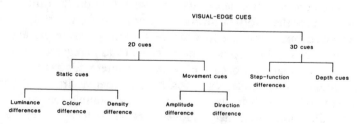

FIG. 10.3. Some probable stimulus correlates (cues) for visual edge.

Visual Size.   Apparent visual size has been largely considered from the standpoint of size–distance relationships (see Kaufman, 1974; Rock, 1975). As a result only scant attention has been paid to stimulus correlates other than those deriving from observer–object distance. At least five other cues for size can be identified, four of which are well documented and one of which is speculative. These five are the stimulus correlates of distance (Hochberg, 1971), the visual angle of the object itself (Epstein & Landauer, 1969; Hastorf & Way, 1952; Rock & McDermott, 1964), the size of an enclosing frame (Rock & Ebenholtz, 1959), the size of adjacent objects (see Gregory & Gombrich, 1973), and the size of the structure of which the feature is a part. The last mentioned cue has yet to be systematically investigated. It is strongly suggested by the Müller-Lyer illusion and its numerous derivatives (see Day & Duffy, 1988) but has not so far been investigated independently of illusory effects.

Proximal Correlates for Other Properties.   The cases of visual distance, auditory direction, visual edge, and visual size are intended simply as examples of physical properties for which there is clear evidence of multiple cues. It is emphasized that the correlates listed for each of these properties are not necessarily complete. There are conceivably others so far unidentified. In this regard, it can be noted that Rosenblum, Carello, and Pastore (1987) recently showed that the Doppler effect and amplitude change along with interaural time differences are correlated with a moving sound source. There are numerous other cases, including visual transparency (Metelli, 1974), visual orientation (see Howard, 1982), and tactile shape (see Gibson, 1968), all of which have yet to be systematically investigated.

PERCEPTUAL INTEGRATION OF MULTIPLE CUES

Perception of a physical property such as size, shape, orientation, or depth is usually effortless, fast, and, under normal full-cue conditions, more or less veridical. The involvement of multiple cues on the one hand and the effortless emergence of a perceptual representation on the other implies a process whereby the information about the property from various cues is not only encoded but combined to produce a unitary perceptual experience. Such a process will be assumed and referred to as *perceptual integration*.

Perceptual integration occurs in respect to intermodal as well as intramodal cues. For example, cues for distance derive from the vergence movements of the eyes as well as from retinal stimulation, and cues for auditory direction from head movements as well as purely auditory stimulation. Therefore, it must be assumed that stimulus correlates derived from different sensory systems are combined in the process leading to an internal representation. It follows that perceptual integration is a higher order process that occurs "upstream" of the various sensory systems transmitting information carried by proximal correlates. Another point to be made in connection with perceptual integration is that the processes appear to be activated regardless of whether the stimulus correlates are varied in number, arranged so that they are in conflict, or contrived in the absence of the properties from which they normally derive. It is argued below that the initiation of perceptual integration by manipulated or "artificial" stimulus correlates is the basis of perceptual illusions.

EXPERIMENTAL MANIPULATIONS OF STIMULUS CORRELATES

Deliberate manipulation of the stimulus correlates of physical properties of objects and events are held to be the basis of most perceptual illusions. Therefore, before discussing the illusions themselves, four types of manipulation that have been identified require explication.

Varying the Number of Cues

Although the number of cues for a particular property of an object or event can in principle be increased or decreased, as far as is known only the effects of the latter have been investigated systematically. Reductions in the number of cues have been made for the most part in studies of visual depth and distance and auditory direction. However, as will be shown below, essentially the same manipulation has been made in experiments concerned with the isolation of particular correlates of object properties.

Cues were systematically removed in the classical experiment by Holway and Boring (1941) on visual size constancy. Binocular disparity, monocular parallax, and various static cues (see Fig. 10.1) were progressively removed by means of monocular viewing, viewing through a small aperture, and viewing in reduced illumination, respectively. The only remaining cue apart from a few patches of reflected light was the retinal image of the object itself, that is, the "visual angle" cue. In the outcome, apparent size approximated closely to visual-angle expectations. Essentially the same result was obtained by Hastorf and Way (1952) and Lichten and Lurie (1950) when they removed all cues for distance, leaving only the size of the retinal image itself.

The number of cues for the direction of a source of sound has also been systematically varied. In an investigation of the role of the pinna cues in the perception of auditory direction. Freedman and Fisher (1968) eliminated head movements, binaural intensity differences, and time differences in order to establish the role of pinna cues in the perception of auditory direction.

Cue reduction was also used in recent experiments by Rosenblum, Carello, and Pastore (1987) in their investigation of the cues involved in the perception of a moving sound source passing the listener. Each of three cues was isolated by removing the other two, and the effect of each compared with that of all three. Whereas all three cues (amplitude change, interaural time differences, and the Doppler effect) reliably indicated the time of the closest approach of a moving sound source, all three together resulted in greater accuracy.

Conflicting Cues and Cue Salience

The proximal stimulus correlates of physical properties can be deliberately arranged so that they are in conflict. In this way their relative salience can be established. In an early experiment Schriever (1925) compared the salience of binocular disparity as a correlate of relative depth with linear perspective, shading, and interposition. This was achieved by presenting stereograms pseudoscopically so that normal binocular disparity was reversed, and then progressively adding three normal cues — linear perspective, shading, and overlay. When perspective was added, the reversed disparity prevailed and the object–depth relationships appeared reversed. When shading was introduced, the appearance of depth was unstable. However, when overlay was also included, the three pictorial cues were predominant, that is, together, they proved to be more salient than the reversed disparity. However, it is to be noted that when McDonald (1962) pitted overlay alone against binocular disparity, the latter proved to be salient.

In an essentially similar way, Wightman, Kistler, and Aruda (1989) compared the relative salience of cues for auditory direction. Listeners indicated the apparent position of a wide-band source when the interaural time differences and pinna cues were at variance with each other. The former proved dominant, influencing both the apparent azimuth and elevation of the sound source.

Contrived Cues

Stimulus correlates can be artificially contrived in the absence of the physical attributes with which they are naturally correlated. The history of visual cue contrivance is closely associated with the history of art (see Gombrich, 1950). Thus apparent depth and distance have for long been convincingly simulated by the skillful and subtle contrivance of linear and aerial perspective, overlay, elevation, and the other static or "pictorial" cues. *Trompe l'oeil art* is a notable case in point (see Hagen, 1980; Pirenne, 1970).

Perhaps the best known and most widely investigated contrived cue for depth is that of binocular disparity by means of disparate figures presented separately to each eye. Wheatstone (1838) was the first to do this by means of his stereograms and mirror stereoscope (see Wade, 1983). Julesz (1960, 1971) extended this procedure using disparate random-dot stereograms in which, unlike conventional stereograms, there was no regular form or structure. The strong impression of depth not only indicated that an average disparity between two regions is sufficient to trigger stereo depth but that recognizable form is not itself a necessary precursor for the emergence of apparent depth.

Monocular parallax has also been artificially contrived. Rogers and Graham (1979, 1982, 1985) generated random-dot patterns on an oscilloscope display. These could be transformed by either movement of the observer or of the display to simulate in a two-dimensional array the parallactic movement of the elements in a three-dimensional array. The outcome was a strong impression of depth similar to that with random-dot stereograms. Indeed, Rogers and Graham's (1979) demonstrations of apparent depth from contrived monocular parallax are similar in principle to Julesz' 1971) demonstrations of depth from contrived binocular disparity.

An effect closely related to monocular parallax and generated by shearing motion in specified regions of two-dimensional random-dot patterns has been described by Royden, Baker, and Allman (1988). In this case, apparent depth depends on the duration of movement of dots relative to the long and short edges of a rectangular region containing them.

The strong impression of depth in the two-dimensional back-projected image of objects moving in depth, the kinetic depth effect or KDE (Miles, 1931; Wallach & O'Connell, 1953), is another instance of contrived stimulus correlates for depth. There is no real depth in the moving pattern on a screen. However, all of the proximal motion characteristics of a three-dimensional object as it moves in depth are preserved.

Stimulus correlates of auditory direction have also been successfully contrived in the absence of an actual source of sound at a specific egocentric location. Wightman and Kistler (1989a, 1989b) presented digitally processed noise bursts via headphones. These bursts from external sources of known direction from the listener had been individually recorded in listeners' ears close to the ear drum. They were then re-presented via headphones, that is, they were contrived in the absence of the external source. Like the KDE, the characteristics of the proximal correlates of the external states of affairs—the direction of the source—were perfectly preserved. Participants perceived the "directions" of the sounds from these contrived correlates as virtually identical to those of the real sources from which they were originally recorded.

Ambiguous Cues

Ittleson and Kilpatrick (1953) demonstrated with mathematical proofs that some of the established proximal correlates of visual depth—those of retinal size (or visual angle), illuminance, motion parallax, and binocular disparity—define an infinite family of equivalent configurations. In the well-known case of retinal size an infinitude of physical sizes at an infinitude of distances can project a retinal image of the same size. Thus retinal size as a cue for object distance is by itself ambiguous in the extreme. In the case of motion parallax the same parallax cue is provided by a family of objects whose spacing varies inversely with the difference between their velocity and that of the observer.

Retinal shape, like retinal size, is ambiguous. An infinite range of object shapes at an infinite range of angles in depth relative to the observer project the same retinal shape. As will be described in detail below, the retinal correlates of some 3D shapes are also ambiguous when viewed with one eye. A particular shape at a particular tilt in depth can project the same retinal form as another shape at another angle.

It is also to be noted that some proximal correlates of auditory direction are by themselves ambiguous (Day, 1968, 1969). A particular interaural time-of-arrival or intensity difference can derive from an infinitude of source locations and head positions.

CUE MANIPULATIONS AND THE BASIS OF PERCEPTUAL ILLUSIONS

For the most part, perception is veridical; there is generally a close accord between physical properties and their perceptual representations. Thus, under everyday conditions, apparent visual size and auditory direction more or less accord with the true state of affairs and representations of postures and movements with physical states. Such veridicality can be reasonably attributed to an adequacy of proximal stimulus correlates for the various properties of environmental situations and bodily states. However, when these correlates are deliberately manipulated in the various ways described above, the accord between the physical states and their perceptual representations breaks down. The four identified classes of manipulation both by themselves and in combination give rise to characteristic perceptual illusions.

Illusions Due to Reduction in Cues

As already noted, the effect on perceptual representation of the removal of cues has been investigated mainly in the context of the perceptual constancies – the tendency for some properties of objects to remain stable and veridical as their *direct* proximal correlates vary. Thus the apparent size of an object remains more or less constant as the observer–object distance varies and, with it, the subtended visual angle. The investigations of Holway and Boring (1941) and later of Hastorf and Way (1952) and Lichten and Lurie (1950) showed that as visual angle varies, perceptual constancy of size is sustained by other cues, including those for observer–object distance. However, with reductions in the number of cues, illusions of size occur; objects appear smaller as distance increases and larger as it decreases. The point to be made is that when the number of cues for size, including those correlated with distance, are systematically removed illusions of size occur. Put another way, the phenomenon of underconstancy of size can be regarded as a perceptual illusion consequent on the reduction of cues that normally sustain veridicality.

Holway and Boring (1941) found that with normal conditions of viewing, that is binocular vision in good light with unrestricted head movement, slight overconstancy occurs; objects appear slightly *larger* as their distance increases. Such overconstancy of size has been confirmed by numerous experiments (Chalmers, 1952; Gilinsky, 1955; Jenkin, 1957). A likely explanation is that in constructed environments such as corridors, roads, and aircraft runways, linear perspective and texture gradients are more precisely delineated than in the natural environments for which the visual system can be presumed to have evolved. This view gains some support from an experiment reported by Leibowitz and Harvey (1967). They found that overconstancy of size with unrestricted viewing was not evident in more natural outside environments.

Visual constancies occur also in respect to object shape, orientation, velocity, luminance, and color (see Day, 1969). The evidence indicates that these are also lost when the relevant cues are eliminated. It can be noted too that perceptual constancy occurs in the auditory mode; apparent direction of a sound source remains more or less stable and veridical with head rotation leading to variations in distance and consequent reduction in sound intensity (Day, 1972; Engell & Dougherty, 1971; Mohrmann, 1939). It can be presumed that were the relevant cues for distance and intensity eliminated, illusions of distance and loudness would occur.

The perceptual constancies are particular instances of veridical perception in the face of a highly variable proximal correlate of the stimulus property itself, for example, its size, shape, luminance, or velocity. This veridicality is dependent on an adequacy of other correlates, and if these are progressively reduced in number underconstancy occurs. In the present context this amounts to a class of illusions due to a particular manipulation, that of cue reduction.

Illusions Due to Conflicting Cues

Cues can also be manipulated so that they are in conflict; some may be devised so that they accord with one state of a physical attribute and others so that they accord with different states. The outcome in perception depends on the relative salience of these conflicting cues. If those according with one state are more salient than those according with another, the perceptual representation is usually that with which the salient cues correlate. So-called visual capture, the over-ruling of haptic by visual cues (Hay, Pick, & Ikeda, 1965; Tastevin, 1937) is a case in point. However, when the cues for different physical states are more or less the same in salience the outcome in perception is usually a compromise. Conflicting cues leading to a compromise representation account for a wide range of visual and haptic illusions in figures and larger scale situations.

Two groups of geometrical illusions can be identified. The first, referred to here as figural illusions, derives from a perceptual compromise between cues provided by the focal, that is, the judged feature, and cues associated with the figure of which the feature is a part. The second group, referred to as figure–ground illusions, derives from compromise between cues provided by the figure and by the ground or field in which it is located. It should be made clear that these two groups of illusions are basically the same in that both are an outcome of perceptual compromise between cues indicating different states of a physical property. The only difference is the source of cues.

Figural Illusions.   The numerous versions of the Müller-Lyer illusion (Müller-Lyer, 1889; see also Robinson, 1972) are examples of figural illusions. One version is shown in Fig. 10.4. The distance between the apex in Fig. 10.4A is the same as that in Fig. 10.4B but the latter appears markedly greater. It has been proposed (Day, 1989) that in each figure interapical extent is one cue for length and the overall extent of the figure another. These two cues are integrated in the usual way and result in a compromise representation of length. Because overall extent of Fig. 10.4A is less than that of 10.4B, the interapical length of the former appears shorter.

This explanation in terms of perceptual compromise between conflicting cues for visual extent applies also to the haptic version of the Müller-Lyer illusion (Over, 1968). It also applies to the occurrence of the illusion when

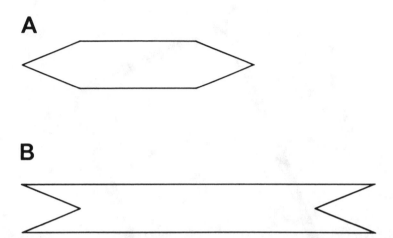

FIG. 10.4.   A version of the Müller-Lyer illusion. The distance between the apexes in A is the same as that in B but appears much less.

the Müller-Lyer figure is viewed when moving behind a narrow slit and its occurrence in the time domain (Day & Duffy, 1988).

Other geometrical illusions can be satisfactorally accounted for in essentially the same terms (Day, 1989). These include the Poggendorff, due to conflicting cues for alignment (Day & Kasperczyk, 1985; Day, Watson, & Jolly, 1986), the visual and haptic Bourdon illusion due to conflicting cues for straightness (Day, 1990) and the newly discovered arc-chevron illusion of alignment due to conflicting cues for axes of alignment (Day, Jee, & Duffy, 1989).

Figure-Ground Illusions.   When the short enclosed line in Fig. 10.5 is vertical it appears to be slightly tilted in the opposite direction to the tilt of the enclosing frame. The illusion occurs more strongly in larger scale arrangements of Fig.10.5 in which a vertical rod is enclosed either by a tilted frame, the rod-and-frame illusion (Witkin & Asch, 1948; see also Wenderoth, 1977), or more completely by a 3D tilted room (Asch & Witkin, 1948a, 1948b). Various cues to line (or rod) orientation are present in these situations. They include the orientation of the line or rod, that of a tilted rectangular field, that of the observer, and conceivably that of the larger space for example, the laboratory in which the arrangement is set up. Assuming that the line or rod, all other structures, and the observer are vertical, and the frame or room is tilted (as in Fig.10.5), there is a conflict between cues for orientation. Whereas the line is upright relative to the gravitational axis, the upright observer, and the upright, larger space, it is tilted relative to the immediately surrounding frame (or room). The

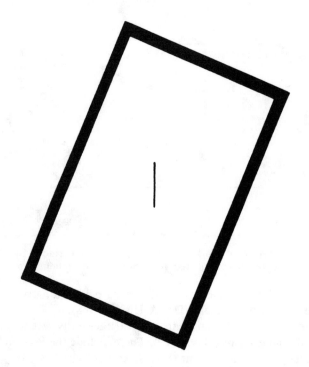

FIG. 10.5. A version of the rod-and-frame illusion. When the short enclosed line is vertical it appears to be slightly tilted in the opposite direction to the enclosing frame.

outcome of the integration of these conflicting cues is apparent tilt of the upright line in the opposite direction to the tilt of the surrounding structure.

The main point to be made about this illusion is that the short line is separate from the structure—the surrounding frame or room—the orientation of which causes the illusion of tilt. In other words, the line is not an *intrinsic* feature of the surrounding structure in the sense that the distance between the apexes in Fig. 10.4 is an intrinsic and inseparable feature of the figure. This distinction between figural and figure–ground illusions is essentially the same as that made by Müller-Lyer (1889) between illusions of confluxion (or assimilation) and illusions of contrast (see also Lewis, 1909). Both are held here to be due to the integration of conflicting cues for a physical attribute of a figure, object, or event with the result that the representation in perception is a compromise between the two states.

Figure–ground illusions occur also in relation to size and movement. A small circle in a much greater circular field appears smaller than when presented alone (Oyama, 1960). In this case it is assumed that the cues for size derive from the circle itself and the circular field in which it is located. It is worth noting that figure–ground illusions have been exploited in the entertainment industry. Individuals are photographed in the context of, for example, an oversized, chair or room and thereby appear markedly smaller than life size (see Day, 1989). Induced movement is another instance of a figure–ground illusion. A small stationary element in an enclosing, moving frame appears to move in the opposite direction to the frame when viewed by a stationary observer (Duncker, 1929; see also Day, 1978). The cues for movement from element, frame and observer are in conflict and so lead to a compromise in the form of an oppositely moving element.

Illusions Due to Contrived Cues

The main purpose of contriving stimulus correlates independently of the physical properties or attributes with which they are normally and naturally associated is to isolate them from other cues, investigate their characteristics, and demonstrate their role in perception. Thus Wheatstone's (1838) contrivance of binocular disparity showed beyond doubt that it is closely involved in the perception of depth and distance. The experiments by Julesz (1971) with random-dot stereograms and those by Rogers and Graham (1979), again with random-dot patterns, were primarily concerned with identifying the essential stimulus conditions for binocular disparity and monocular parallax, respectively. However, the point of these experiments in the present context is that when proximal correlates are so contrived, illusions of depth in the absence of real depth occur. Likewise, the contrivance on a surface of motion cues for depth, the kinetic depth effect (Wallach & O'Connell, 1953), results in a singularly convincing illusion of a 3D object moving in depth.

Cues can also be contrived so that depth relationships are apparently reversed; far objects can be contrived to look near and vice versa. Gibson (1950) did so by contriving the elevation cue—far objects higher in the visual field than near ones. The nearer of the two planar rectangles was raised above a patterned surface so that the line of regard through its lower edge intercepted the surface further away than that through the lower edge of the farther rectangle. When viewed monocularly through a small aperture the physically nearer object appeared faether and vice versa. In an essentially similar vein the apparent distance of objects has been reversed by contriving overlay (interposition) opposite to that of the actual depth relations (see Kilpatrick, 1953). This is achieved by cutting out sections of rectangles and arranging the latter so that when viewed monocularly from one position only part of the near card and all of the far card are visible.

The stimulus correlates for edge have also been contrived so that edges appear where none are actually present. Some of the multiple 2D and 3D cues for edge are set out in Fig. 10.3. It has been argued (Day, 1987) that the basis of illusory edges is the contrivance of one or more of these cues for edge in the absence of real edges. Thus in Fig. 10.6 (Kanizsa, 1979) there is a strong impression of a continuously edged bright annulus overlaying the black lines. Both the inner and the outer edges of the annulus appear to extend across the gaps between the black lines.

The cues for edge in the figure include an apparent step-function difference in brightness between the annulus and its white ground. This is due to induced enhancement of brightness between the ends of the black lines, that is, in the gaps, and induced reduction in brightness between the irregular lines (Day & Jory, 1978). The induced-brightness effects spread to partially delineated borders (Day & Jory, 1980). Another cue is the apparent overlay of the lines by the annulus, a cue emphasized in Kanizsa's (1979) explanation.

There are numerous and varied instances of illusory contours and much debate about their origins (see Petry & Meyer, 1987). The view adopted here is that when one or more of the motion or static cues for edge are artificially contrived, an illusory edge will emerge. From this standpoint illusory contours fall into the same category of perceptual illusions as illusory depth in laboratory demonstrations and pictures, and illusory directions of a source of sound through headphones. Although none of the cues for edge is by itself necessary for the occurrence of the illusion, for example, induced

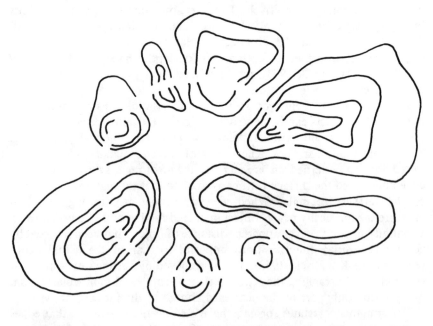

FIG. 10.6. Example of illusory contours. The physically continuous edges of the white annulus appear to be continuous. From Kanizsa (1979). Reprinted by permission.

contrast as in Fig. 10.6 (see Halpern, 1981), it seems that one by itself is sufficient. It is conceivable, but not yet confirmed, that cues for edge, like cues for visual depth and auditory direction, also vary in salience.

Stimulus correlates for both body orientation and limb position and movement have also been contrived with consequent illusory effects. Centrifugation of the whole body generates a gravito-inertial force different in both direction and magnitude to that of gravity. If the individual is facing in the direction of movement the direction of the force acting on the labyrinthine otoliths accords with that which normally occurs when the body is tilted laterally. In the dark the gravitationally upright individual undergoes an experience of lateral tilt (Graybiel, 1952; see also Howard, 1982).

Experiments by Goodwin, McCloskey, and Mathews (1972a, 1972b) have shown that if a muscle is vibrated at 100 Hz then the joint about which the muscle operates appears to move as if the muscle were lengthening. Furthermore, the position of the joint at any moment is perceived to be as if the vibrated muscle is stretched. Thus a kinesthetic illusion follows activation of a muscle system by means of externally applied vibration. Presumably the pattern of stimulation at the receptors accords with that occurring during limb movement and when the limb is in a particular position.

Illusions Due to Ambiguous Cues

Certain stimulus correlates can be deliberately contrived so that together they are equally representative of two or more physical states of affairs. The outcome of this arranged ambiguity is repeated fluctuations in perception between the physical states of which the cues are representative. Mach described such unstable perception in a card bent to resemble a book as illustrated in Fig. 10.7: "The card . . . whose edge *b e* when turned outwards towards me is in a vertical position, assumes, when I succeed in seeing *b e* depressed, a recumbent position, like that of a book lying open upon my table, with the result that *b* appears further away from *e*" (Mach, 1887/1959, p. 223 [italics added]).

Thus the object in Fig. 10.7 can be seen as upright with the central ridge b e near relative to the edges a d and c f or as nearly horizontal with b e relatively far. The cues for relative depth and orientation are the same for these two physical states with the result that the figure alternates between the two possible forms. That is to say, perception is rendered unstable.

Although the unstable perceptual effects are commonly demonstrated with 2D figures like that in Fig. 10.6, they occur also with the 3D objects from which the former derive. Fluctuations between veridical and illusory forms occur with 3D "skeletal" cubes, rhomboids, and "staircases." They

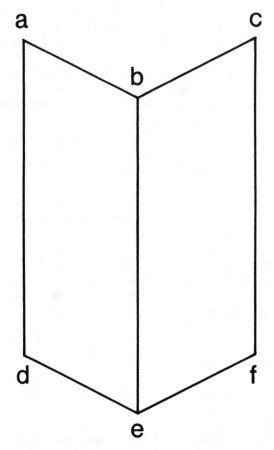

FIG. 10.7. A two-dimensional version of Mach's bent card in which the apparent depth relationships appear to fluctuate. The same fluctuations occur with a three-dimensional bent card when it is viewed with one eye.

occur also with transparent glass cubes, as Mach himself pointed out, and with prisms. Fisher (1968) assembled various "skeletal" forms that in 2D and presumably 3D forms fluctuate in a manner similar to Fig. 10.7.

Perceptual instability is not confined to combinations of cues for depth and orientation, as in the 2D or 3D forms of Fig. 10.6. It occurs also with ambiguous combinations of cues for direction of movement and orientation. The Sinsteden "windmill" (see Boring, 1942) is a case in point; the vanes of a silhouetted windmill seem to rotate clockwise when they are apparently orientated in one plane in depth and counterclockwise when orientated in another.

A point to be stressed is that these fluctuations between veridical and illusory perception occur for the most part in highly contrived situations from which all but the ambiguous combination of cues have been excluded. The addition of other cues for depth or orientation to 3D structures like that in Fig. 10.6 straightaway restore stability. For example, the fluctuations between the two states cease when the 3D objects are viewed with two eyes, suggesting that binocular disparity removes any ambiguity in depth relationships and so renders the perceptual representation stable and veridical. It can therefore be expected that 2D figures will also be stabilized by the addition of cues for depth. That this is so was shown by Wong (1970; see also Day, 1969), who stabilized figures like that in Fig. 10.6 by the addition of texture gradients consonant with b e being either relatively near or far.

Perceptual stabilization does not necessarily result in veridical perception; the stabilized outcome can also be illusory. Day and Power (1963; see also Day, 1969) showed that when a planer ellipse rotating in depth is viewed with one eye its apparent direction of rotation fluctuates between a clockwise and counterclockwise movement. It is held that this is because the stimulus correlate for rotary movement—expansion and contraction of the retinal projection—is the same for the two directions of rotation. Power and Day (1973) went on to show that apparent direction can be stabilized to accord with the true or illusory direction of rotation by means of a perspective pattern on the two surfaces of the ellipse.

STIMULUS CORRELATES AND COGNITIVE PROCESSES

None of the preceding argument is meant to imply that perception occurs independently of cognition. The question is not whether cognition is implicated in perception, but rather with how it is implicated. Evidence from three sources suggests an answer to this question.

It is commonly found that illusions associated with geometrical figures decline in magnitude with repeated judgments, especially when it is required to adjust the figure to eliminate the illusion (Judd, 1902; see also Coren & Girgus, 1978). This outcome is usually referred to as the "practice effect." However, closer consideration of the data shows that progressive decrement does not occur for *all* participants. For some there is no change in the size of the illusion over trials, for some an increase, and for others a decrease (see Day, 1962). Illusions in geometrical figures are interpreted here in terms of conflicts between cues for a particular attribute. If, as suggested earlier (Day, 1989), the individual learns by appropriate and possibly implicit reinforcement to use one cue rather than another, a progressive change in the size of the illusion can be expected. If the reinforced cue is valid then the direction of change will be toward veridicality—the usual practice effect. If, on the other hand, the reinforced cue is invalid the change will be in the direction of greater illusion. It can also be presumed that if neither cue comes to be favored over the other, no change on the magnitude of the illusion would occur.

Some illusions, notably the Müller-Lyer and Poggendorff, decrease with age, others, including the Ponzo, increase, and others remain more or less stable (see Coren & Girgus, 1978, for a review). Changes in illusions with age can be interpreted in essentially the same way as changes due to repeated judgment. It is reasonable to expect that when there are valid and invalid cues for the state of a physical property the former will come to be favored over the latter during the course of perceptual development. Put another way, it can be expected that valid cues will be reinforced and so come to be used to a greater degree than invalid ones. Essentially the same reasoning can be applied to the increase in visual size constancy with age as found by Leibowitz & Heisel (1958), Leibowitz and Judisch (1967), and Farquar and Leibowitz (1971).

Finally, marked differences occur in the size of some illusions between individuals reared in different cultures (see Segall, Campbell, & Herskovits, 1966). Again it can be expected that the conflicting cues associated with geometrical and other illusions vary between different physical environments and in the course of development come to be differentially reinforced.

In summary, if the physical attributes of objects, situations, and events give rise to a multiplicity of proximal correlates, individuals are likely to come to favor the valid over the less valid correlates as a result of reinforcement. In other words, we learn which cues are the more valid and which are less so.

SUMMARY AND CONCLUDING COMMENTS

Hochberg (1988) distinguished between attempts to explain perception primarily in terms of stimulus patterns, neurophysiological processes, and psychological principles that cannot be derived from the first two. The explanation set out here belongs in the first class but has a dash of the second. The starting point for the argument is that many physical attributes of situations and events in the physical world, including those of individuals themselves, are numerously and variously characterized in the proximal stimulus. In other words, numerous features of the proximal patterns of stimulation are correlated with a particular property of a situation or event in the physical world. A good deal of research on perception has been devoted to verifying and contriving these proximal correlates – or cues as they have come commonly to be called. Cues have been systematically varied – usually reduced – in number, thrown into conflict so that some represent one value of an attribute and others another value, contrived in the absence of the attribute with which they normally correlate, and selected so that together they are correlated with two or more situations, that is, contrived to be ambiguous.

All of these clever manipulations result in nonveridical perception — things appear smaller as they get further away, lines appear to be longer or shorter than they really are, sounds seem to come from the wrong direction, an arm appears to be moving when it is stationary, and the observer feels to be tilted when gravitationally upright. What these outcomes indicated is that no matter how cues are selected, contrived, or arranged they are integrated to produce a unitary and meaningful representation of the state of affairs. Whether that representation is veridical or nonveridical depends largely on whether the stimulus correlates are those naturally available or artificial in the sense of being deliberately manipulated in the ways described here. Incidentally, it is not claimed that the four types of manipulation and the illusions that occur in consequence of these are the only types; there may well be others.

The data from experiments on the effects of repeated judgments of illusions, in particular illusions in geometrical figures, and on the difference in the variations in the magnitude of illusions with age and cultural affiliation suggest certain stimulus cues come to be preferred to others. It can be presumed that cue preferences leading to change of illusion magnitude with practice, decreases or increases in illusions with age, differences in illusions and perceptual constancy between cultural groups result from learning by reinforcement to favor certain cues and not others. The nature of the reinforcement — whether it derives from unrecognized responses by the experimenter, from the actions of the individual following perception, or other sources — is for the time being a matter for conjecture. It is also one of considerable significance for a more complete understanding of perception and, therefore, an issue for sustained inquiry.

Finally, there is the question of whether perception is direct, as Gibson has so forcefully contended, or mediated in the manner originally proposed by von Helmholtz. The data from experiments on perceptual illusions indicates that both these views are valid. Whether one rather than the other view is adopted seems to depend on the angle from which perception is approached. If it is approached entirely by way of the proximal stimulus array and its intrinsic correlates, its directness is immediately evident. Regardless of whether the correlates are natural and numerous, natural and limited in number, contrived, that is, artificial, or selected so that they are ambiguous, a unitary and meaningful representation results. All that appears to be necessary is an impingent pattern of energy carrying natural or artificial correlates. On the other hand, certain correlates can as a result of practice, age, or cultural background come to be favored over others. In short, perception appears to be direct in the sense of resulting from the stimulus correlates that are integrated but mediated from the standpoint of those that as a result of experience come to be more or less salient than others.

ACKNOWLEDGMENTS

Almost all of the research by the author and his colleagues cited in this chapter was funded by the Australian Research Council, whose assistance is gratefully acknowledged. I also acknowledge with thanks the considerable help given by Erica Stecher and Greg Savage in the preparation of the chapter for publication, and Vladimir Kohout and Rosemary Williams in preparation of the figures.

REFERENCES

Asch, S. E., & Witkin, H. A. (1948a). Studies in space orientation: I. Perception of the upright with displaced visual fields. *Journal of Experimental Psychology, 38*, 325–337.

Asch, S. E., & Witkin, H. A. (1948b). Studies in space orientation. II. Perception of the upright with displaced visual fields and with body tilted. *Journal of Experimental Psychology, 38*, 455–477.

Boring, E. G. (1942). *Sensation and perception in the history of experimental psychology*. New York: Appleton-Century.

Chalmers, E. L. (1952). Monocular and binocular cues in the perception of size and distance. *American Journal of Psychology, 65*, 415–423.

Coren, S., & Girgus, J. S. (1978). *Seeing is deceiving: The psychology of visual illusion*. Hillsdale, NJ: Lawrence Erlbaum Associates.

Davson, H. (1980). *Physiology of the eye*. Edinburgh: Churchill Livingston.

Day, R. H. (1962). The effects of repeated trials and prolonged fixation on error in the Muller-lyer figure. *Psychological Monographs: General and Applied, 76* (14, Serial No. 533).

Day, R. H. (1968). Perceptual constancy of auditory direction with head rotation. *Nature, 219*, 501–502.

Day, R. H. (1969). *Human perception*. Sydney: Australia: Wiley.

Day, R. H. (1972). Visual-auditory distance constancy. *Nature, 238*, 277–228.

Day, R. H. (1978). Induced visual movement as nonveridical resolution of displacement ambiguity. *Perception and Psychophysics, 23*, 205–209.

Day, R. H. (1987). Cues for edge and the origin of illusory contours: An alternative approach. In S. Petry & G. E. Meyer (Eds.), *The perception of illusory contours* (pp. 53–61). New York: Springer-Verlag.

Day, R. H. (1989). Natural and artificial cues, perceptual compromise and the basis of veridical and illusory perception. In D. Vickers & P. L. Smith (Eds.), *Human information processing: Measures and mechanisms* (pp. 107–129). North-Holland: Elsevier Science Publishers.

Day, R. H. (1990). The Bourdon illusion in haptic space. *Perception and Psychophysics, 47*, 400–404.

Day, R. H., & Duffy, F. M. (1988). Illusions of time and extent when the Muller-Lyer figure moves in an aperture. *Perception and Psychophysics, 44*, 205–210.

Day, R. H., Jee, F. M., & Duffy, F. M. (1989). Visual misalignment in arc and chevron figures. *Journal of Experimental Psychology, 15*, 762–770.

Day, R. H., & Jory, M. K. (1978). Subjective contours, visual acuity, and line contrast. In J. C. Armington, J. Krauskopf, & B. R. Wooten (Eds.), *Visual psychophysics and physiology* (pp. 331–340). New York: Academic Press.

Day, R. H., & Jory, M. K. (1980). A note on a second stage in the formation of illusory contours. *Perception and Psychophysics, 27,* 89–91.

Day, R. H., & Kasperczyk, R. T. (1985). Apparent displacement of lines and dots in a parallel-line figure: A clue to the basis of the Poggendorff effect. *Perception and Psychophysics, 38,* 74–80.

Day, R. H., & Parks, T. E. (1989). To exorcise a ghost from the perceptual machine. In M. Hershenson (Ed.), *The moon illusion* (pp. 343–350). Hillsdale, NJ: Lawrence Erlbaum Associates.

Day, R. H., & Power, R. P. (1963). Frequency of apparent reversal of rotary motion in depth as a function of shape and pattern. *Australian Journal of Psychology, 15,* 162–174.

Day, R. H., Watson, W. L., & Jolly, W. J. (1986). The Poggendorff displacement effect with only three dots. *Perception and Psychophysics, 39,* 351–354.

Duncker, K. (1929). Uber induzierte Bewegung (ein Beitrag zur Theorie Optisch Wahrgenommener (On induced movement: A contribution to the theory of visual perception). *Psychologische Forschung, 12,* 180–259.

Engel, G. R., & Dougherty, W. G. (1971). Visual-auditory distance constancy. *Nature, 234,* 308.

Epstein, W., & Landauer, A. A. (1969). Size and distance judgments under reduced conditions of viewing. *Perception and Psychophysics, 6,* 269–272.

Farquar, M., & Leibowitz, H. W. (1971). The magnitude of the Ponzo illusion as a function of age for large and for small stimulus configurations. *Psychonomic Science, 25,* 97–99.

Fisher, G. H. (1968). *The frameworks for perceptual localization.* Newcastle-Upon-Tyne, Department of Psychology. (Library of congress, catalogue card no. 68–8554).

Fisher, S. K., & Cuiffreda, K. J. (1988). Accommodation and apparent distance. *Perception, 17,* 609–621.

Freedman, S. J., & Fisher, H. G. (1968). The role of the pinna in auditory localization. In S. Freedman (Ed.), *The neuropsychology of spatially oriented behavior* (pp. 135–152). Homewood, IL: Dorsey Press.

Gibson, J. J. (1950). *The perception of the visual world.* Boston: Houghton Mifflin.

Gibson, J. J. (1959). Perception as a function of stimulation. In Sigmund Koch (Ed.), *Psychology: A study of science* (pp. 456–501). New York: McGraw-Hill.

Gibson, J. J. (1968). *The senses considered as perceptual systems.* London: George Allen & Unwin LTD.

Gibson, J. J. (1979). *The ecological approach to visual perception.* Boston: Houghton Mifflin.

Gilinsky, A. S. (1955). The effect of attitude upon the perception of size. *American Journal of Psychology, 68,* 173–192.

Gombrich, E. H. (1950). *The story of art.* New York: Phaidon Publishers.

Goodwin, G. M., McCloskey, D. I., & Mathews, P. C. B. (1972a). Proprioceptive illusions induced by muscle vibration: Contribution by muscle spindles to perception? *Science, 175,* 1382–1384.

Goodwin, G. M., McCloskey, D. I., & Mathews, P. C. B. (1972b). A systematic distortion of position sense produced by muscle vibration. *Journal of Physiology 221,* 8–9.

Graybiel, A. (1952). The oculograsic illusion. *AMA Archives of Ophthalmology,* 48, 605–615.

Gregory, R. L., & Gombrich, E. H. (Eds.). (1973). *Illusion in nature and art.* London: Gerald Duckworth.

Gulick, W. L. (1971). *Hearing, physiology and psychophysics.* New York: Oxford University Press.

Hagen, M. A. (1980). *Alberti's window: The projective model of pictorial information. The perception of pictures* (Vol. 1, E. C. Carterette & M. P. Friedman, Eds.). New York: Academic Press.

Halpern, D. F. (1981). The determinants of illusory-contour perception. *Perception, 10,* 199-213.

Hastorf, A. H., & Way, K. S. (1952). Apparent size with and without distance cues. *Journal of General Psychology, 47,* 181-188.

Hay, J. C., Pick, H. L., & Ikeda, K. (1965). Visual capture produced by prism spectacles. *Psychonomic Science, 2,* 215-216.

Hochberg, J. (1988). Visual perception. In R. C. Atkinson, R. J. Herrnstein, G. Lindzey, & R. D. Luce (Eds.), *Steven's handbook of experimental psychology: Vol. 1. Perception and motivation* (2nd ed., pp. 195-276). New York: Wiley.

Hochberg, J. E. (1971). Perception, space and movement. In J. W. Kling & Lorrin A. Riggs (Eds.), *Woodworth & Schlosberg's experimental psychology* (pp. 475-550). London: Methuen & Co.

Holway, A. F., & Boring, E. G. (1941). Determinants of apparent visual size with distance variant. *American Journal of Psychology, 54,* 21-37.

Howard, I. P. (1982). *Human visual orientation.* New York: Wiley.

Irvine, D. R. F. (1986). *The auditory brainstem.* Berlin: Springer-Verlag.

Ittelson, W. H., & Kilpatrick, F. P. (1953). Equivalent configurations and the monocular and binocular distorted rooms. In F. P. Kilpatrick (Ed.), *Human behavior from the transactional point of view* (pp. 41-55). Princeton: Institute for Associated Research.

Jenkin, N. (1957). Effects of varied distance on short-range size judgments. *Journal of Experimental Psychology, 54,* 327-331.

Judd, C. H. (1902) Practice and its effects on the perception of illusions. *Psychological Review, 8,* 27-39.

Julesz, B. (1960). Binocular depth perception of computer-generated patterns. *Bell System Technical Journal, 39,* 1125-1162.

Julesz, B. (1971). *Foundations of cyclopean perception.* Chicago: The University of Chicago Press.

Kanizsa, G. (1979). *Organization in vision: Essays on gestalt perception.* New York: Praeger Publishers.

Kaplan, G. A. (1969). Kinetic disruption of optical texture: The perception of depth at an edge. *Perception and Psychophysics, 6,* 193-198.

Kaufman, L. (1974). *Sight and mind: An introduction to visual perception.* Oxford: Oxford University Press.

Kilpatrick, F. P. (1953). *Human behavior from the transactional point of view.* Princeton: Institute for associated research.

Künnapas, T. (1968). Distance perception as a function of available visual cues. *Journal of Experimental Psychology, 77,* 523-579.

Leibowitz, H. W., & Harvey, L. O. (1967). Size matching as a function of instructions in a naturalistic environment. *Journal of Experimental Psychology, 74,* 378-382.

Leibowitz, H. W., & Heisel, M. A. (1958). L'evolution de l'illusion de Ponzo en fonction de l'age. [Development of the Ponzo illusion as a function of age]. *Archives de Psychologie, 36,* 328-331.

Leibowitz. H. W., & Judisch, J. M. (1967). The relationship between age and the magnitude of the Ponzo illusion. *American Journal of Psychology, 80,* 105-109.

Lewis, E. O. (1909). Confluxion and contrast effects in the Müller-Lyer illusion. *British Journal of Psychology, 3,* 21-41.

Lichten, W., & Lurie, S. (1950). A new technique for the study of perceived size. *American Journal of Psychology, 63,* 280-282.

Mach, E. (1959). *The analysis of sensations* (C. M. Williams, Trans.). New York: Dover. (Original work published 1887)

McDonald, R. P. (1962). An artifact of the Brunswick ratio. *American Journal of Psychology, 75,* 152-154.

Metelli, F. (1974). Achromatic color conditions in the perception of transparency. In R. B. MacLeod & H. L. Pick, (Eds.), *Perception: Essays in honor of James J. Gibson* (pp. 95–116). New York: Cornell University Press.

Miles, W. R. (1931). Movement interpretation of the silhouette of a revolving fan. *American Journal of Psychology, 78,* 145–147.

Mohrmann, K. (1939). Lautheitskonstanz im Entfernungswechsel [Loudness constancy with change in distance]. *Zeitschrift für Psychologie, 145,* 149–199.

Müller-Lyer, F. C. (1889). Optische Urteilstauschungen. *Archiv für Anatomie und Physiologie, Physiologische Abetilung, 2,* 263–270.

Over, R. (1968). Explanations of geometric illusions. *Psychological Bulletin, 70,* 545–562.

Oyama, T. (1960). Japanese studies on the so-called geometrical-optical illusions. *Psychologia, 3,* 7–20.

Pastore, N. (1971). *Selective history of theories of visual perception 1650–1950.* New York: Oxford University Press.

Petry, S., & Meyer, G. E. (1987). *The perception of illusory contours.* New York: Springer-Verlag.

Pirenne, M. H. (1970). *Optics, painting & photography.* London: Cambridge University Press.

Power, R. P. (1967). Stimulus properties which reduce apparent reversal of rotating rectangular shapes. *Journal of Experimental Psychology, 73,* 359–399.

Power, R. P., & Day, R. H. (1973). Constancy and illusion of apparent direction of rotary motion in depth: Tests of a theory. *Perception and Psychophysics, 13,* 217–223.

Robinson, J. O. (1972). *The psychology of visual illusion.* London: Hutchinson.

Rock, I. (1975). *An introduction to perception.* New York: Macmillan.

Rock, I., & Ebenholtz, S. (1959). The relational determination of perceived size. *Psychological Review, 66,* 387–401.

Rock, I., & McDermott, W. (1964). The perception of visual angle. *Acta Psychologica, 22,* 119–134.

Rogers, B., & Graham, M. (1979). Motion parallax as an independent cue for depth perception. *Perception, 8,* 125–134.

Rogers, B., & Graham, M. (1982). Similarities between motion parallax and stereopsis in human depth perception. *Vision Research, 22,* 261–270.

Rogers, B., & Graham, M. (1985). Motion parallax and the perception of three dimensional surfaces. In D. J. Ingle, M. Jeannerod, & D. N. Lee (Eds.), *Brain mechanisms and spatial vision* (pp. 95–111). Hingham, MA: Nifhoff.

Rosenblum, L. D., Carello, C., & Pastore, R. E. (1987). Relative effectiveness of three stimulus variables for locating a moving sound source. *Perception, 16,* 175–186.

Royden, C. S., Baker, J. F., & Allman, J. (1988). Perceptions of depth elicited by occluded and shearing motions of random dots. *Perception, 17,* 289–296.

Segall, M. H., Campbell, D. T., & Herskovits, M. J. (1966). *The influence of culture on visual perception.* Indianapolis, IN: Bobbs-Merrill.

Sekuler, R., & Blake, R. (1985). *Perception.* New York: Alfred A. Knopf, Inc.

Schriever, W. (1925). Experimentelle Studien uber stereoskopisches Sehen [Experimental study of the stereoscopic sense]. *Zeitschrift fur Psychologie, 96,* 113–170.

Tastevin, J. (1937). En partant de l'experience de'Aristotle [On Aristotle's experiment]. *L'Encephale, 1,* 57–84, 140–158.

Wade, N. J. (Ed.). (1983). *Brewster and Wheatstone on vision.* London: Academic Press.

Wallach, H. (1939). On sound localization. *Journal of the Acoustic Society of America, 10,* 270–274.

Wallach, H. (1940). The role of head movements and vestibular and visual cues in sound localization. *Journal of Experimental Psychology, 27,* 339–368.

Wallach, H., & O'Connell, D. N. (1953). The kinetic depth effect. *Journal of Experimental Psychology, 45,* 205–217.

Wenderoth, P. (1977). An analysis of the rod-and-frame illusion and its variants. In R. H. Day & G. V. Stanley (Eds.), *Studies in perception* (pp. 95–141). Perth: University of Western Australia Press, Monash University Publications Committee.

Wheatstone, C. (1838). On some remarkable and hitherto unobserved, phenomena of binocular vision. *Philosophical Transactions Royal Society of London, 128*, 371–394.

Wightman, F. L., & Kistler, D. J. (1989a). Headphone simulation of free-field listening. I: Stimulus synthesis. *Journal of the Acoustic Society of America, 85*, 858–867.

Wightman, F. L., & Kistler, D. J. (1989b). Headphone simulation of free-field listening. II: Psychophysical validation. *Journal of the Acoustic Society of America, 85*, 868–878.

Wightman, F. L., Kistler, D. J., & Aruda, M. (1989). The hierarchy of sound localization cues revealed by experiments in a simulated-free field. *Abstract of the Association for Research in Otolaryngology* Twelve midwinter research meeting.

Witkin, H. A., & Asch, S. E. (1948). Studies in space orientation: IV. Further experiments on perception of upright with displaced visual fields. *Journal of Experimental Psychology, 38*, 762–782.

Wong, T. S. (1970). *Some studies in perceptual instability.* Unpublished master's thesis, Monash University, Melbourne, Australia.

11 Perceptual Theory and Visual Cognition

Julian Hochberg
Columbia University

Theories of perception, especially of early vision and of late visual cognition, have burgeoned in the last three decades, but I think they are almost entirely unrelated to each other. I think that the case can be made (and was made by Helmholtz) that mental structures, opaque to the processes of early vision, intervene between sensory input and our reportable knowledge of the visual world. Nakayama (1990) used a title that I wish were free for me to use here: "The Iconic Bottleneck and the Tenuous Link Between Early Visual Processing and Perception" (although actually I discuss a somewhat higher level bottleneck).

Because they can be defined locally within the retinal image, the attributes of color and motion have seemed easier to explain without drawing on deeply postretinal or cognitive processes. It is therefore about achromatic color (specifically, lightness) and about simple motions that I will ask whether even for these attributes mental structures thoroughly transform and perhaps obscure the contribution of early vision. I hang this discussion on the framework of the classical theory, which is best for that purpose, and which is still probably the explicit or implicit approach of most perception psychologists.

What I consider the classical theory, as epitomized by Helmholtz a century past, has two distinct stages: analytic and synthetic. Brief reminders of each follow in turn.

ANALYSIS

From the objects in the world, which are the *distal stimuli*, patterns of different forms of *proximal stimulus* energy affect those sense organs specialized to respond to them. Within each sense organ are individual receptor cells that are specialized by evolution to respond as *independent* neutral units to such aspects of the impinging energy as will suffice, in proper combination, to account for all possible perceptions within that modality; the responses of those units, the *fundamental sensations,* were not in general thought to be reportable as such. Until the 1950s this picture seemed in good correspondence with what we could observe in the nervous system itself. Although it could be tested against difference-threshold and color-matching data obtained with small homogeneous patches of light, this set of theories is mute concerning most of the perceptual properties that viewers do report about the world, and mute too about interaction effects, for example, the effect of steep luminance-contours on luminance-difference matches. There had always been two ways to go in order to accommodate such omissions: to explain them in terms of postsensory or cognitive processes, or to posit different or additional classes of sensory receptors, specialized for aspects of the stimulus pattern more extended than the individual punctiform rods and cones.

All of the attributes of distal objects and events that viewers report they are able to perceive—distance, form, surface-reflectance, motion, cause, purpose, gracefulness, and so forth—could simply be compound properties and expectations about what sensory events will next occur together. Centuries of Associationist philosophy provide the framework here. This line of explanation, as we will see, strongly calls for *mental representations* and *mental operations*; gives cognitive processes causal status in perception; and, reciprocally, provides perceptual outcomes with what I call *cognitive consequences*. Well represented within current theories of perception and visual cognition, we discuss this general explanation under *Synthesis*, later.

First we consider the alternative, the search for pattern-sensitive neural units that transcend punctiform analysis, and that at the cost of reducing the independence of the individual receptors respond only to relatively extended aspects of the retinal image. Such search has been pursued within two quite different reference systems, those of proximal stimulus measures and those of distal object attributes: It is with the attributes of the retinal image (or of the optic array that it samples) that research in the field of *visual science*, or sensation, is chiefly concerned. And because the same proximal display could be produced by any number of very different distal stimulus arrangements, having very different distal attributes, the experimenter in the field of *visual perception* is primarily interested in the viewer's report of which distal arrangement is perceived and what its attributes seem to be.

We therefore distinguish two reference frames within the general reexamination of early sensory processing ("early" on the chain of processing, that is): (a) proximal reference, concerned with the psychophysical effects of patterning in the retinal image, that is, the nonindependence of the elements of a sensory mosaic; and (b) distal reference, which seeks ways in which sensitivity to relationships within the patterned retinal stimulus distribution might provide sensory or cortical responses that correspond directly and *without any intervening cognitive processes* to the distal properties of objects and events in the world. Despite some efforts, the two lines of inquiry have not yet convincingly converged, as I consider after very briefly outlining them.

PROXIMAL REFERENCE

We have come a long way from thinking of the retina as a mosaic of independent receptor elements, with only the associations formed in the brain as the means of dealing with extended patterns. There are now many different theories that use models about receptor networks or receptive fields, frequency channels, or dynamic cortical networks, which explain observers' thresholds for detecting changes in the extended pattern of retinal stimulation. There are also theories about how the visual system, or some computer simulation of it, might analyze the retinal image into primitives for the analysis of larger patterns; Adelson and Bergen (1991) offered what is probably the most general and principled attempt to derive the possible visual elements that will characterize the structure of what they call the *plenoptic function*, which describes everything that can be seen in the sense that, if some information in the light impinging on the organism is not picked up by early vision, it can have no further consequences. And although most theories that deal with proximal variables measure some form of detection thresholds, some few theories aim at predicting above-threshold, reportable attributes, such as the smoothness of apparent motion between successively presented spots of light. These impressive lines of research are clearly useful in probing the receptive machinery of the visual system. But I think that they may not contribute in any direct way to our understanding of visual perception, as their proponents quite generally imply, and I think that they contribute even less to our understanding of visual cognition.

I say this because theories about the attributes of the retinal image (edges, contours, luminances, grating-spacing, motions, etc.) are not theories about visual perception, which is concerned with distal, not proximal properties. There is no one-to-one relationship between these two sets of attributes. Although no longer punctiform, the sensory elements of analysis generally have no direct implication about such distal attributes as perceived depth, form, surfaces' reflectances, and so on, and the task of getting from proximal to distal attributes is still left to higher processes (if considered at all).

There are, however, sweeping proposals that endow the retina with analytic sensitivities to *distal* attributes, contradictory as that may sound at first hearing; we consider these next.

DISTAL REFERENCE: PERCEPTION WITHOUT COGNITIVE PARTICIPATION

The point is, the local attributes of the retinal pattern of stimulation are not generally in 1:1 correspondence with the attributes of their distal objects: The size of the image that some object provides the retina will fit as well any number of different sized objects if their distance is free to vary; the square perpendicular to the line of sight, and the trapezoid at a slant, subtend the same image. The free variable in these particular examples is distance: Three dimensions cannot be specified in two, an incontestable point that as we shall see remains nevertheless in contest.

But that is not the only variable not specified in the local retinal image: The same luminance may mean snow in the shade or coal in sunlight, because the distal illumination on the distal reflecting surface is not specified in the retinal image we receive from that reflecting surface. The same retinal motion or lack of it is provided by a stationary point and by a moving point that is pursued by a moving eye or head, or that is provided by a moving point with stationary viewpoint and by a stationary point and an appropriately moving viewpoint, because the viewpoint is not specified in the retinal image of the point itself. And the retinal image provided by an upright line and a tilted head is the same as that provided by a tilted line and an upright head, for the same reasons.

How then do we ever perceive any object, scene, or event in the world? The classical answer was that we have learned to take the conditions of seeing into account, an answer we will return to shortly. For now, note only that this would generally require that in order to assign distal attributes to an object that is projected in one localized part of the retinal image, our visual systems must consult other parts of the retinal image for information about distance and illumination, must draw upon extended sources of proprioceptive information about movements of the eye and head, and so on, and in each case reach a solution consistent with these converging sources of information. And that suggests a radically different alternative: that our *sensory systems* are structured as *perceptual systems*, responding not to local independent stimulation, but to just such variable aspects of extended proximal stimulation as are in fact in 1:1 correspondence, given some constraints, with distal attributes of the objects and layouts in the world. Once alerted to that possibility, it is not hard to find candidates for such variables:

Perhaps the oldest of these were Hering's proposals that we possess binocular depth receptors, and that lateral inhibition between extended retinal regions works to offset the effect of changes in overall illumination. Both proposals have been vindicated by microelectrode recording and are strongly represented in contemporary theory. As to binocular depth receptors: postretinal cells with binocular receptive fields are found as early as the lateral geniculate and grouped by disparity in cortical columns; Sperling (1970) has since advanced a fairly explicit theory of cooperation and competition between hypothetical network elements that correspond to different points of depth in binocular space; in that model, and in the subsequent variations (like that of Marr & Poggio, 1976) that have been offered and tested computationally, perceived depth, which is of distal reference, rests on the output of that network.

With respect to Hering's proposal that compensation for increased illumination might come from lateral inhibition: Wallach and others argued that our visual systems respond not to the luminance of a given part of the retinal image but to the *ratio* of adjacent luminances. A sensitivity to luminance-ratios would not only explain many of facts of brightness-contrast, but would explain the constancy of perceived surface-lightness under different illuminations, as well: The ratio of luminances provided by an object and its surroundings remains invariant despite any changes in illumination that the scene may undergo; sensitivity to that invariant ratio could be the basis for perceptions of reflectance that would themselves remain invariant, regardless of changes in the local retinal image. Receptive fields with just such properties have been reported, and more complex patterns have been modeled without specific neurophysiological underpinning.

No "taking into account" of the conditions of seeing is needed in either of these examples. If we could find the variable of proximal stimulation that stands in 1:1 correspondence with each of the distal properties of the environment that we can perceive, if we could be sure that our perceptions are in fact based on that variable, and if we could uncover the neurophysiology of the matter, we would have explained the perception of our environment with no appeal to vague inference-like processes.

The first of these three tasks comprised the heart of J. J. Gibson's very general and revolutionary program. That program, varying though it did (Gibson, 1950, 1966, 1979), may be paraphrased as the search for, and study of, the informative variables of stimulation that in the normal visual ecology remain *invariant* under changes (especially those that are self-produced) in the seeing conditions. In the strong form of this *direct theory*, no inferential processes are involved in perception, no cognitive computations, no mental structures, no internal representations of the world: Perceptual learning (where any is needed) consists only of coming to respond to the appropriate informative variables. There are now several energetic and productive lines of inquiry pursuing this approach to visual perception and visuomotor performance (R. Warren, & Wertheim, 1990; W. Warren, Mestre, Blackwell, & Morris, 1991; Todd, 1985), and they must be taken seriously. But it has problems that have not been squarely faced and that may severely limit its consequences:

First, as to programmatic problems: There is a vast number of distal variables that we could measure within each scene or layout, and for each of these there are, as Cutting (1983, 1986) and others (e.g., Hochberg & Smith, 1955) have pointed out, many different informative proximal variables. Which of these are important in perception and cognition? Helmholtz had taken as the fundamental variables of proximal stimulation a set both sufficient to specify every possible retinal image, and plausible as adequate stimuli for independent local receptors. No equivalent principle has been offered for these newer approaches. There is a continuing assertion, from Gibson on, that the visual demands imposed by our ecological niche tell us what stimulus information is important, but that assertion neither distinguishes the new approach from the old (no modern-day "ecolological realist" prescription for assessing ecological validity is a tiny fraction as explicit as Brunswik's Helmholtzean method and theory; see Brunswik, 1956), nor faces up to the repeated arguments by evolutionary biologists against using environmental structure alone as grounds for such prediction. (The same criticism applies when modern Helmholtzean theorists claim that some specific perceptual phenomenon supports their view because they can find some plausible and corresponding co-occurrence in the environment.)

Furthermore, although what has been designated as an informative variable of proximal stimulation sometimes does indeed appear to serve as such (R. Warren, 1976; W. Warren, Blackwell, & Kurtz, 1991), more often we find that even when proximal and distal variables are in perfect correspondence, the former is not used by viewers (Cutting, 1986; Hochberg, 1988; Todd, 1985). Even if we should become convinced that the program is valid, we will need some principled way of knowing when its invariance rubric works and when it doesn't.

As to theoretical and metatheoretical problems, although none seem inherently unanswerable, some are critical to the theory's survival but remain, quite astonishingly, completely unaddressed. The most serious problem is that in fact *no* proximal stimulus variable stands in 1:1 correspondence with *any* distal variable unless additional constraints are added, unless additional assumptions are made. Thus, whenever depth is involved, the truism that two dimensions does not specify three is not answered by the glib slogan that time (i.e., change or motion) restores a third dimension to the D. proximal stimulus information: An infinity of changing (i.e., nonrigid) arrangements, such as motion pictures or objects undergoing rubbery deformation, will fit the changing proximal pattern received by a moving viewer in a rigid scene. Prediction demands an additional constraint: For example, of the many possible distal structures that fit a given changing proximal pattern, viewers will perceive only the rigid one—if such there is. But convenient as such a rigidity constraint would be (many recent theories assume it), we have known for years that rigid, moving (a) skeletal cubes, (b) Ames "windows," and (c) facial masks all appear to reverse direction spontaneously, deforming nonrigidly when they do so (respectively, (a): Hochberg, Amira, & Peterson, 1984; Schwartz & Sperling, 1983; van Hornbostel, 1922); (b) Ames, 1951; Hochberg, 1987; (c) Klopfer, 1991); indeed, reversals to nonrigidity come to dominate such objects' appearances as one's experience with them increases (at least for the rotating skeletal cube: Cooper, 1988, personal communication), which is hardly what one would expect from a strong rigidity constraint. Most damaging of all, a perfectly rigid and stationary Ames window will, when its large end appears incorrectly as the nearer, undergo illusory concomitant motion and apparent rubbery deformation as the viewer moves (Hochberg & Beer, 1991), even though the optic transformations provided by self-movement are supposed to be definitive within the Gibsonian approach. We might still entertain *local* rigidity constraints that interact with other misleading depth cues, as Ullman has suggested (Ullman, 1984), but it is unclear whether that returns us in practice to some cognitive, inferential process or whether the approach can remain stimulus-determined and "direct."

A second and equally serious set of problems centers on the notion that the information in the optic array specifies not only what is out there, but determines what we perceive. This formula requires, of course, that we perceive veridically, without mistakes or illusions. In fact, illusions obviously do occur. To Helmholtzeans (Gregory, 1963, 1980; Rock, 1977, 1983), these are misapplication in abnormal circumstances of just those inferential rules and premises that would normally provide veridical perceptions by taking the conditions of seeing into account. To Gibsonians (Gibson, 1966; Michaels & Carello, 1981), very similarly, illusions occur only under abnormally uninformative seeing conditions, for example, line drawings, static viewing, and so on. In fact, illusions do occur under what appear to be quite normal conditions, as well (DeLucia & Hochberg, 1991; Leibowitz & Pick, 1972; Nijhawan, 1991). This central issue obviously demands a rigorous and noncircular discussion of what is meant by "normally informative," without which the program seems invulnerable and inapplicable as well (except by intuition).

What aggravates this last problem is that the objective stimulus information in the optic array does not itself determine what information the viewer receives or uses. As we discuss shortly, where the viewer attends, what the viewer knows, and what the viewer seeks are strong factors (except, perhaps, in uniformly informative displays). These variables have no explicit provision within the direct program. It will be difficult to specify what "normally informative" — or any other — stimulus information might mean unless such provision can be made.

Even with all these problems solved, this direct — and indeed behaviorist — approach would remain isolated from the rest of visual cognition. That might be considered as merely a metatheoretical issue, except that there are at least three kinds of evidence of *mental structure*, and of stages of synthesis beyond the visual analysis we have been discussing, within perception itself. We consider these next.

SYNTHESIS

If we start with punctiform receptors, or with any other channels that analyze proximal stimulation into independent attributes, we will need some postsensory structure to explain responses that depend on the convergence of information from more than one such channel. Although always present, this need is most conspicuous when individual sources of information, with very different sensory origins, contribute interchangeably to the perception of the same distal attribute that, like depth, is not found at all in the local proximal stimulation.

The point is that depth, and other distal attributes, cannot be equated with information from individual local proximal channels. Thus, as noted earlier, although it is true that receptive fields sensitive to binocular retinal disparity seem to provide information that specifies relative stereoscopic depth, stereopsis will arise as well from the noncorresponding occlusions that an object affords the two eyes' views, even with no shared disparate points (see Nakayama, 1990; Nakayama & Shimojo, 1990, on "the Leonardo effect"). And we can also provide the same depth monocularly, through motion parallax, by dynamic occlusion, and so on. I should stress that it is not only depth that poses this problem: Quite generally, *different sensory paths converge to the same final perceptual consequence* (cf. H. Wallach, 1990). But in what sense is it "the same depth" (or, in other cases, motion, position, etc.) to which these extremely different sensory analyses contribute? We can say that they refer to the same *distal* depth, specified by different sensory channels, but that (except for Gibsonians) begs the question completely. Or we can show that they provide the same *conse-*

quence wherever perceived depth is a *causal variable*, a mentalistic point to which I return in a moment.

First, I compare a complex, mentalistic cognitive explanation and a simple noncognitive explanation of why a region in the proximal stimulus pattern appears to change in lightness even though its luminance remains invariant. Then I describe an old experiment which, by adding depth-based information, yields lightness changes that essentially mandate the cognitive explanation. This is followed by a very widespread set of new examples that also appear, on somewhat different reasoning, to require a similar (and perhaps stronger) conclusion. And finally, I note briefly some difficulties that must be faced before adopting and using that conclusion.

Two Explanations of Perceived Lightness Contrast: Mental Structure Versus Lateral Interaction

Imagine a luminous target patch (a) with a surrounding annulus (b) of independently varying luminance (in Fig. 11.1). With no change in the target itself, increasing the annulus' luminance results in a decrease in the target's apparent brightness. Because he assumed our retinal receptors to respond independently to local luminances, to Helmholtz this phenomenon of *brightness contrast* required special explanation as a case of *misapplied lightness constancy*: He argued that at some postsensory, cognitive level, the annulus reveals the level of illumination received by both it and the target, and the unchanged luminance of the target must "therefore" (according to the premises of unconscious inference, learned from the physics of our visual ecology) be less if the illumination is more. That is, *we do not "see our sensations"*—we perceive that distal situation that would in the normal world most probably have provided them. Notice that this requires not only a mental representation of the object on its background, but the *mental structure* that relates illuminance, reflectance, and luminance. And that mental structure lies, irremovable, between early response to stimulation and what I will call the "final common path" to reportable or potentially reportable appearance.

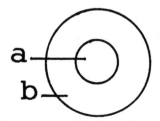

FIG. 11.1. Contrast: Target (a) appears darker as the luminance of surround (b) increases.

In place of this elaborate and uncomfortably mentalistic account, it seems far more economical to ascribe the contrast, and indeed much of lightness constancy as well, to the direct response of a network that includes lateral inhibitory connections. As we noted earlier, a simple hypothesis might be that our perception of adjacent lightnesses depends on our sensory response to the ratio of adjacent luminances. And, as we also noted earlier, there is no need for mental representation within this explanation. But that is only because of the way in which we have set up the situation and the task.

An Experiment that Seems to Mandate an Explanation in Terms of Mental Structure

In particular, let us introduce depth, as revealed through very different sensory channels, as an explicit variable: Viewed monocularly, an upright trapezoidal target (if properly made) is compellingly perceived as a square lying flat on the table, as at (a) and (b) in Fig. 11.2. When the target (a) is made to appear upright, by any of four manipulations that are *proximally very different but are equivalent in the perceived depth they reveal* (i.e., manipulations providing (i) binocular vision, (ii) viewer movement that

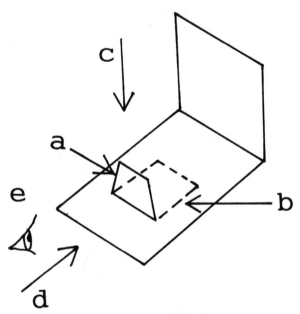

FIG. 11.2. Perceptual lightness of upright target (a) is perceptually coupled to the apparent source of illumination (c,d) and the spatial arrangement (a,b) as construed by the viewer (e), regardless of the basis of the reconstrual. See text.

imparts motion parallax, (iii) and (iv) a black rod, or a white rod, waving behind the target), it should then appear to receive less illumination if an apparent light source is overhead (c), and increased illumination if the apparent light source is from in front (d). If viewing conditions are being taken into account, the target should therefore appear to be lighter—more reflective—in the first case, and darker in the second, even though the light (and the luminance-ratio) it receives and reflects remains unchanged in either case.

This in fact is what all viewers reported when they matched the trapezoid to a scale of gray test patches (Hochberg & Beck, 1954). Because the different means of changing the apparent 3D orientation of the target had only one thing in common, that is, the perceived slant that in turn determined what the perceived illumination should be, we must grant that mental state a causal status, whether direct or indirect, in the perception of reflectance. I see these results as evidence of a cognitive process involving a specific mental structure (relating perceived slant, perceived illumination, and perceived reflectance), but I want to limit this term: When I use the term *mental structure* or *mental representation*, I try to mean only that we can observe structured interresponse constraints, *conforming to some relationship between distal properties*, which cannot be attributed to specific proximal stimulation or to known neurophysiological structures.

In the almost four decades that have passed, two partial replications have failed (Epstein, 1961; Flock, & Freedberg 1970) and four succeeded (Beck, 1965; Coren & Komoda, 1973; Gilchrist, 1977; Gogel & Mershon, 1969); all the replications used only one method (binocular vision) to change apparent slant, however, thus lending somewhat less support for the existence of an R-R rather than an S-R coupling. Furthermore, because all of these experiments used real surfaces, one might argue that where positive findings were obtained they might result because the viewer attends different informative features, such as microhighlights (Beck, 1972), or engages in different looking and comparison behavior (Flock, Wilson, & Poizner, 1966; Hochberg, 1972), when perceiving the depth correctly. Finally, and most important for the central theoretical question with which I started, the question of cognitive transparency (do intervening inference-like cognitive processes make perception opaque to the contributions of early vision), we might admit that although some part of the surface lightness that we perceive is determined by the cognitive process, the remainder (perhaps the greater part) is predictable from retinal measures alone.

Concerns about microhighlights and about the need for replication with alternative equivalent depth information are allayed by experiments using computer-generated alternative-cue binocular displays that offer no micro-highlights (Hochberg & Beer, in preparation). Perhaps more importantly, the research task drew on a method that applies over a wide range of perceptual phenomena and brings us closer to answering the question of cognitive transparency to sensory input: When no binocular disparity was used, and observers were *instructed* to reconstrue the objects' spatial orientations, both the objects' arrangements in space *and their apparent lightnesses* were reported to change accordingly, although there was no change at all in the stimulus display.

Perceptual Coupling as a Function of Intended and Spontaneous Construal: When Familiarity and Intention Determine the Structure We Perceive.

This last phenomenon, noted anecdotally by Mach in 1906 (1906/1959), offers a more widely applicable method by which we can identify the operation of a mental structure and of the inferential process that, in Helmholtz's account, *underlies all perception*: What is changing when the viewer deliberately or spontaneously reconstrues the spatial arrangement is not any proximal stimulus information, but a mental representation that is fitted to it, which in turn provides for a difference in perceived lightness. For possible specific algorithms, see Adelson & Pentland (1991).

And other examples, in which the changes are more clearly categorical, abound. These phenomena that I reviewed earlier in connection with the rigidity constraint all showed strong interresponse constraints: When the rear face (Fig. 11.3a) of a wire cube rotating in one direction (3b) is perceived as nearer, or the concave side (4a) of a rotating face mask appears convex, each is perceived to rotate in the opposite direction (Fig. 11.3c and 11.4c, respectively); when the large, more distant side of a *stationary* Ames trapezoid (shown from the front in Fig. 11.5a, from above in Fig. 11.5b) appears to be the nearer, it is perceived in illusory concomitent motion when the observer moves (as in Fig. 11.5c). In each case, reconstruals (whether they are spontaneous or follow the experimenter's instructions) that occur without any change in the external situation are accompanied by the appropriate illusory motion. In each case, one stimulus attribute varies with the perceived state of another, even when stimulus conditions remain unchanged.

I think that such perceptual coupling in reconstrual is a strong indication of mental structure (although by no means a conclusive one: see Hochberg, 1982). Moreover, whether or not it is such, it is evidence that perception is not transparent to early vision. That point applies to Figs. 11.3–11.5, but is most clear in Fig. 11.6, the "vector analysis" demonstration of Johansson (1950): Although Johansson did not report the fact, when such patterns are seen within a visible framework, perceptions alternate sharply between the construals of 6b and 6a, where 6a is the actual display (Hochberg & Beer, 1990; Hochberg, Fallon, & Brooks, 1977). In each case in Figs. 11.3–6, one construal is close enough to the proximal distribution—for example, a dot

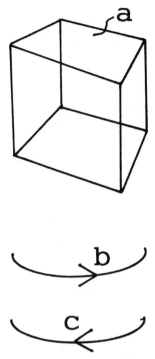

FIG. 11.3.   Skeletal object rotating in direction (b) is perceived in direction (c) if reconstrued so that its rear (a) appears the nearer. See text.

moving diagonally in the retinal image in Fig. 11.6a — to invite an explanation in terms of some sensory mechanism, such as the direction-specific motion detectors modeled by Burt and Sperling (1981); but the other construals are very different from the proximal event — for example, a dot moving diagonally, as in Fig. 11.6a within a framework is (weakly and unreliably) seen to move vertically.

Observers normally see only one of these two movements at any time, usually with 11.6b predominating, and are indeed generally surprised when they see the diagonal (true) motion for the first time. *While 6b prevails, there is no discernible trace of 6a*: We do then appear to be blind in some sense to the diagonal motion on the retina. Indeed, some evidence suggests that viewers cannot distinguish the illusory from a true (approximately) vertical motion (Hochberg & Fallon, 1976), perhaps making it possible to use signal detection procedures. One might argue that the construal that is close to the proximal stimulus distribution is a relatively direct window to the sensory processing, and that only the other alternatives involve an intervening mental structure. It would be interesting to see such an argument, and ways of testing it, developed in appropriate detail. As of

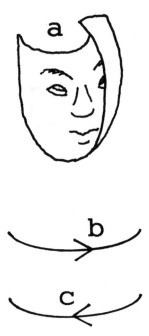

FIG. 11.4. The rotation (b) of concave mask (a) is perceived in direction
(c) if (a) is misconstrued as convex. (Klopfer, 1991).

now, I do not find that argument more plausible than the proposal that all
construals are equally opaque to early processing.

If that is true, the phenomena that I have described are at least as
important to any theory of how we see as are any of the issues that more
concern visual scientists and computational neurophysiologists. Models,
and a nonmentalistic taxonomy, would probably make the area more
popular but we still have to much to find out about what there is to model.
I don't think that purely local "smart instruments" (Runeson, 1977) will do.
One might easily imagine independent and indeed mutually exclusive
networks that respond to the same proximal distribution, and that provide
for each of the alternative construals and for the competition between them
(cf. Hebb, 1949, 1958) but, as we consider next, such models must also
provide as well for the effects of familiarity and intention. Reconstruals are
to some degree spontaneous and mandatory, but they also depend strongly
on the viewer's prior knowledge of the alternatives (Girgus, Rock, & Egatz,
1977) and on the familiarity and meaningfulness of the alternatives
(Peterson, Harvey, & Weidenbacher, in press; Peterson & Hochberg, 1989).
In figure-ground perception, a single physical pattern may provide
two alternative construals of shape so different that a viewer cannot

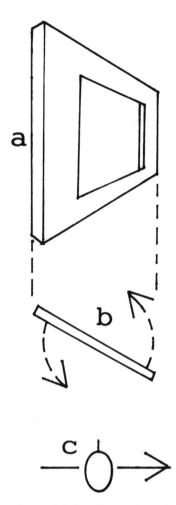

FIG. 11.5. Stationary Ames "window," seen from in front at (a) and from above at (b), with its large edge further from the viewer (c), appears in illusory concomitent motion when (c) moves (arrows). (Gogel & Tietz, 1992; Hochberg & Beer, 1991)

recognize that one is related to the other (Davis, 1985; Rubin, 1915/1958), and it has been persuasively argued (Peterson & Gibson, 1991, in press) that shape memories can determine the earliest, initial figure-ground organization. Moreover, in both shape perception and the perceptual couplings quite generally, construals depend on the viewer's *intentions* to perceive one or the other alternative (Hochberg & Beer, 1990, 1991; Hochberg & Peterson, 1987, in press; Peterson, 1986; Peterson & Hochberg, 1983). (The viewer is

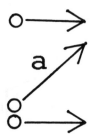

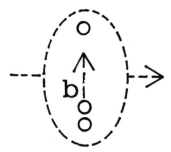

FIG. 11.6. Three lights moving (arrows) as shown at (a) are dominantly seen as the vertically moving light (b), plus a weakly seen horizontal resultant (Johansson, 1950). These events undergo categorial alternation. See text.

probably not merely making the verbal response being requested, e.g., naming one orientation of a cube, because what is reported is the perceptually coupled attribute, e.g., apparent direction of motion.)

Some Refractory Problems in Definition and Application.

If these structures stand athwart the line from sense to experience, they are worth the effort to investigate, and that effort will have to be substantial. The two most serious problems, as I see it, are to specify the characteristics of mental structures so that they can be tested and modeled, and to set them in a chain of consequence that leads to other cognitive processes—to thinking, imagining, remembering.

As to their characteristics, it is generally asserted by most who use the concept that mental structures reflect those of the visual ecology, as filtered through the constraints of our processing limits and our opportunities to learn. That is Helmholtz's *likelihood principle*: We perceive the distal arrangement that would normally have produced the same sensory effect as the stimulus distribution we have received. I have sometimes been named as an adherent of this principle, but I must demur: There are simply too many examples, including those I have discussed here, that are not generated by that rule as it stands (nor, for that matter, by a *minimum principle*, that contemporary survivor from Gestalt theory; see Hochberg, 1987, and Peterson & Hochberg, 1989). For example, as noted earlier, the Müller-Lyer illusion continues to be explained as an example of unconscious inference based on misinterpreting converging lines on paper for the perspective provided when parallel edges recede, or for the angles presented when two walls meet in a corner, but this explanation does not deal with the long-known fact that the illusion also occurs with three-dimensional arrangements in the real world (most recently, DeLucia & Hochberg, 1991; Massaro & Anderson, 1970; Nijhawan, 1991).

Moreover, the mental structures that are manifest in perceptual couplings like those I have described are far less complete and consistent than those of objects in the world: Information is effective only over some limited span, and that depends on the viewer's attention (as discussed in connection with Fig. 9.1A, in chapter 9). We tolerate inconsistencies and implausibilities according to some unknown calculus, as when the cost of perceiving the stationary trapezoid of Fig. 11.5 in the wrong orientation is that it undergoes weird nonrigid deformations during its illusory concomitent motions, without instigating a reconstrual of its orientation. Without ways to take into account our processing limits and how they are deployed in the course of perceptual inquiry, and to know in advance what implausibilities will be tolerated without forcing a reconstrual, no principled prediction of what we actually see in any case is possible.

I think that perceptual construal proceeds over short spans of time and space (or time and structure), although it is constrained by the more purposive and conceptual context of the perceptual question being asked, and that the construal draws readily on only *minimal inferences* (to borrow a term applied by McKoon & Ratcliff, 1992, to the reading process). The phenomena I described do not warrant the notion of an extended inferential construction (I agree in this respect with what has been argued by Gogel, 1990), and in any case the bare notion will not by itself predict what we perceive. We do not now have any general rule, then, by which to predict the characteristics of these structures with any confidence.

As to cognitive consequence, it is often argued that our ideas, the elements of thinking and imagining, are the same structures I have been discussing, stripped of their sensory input. There are some examples in visual thinking and recognition of what we must call structures that do indeed appear to display interattributive coupling (Cooper, 1976; Kosslyn, 1980). But interattributive coupling dominated this chapter only because it made the phenomena that I have been discussing suitable tools with which to test perceptual consequences of early sensory analysis: There are many examples of cognitive structure that do not share this property (Biederman, 1987; Reisberg & Chambers, 1991; see Cooper, chapter 8, this volume). The nature of the mental structures that are suggested by the regularities of visual thinking and remembering seem to depend greatly on the tasks they serve, with a major division into those with explicit or declarative consequence, and those with implicit consequence that affect the performance of cognitive tasks but that cannot be reported or used explicitly in visual thinking (see Cooper, this volume). The structures of visual perception face different tasks and fates within the flow of visual cognition, and dissociation according to those differences seems like a promising start at dealing with the first problem, that is, starting to describe systematically the characteristics of the inferred perceptual structures.

I hope that we can replace "mental structures" as soon as possible with more specific descriptors and theories. We probably have enough conceptual tools, in the form of sensory networks and acquisitive neural nets, to do the job in the language of neurophysiological structure and function if that is most congenial, but not in the categories of early vision. We need to start with the observable regularities and limitations of the perceptual structures that we know exist but have yet to take seriously.

REFERENCES

Adelson, E. H., & Bergen, J. R. (1991). The plenoptic function and the elements of early vision. In M. Landy & J. Movshon (Eds.), *Computational models of visual processing* (pp. 3–20). Cambridge, MA.: MIT Press.

Adelson, E. H., & Pentland, A. P. (1991). The perception of shading and reflectance. In B. Blum (Ed.), *Channels in the visual nervous system* (pp. 105–123). London: Freund.

Ames, A. (1951). Visual perception and the rotating trapezoidal window. *Psychological Monographs, 65* (Whole No. 324).

Beck, J. (1965). Apparent spatial position and the perception of lightness. *Journal of Experimental Psychology, 69*, 170–179.

Beck, J. (1972). *Surface color perception.* Ithaca, NY: Cornell University Press.

Biederman, I. (1987). Recognition by components: A theory of human image understanding. *Psychological Review, 94*, 115–147.

Burt, P., & Sperling, G. (1981). Time, distance, and feature-trade-offs in visual apparent motion. *Psychological Review, 88*, 171–195.

Brunswik, E. (1956). *Perception and the representative design of psychological experiments.* Berkeley: University of California Press.

Cooper, L. A. (1976) Demonstration of a mental analog of an external rotation. *Perception & Psychophysics, 19*, 296–302.

Coren, S. C. & Komoda, M. K. (1973). The effect of cues to illumination on apparent brightness. *American Journal of Psychology, 86,* 345–349.

Cutting, J. E. (1983). Four assumptions about invariance in perception. *Journal of Experimental Psychology: Human Perception and Performance, 9,* 310–317.

Cutting, J. E. (1986). *Perception with an eye for motion.* Cambridge, MA: Bradford.

Davis, J. M. (1985). An examination of the status of the ground in figure-ground perception. Unpublished doctoral dissertation. Rutgers, The State University of New Jersey.

DeLucia, P. R., & Hochberg, J. (1991). Geometrical illusions in solid objects under ordinary viewing conditions. *Perception & Psychophysics, 50,* 547–554.

Epstein, W. (1961). Phenomenal orientation and perceived achromatic color. *Journal of Psychology, 52,* 51–53.

Flock, H., & Freedberg, E. (1970). Perceived angle of incidence and achromatic surface color. *Perception & Psychophysics, 8,* 251–256.

Flock, H., Wilson, A., & Poizner, S. (1966). Lightness matching for different routes through a complex scene, *Perception & Psychophysics, 1,* 382–384.

Gibson, J. J. (1950). *The perception of the visual world.* Boston: Houghton Mifflin.

Gibson, J. J. (1966). *The senses considered as perceptual systems.* Boston: Houghton Mifflin.

Gibson, J. J. (1979). *The ecological approach to visual perception.* Boston: Houghton Mifflin.

Gilchrist, A. (1977). Perceived lightness depends on perceived spatial arrangement. *Science, 195,* 185–187.

Girgus, J. J., Rock, I., & Egatz, R. (1977). The effect of knowledge of reversibility on the reversibility of ambiguous figures. *Perception & Psychophysics, 22,* 550–556.

Gogel, W. C. (1990). A theory of phenomenal geometry and its applications. *Perception and Psychophysics, 48,* 105–123.

Gogel, W., & Mershon, D. H. (1969). Depth adjacency in simultaneous contrast. *Perception & Psychophysics, 5,* 13–17.

Gogel, W. C., & Tietz, J. D. (1992). Absence of computation and reasoning-like processes in the perception of orientation in depth. *Perception and Psychophysics, 51,* 309–318.

Gregory, R. L. (1963). Distortion of visual space as inappropriate constancy scaling. *Nature, 199,* 678–680.

Gregory, R. L. (1980). Perceptions as hypotheses. In H. C. Longuet-Higgins & N. S. Sutherland (Eds.), *The psychology of vision* (pp. 137–149). London: The Royal Society.

Hebb, D. (1949). *The organization of behavior.* New York: Wiley.

Hebb, D. (1958). *A textbook of psychology.* Philadelphia: Saunders.

Hochberg, J. (1972). Perception, I. Color and shape. II. Space and movement. In J. W. Kling & L. A. Riggs (Eds.), *Woodworth & Schlosberg's Experimental Psychology* (3rd ed.). NY: Holt, Rinehart & Winston.

Hochberg, J. (1982). How big is a stimulus? In J. Beck (Ed.), *Organization and representation in perception* (pp. 191–217). Hillsdale, NJ: Lawrence Erlbaum Associates.

Hochberg, J. (1987). Machines should not see as people do, but must know how people see. *Computer Vision, Graphics, and Image Processing, 37,* 221–237.

Hochberg, J. (1988). Visual perception. In R. Atkinson, R. Herrnstein, G. Lindzey, & D. Luce (Eds.), *Stevens' handbook of experimental psychology* (Vol. I, pp. 295–375). New York: Wiley

Hochberg, J., Amira, L., & Peterson, M. A. (1984). Extensions of the Schwartz/Sperling phenomenon: Invariance under transformation fails in the perception of objects' moving pictures. [Abstract] *Proceedings of the Eastern Psychological Association,* p.44.

Hochberg, J., & Beck, J. (1954). Apparent spatial arrangement and perceived brightness. *Journal of Experimental Psychology, 47,* 263–266.

Hochberg, J., & Beer, J. (1990). Alternative movement organizations: Findings and premises for modeling [Abstract]. *Proceedings of the Psychonomic Society,* p. 25.

Hochberg, J., & Beer, J. (1991). Illusory rotations from self-produced motion: The Ames window effect in static objects [Abstract]. *Proceedings of the Eastern Psychological Association*, p. 34.

Hochberg, J., & Beer, J. (in preparation). *Virtual reflectance in virtual space.*

Hochberg, J., & Fallon, P. (1976). Perceptual vector analysis of moving patterns. *Science, 194,* 1081–1083.

Hochberg, J., Fallon, P., & Brooks, V. (1977). Motion organization in "stop action" sequences. *Scandinavian Journal of Psychology, 18,* 187–191.

Hochberg, J., & Peterson, M. A. (1987). Piecemeal organization and cognitive components in object perception: Perceptually coupled responses to moving objects. *Journal of Experimental Psychology: General, 116,* 370–380.

Hochberg, J., & Peterson, M. A. (in press). Mental representations of occluded objects: Sequential disclosure and intentional construal. *Italian Journal of Psychology.*

Hochberg, J., & Smith, O. W. (1955). Landing strip markings and the "expansion pattern": 1. Program, preliminary analysis and apparatus. *Perceptual and Motor Skills, 5,* 81–92.

Johansson, G. (1950). *Configurations in event perception.* Uppsala, Sweden: Almqvist & Wiksell.

Klopfer, D. S. (1991). Apparent reversals of a rotating mask: A new demonstration of cognition in perception. *Perception & Psychophysics, 49,* 522–530.

Kosslyn, S. M. (1980). *Image and mind.* Cambridge, MA: Harvard University Press.

Leibowitz, H. W., & Pick, H. L. (1972). Cross-cultural and educational aspects of the Ponzo illusion. *Perception & Psychophysics, 12,* 403–432.

Mach, E. (1959). *The analysis of sensation and the relation of the physical to the psychical.* (S. Waterlow, Trans). New York: Dover. (Original work published 1906)

Marr, D., & Poggio, T. (1976). Cooperative computation of stereo disparity. *Science, 194,* 283–287.

Massaro, D., & Anderson, N. (1970). A test of a perspective theory of geometrical illusions. *American Journal of Psychology, 84,* 565–575.

McKoon, G., & Ratcliff, R. (1992). Inference during reading. *Psychological Review, 99,* 440–466.

Michaels, C. F., & Carello, C. (1981). *Direct perception.* Englewood Cliffs, NJ: Prentice-Hall.

Nakayama, K. (1990). The iconic bottleneck and the tenuous link between early visual processing and perception. In C. Blakemore (Ed.), *Vision: Coding and efficiency* (pp. 411–422). Cambridge: Cambridge University Press.

Nakayama, K., & Shimojo, S. (1990). Toward a neural understanding of visual surface representation. *Cold Spring Harbor symposium on quantitative biology, LV,* 911–924.

Nijhawan, R. (1991). Three-dimensional Muller-Lyer illusion. *Perception & Psychophysics, 49,* 333–341.

Peterson, M. A. (1986). Illusory concomitant motion in ambiguous stereograms: Evidence for nonsensory components in perceptual organization. *Journal of Experimental Psychology: Human Perception and Performance, 12,* 50–60.

Peterson, M. A., & Gibson, B. S. (1991). The initial identification of figure-ground relationships: Contribution from shape recognition processes. *Bulletin of the Psychonomic Society, 29,* 199–202.

Peterson, M. A., & Gibson, B. S. (in press). Shape recognition inputs to figure-ground organization in three-dimensional displays. *Cognitive Psychology.*

Peterson, M. A., Harvey, E. H., & Weidenbacher, H. L. (in press). Shape recognition inputs to figure-ground organization: Which route counts? *Journal of Experimental Psychology: Human Perception and Performance.*

Peterson, M. A., & Hochberg, J. (1983). Opposed-set measurement procedure: A quantitative analysis of the role of local cues and intention in form perception. *Journal of Experimental Psychology: Human Perception and Performance, 9,* 183–193.

Peterson, M. A., & Hochberg, J. (1989). Necessary considerations for a theory of form perception: A theoretical and empirical reply to Boselie and Leeuwenberg. *Perception, 18*, 105–119.

Reisberg, D., & Chambers, D. (1991). Neither pictures nor propositions: What can we learn from a mental image? *Canadian Journal of Psychology, 45*, 288–302.

Rock, I. (1977). In defense of unconscious inference. In W. Epstein (Ed.), *Stability and constancy in visual perception* (pp. 321–373). New York: Wiley.

Rock, I. (1983). *The logic of perception.* Cambridge, MA: MIT Press.

Rubin, E. (1958). Figure and ground. In D. Bearslee & M. Wertheimer (Eds. M. Wertheimer, Trans.), *Readings in perception* (pp. 35–101). New York: Van Nostrand. (Original work published 1915)

Runeson, S. (1977). On the possibility of "smart" perceptual mechanisms. *Scandinavian Journal of Psychology, 18*, 172–179.

Schwartz, B. J., & Sperling, G. (1983). Non-rigid 3D percepts from 2D representations of rigid objects. *Investigative Ophthalmology and Visual Science. ARVO Supplement, 24*, 239. (Abstract)

Sperling, G. (1970). Binocular vision: A physical and neural theory. *American Journal of Psychology, 84*, 461–534.

Todd, J. (1985). Perception of structure from motion: Is projective correspondence of moving elements a necessary condition? *Journal of Experimental Psychology: Human Perception and Performance, 11*, 689–710.

Ullman, S. (1984). Maximizing rigidity: The incremental recovery of 3-D structure from rigid and nonrigid motion. *Perception, 13*, 255–274.

von Hornbostel, E. M. (1922). *Ueber optische Inversion.* [On optical inversion]. *Psychologische Forschung, 1*, 130–156.

Wallach, H. (1990). The role of eye movements in the perception of motion and shape, In E. Kowler (Ed.), *Eye movements and their role in visual and cognitive processes* (pp. 289–305). New York: Elsevier.

Warren, H. H., Blackwell, A. W., & Kurtz, K. J. (1991). On the sufficiency of the velocity field for perception of heading. *Biological Cybernetics, 65*, 311.

Warren, R. (1976). The perception of egomotion. *Journal of Experimental Psychology: Human Perception and Performance, 2*, 448–456.

Warren, W. H., Mestre, D., Blackwell, A., & Morris, M. (1991). Perception of circular heading from optical flow. *Journal of Experimental Psychology: Human Perception and Performance, 17*, 28–43.

Warren, R., & Wertheim, A. H. (Eds.) (1990). *Perception and control of self motion.* Hillsdale, NJ: Lawrence Erlbaum Associates.

Author Index

A

Abrahamsen, A., 92, *119*
Adelson, E. E., 271, 280, *286*
Ahuir, F., 114, *119*
Albright, T. S., 2, *17*, 200, *220*
Algarabel, S., 114, *119*
Allman, J., 251, *267*
Allport, A. D., 5, *15*, 164, *195*
Ames, A., 15, 275, *286*
Amira, L., 275, *287*
Amrhein, P. C., 161, 162, 164, 165, *198*
Amsel, A., 2, *16*
Amsterdam, J. B., 199, 200, *220*
Andersen, R. A., 200, *219*
Anderson, D. R., 63, *66*
Anderson, N., 285, *288*
Anderson, S. H., 63, *67*
Antes, J. R., 46, *64*
Aruda, M., 246, 250, *268*
Asch, S. E., 255, *264, 268*
Attneave, F., 227, *237*
Avery, G. C., 15, *16*

B

Badcock, D. R., 86, *89*
Badcock, J. C., 86, *89*
Baddeley, A., 230, *237*
Bagnara, J., 52, *67*

Baird, J. C., 73, 80, *89*
Baker, J. F., 251, *267*
Baker, M. A., 91, *119*
Ballard, D. H., 92, *120*
Ballesteros, S., 8, 11, 12, 13, *16*, 47, 48, 49,
    51, 55, *64*, 202, 212, 213, 214, 215, 217,
    218, *219*, 229, *237*
Balota, D. A., 158, 161, *195, 196*
Barlow, D. H., 92, *119*
Baro, J. A., 86, *89*
Bauer, D. W., 48, *66*
Baylis, G. C., 44, 45, *65*
Bechtel, W., 2, *17*, 92, *119*
Beck, J., 226, *238*, 279, *286, 287*
Becker, C. A., 158, 163, 164, *195*
Beer, J., 275, 279, 280, 283, *287, 288*
Ben-Av, M., 34, *40*
Bergen, J. R., 271, *286*
Besner, D., 48, 49, 50, 52, *64, 66*
Biederman, I., 2, 9, 10, *17, 18*, 46, *64*, 201,
    202, *219, 286*
Biggs, T. C., 156, 161, 163, 165, 193, *195*
Bjork, R. A., 9, *19*
Blackwell, A. W., 274, *289*
Blake, R., 246, *267*
Blakemore, C., 83, *89*
Blaxton, R. A., 14, *19*
Boer, L. C., 6, *17*, 73, 78, 80, *89*
Bohdanecky, Z., 91, *119*
Boles, D. B., 59, *64*

291

Subject Index

A

Artificial neural networks, 8, 9, 94–96
  simulations, 94–97, 106, 107
Attention,
  see Perceptual organization,
  see Selective attention

C

Cognitive processes, 270
Configural stimuli, 130–148
  definition of, 130
Connectionism,
  see Artificial neural networks,
Context effects,
  in letter perception, 54–61
  in scene perception, 46, 47
  see also Irrelevant information

D

Direct theory of perception, 273–276
  problems of the, 274–276
Distal vs. proximal stimuli, 269, 270
Divided attention, 26, 27
  see also Selective attention

E

Early processing,
  see Low-level processing,
Electro-oculography,
  see Eye movements,
Encoding conditions,
  number of exposures, 209
  structural vs. elaborative encoding,
    203–208
Eye movements measures of form percep-
    tion, 91–119
  fixation indices, 93–94
    cumulative fixation time, 93
    scanpath order, 93
  K means cluster analysis, 101, 102
  connectionist models, 92, 93

F

Facilitation, 155
  see also Priming,
  see also Stroop facilitation,
  in naming and categorization tasks,
    161–195
    stimulus onset asyncrony, 163, 164
Feature-weighting,
  in complex form perception, 94–106
  in simple form perception, 106–111